# The
# Little Mac
# Book

**THIRD**

Robin Williams

Peachpit Press
Berkeley ▼ California

**The Little Mac Book** third edition
© 1990, 1991, 1993 by Robin Williams
  (previously published under the title *Macintosh Basics;*
  *An informal guide to using the Mac,* by Performance Enhancement Products)


· Peachpit Press, Inc.
· 2414 Sixth Street
· Berkeley, California 94710
· 510.548.4393
· 510.548.5991 fax

**Notice of Liability**
The information in this book is distributed on an "As is" basis, without
warranty. While every precaution has been taken in the preparation of this
book, neither the author nor Peachpit Press, Inc. shall have any liability to any
person or entity with respect to any liability, loss, or damage caused or alleged
to be caused directly or indirectly by the instructions contained in this book or
by the computer software and hardware products described herein.

**Trademarks**
Throughout this book trademarked names are used. Rather than put a
trademark symbol in every occurrence of a trademarked name, we state
we are using the names only in an editorial fashion and to the benefit
of the trademark owner with no intention of infringement of the trademark.

ISBN 1-56609-052-0

0 9 8 7 6 5 4 3 2
Printed and bound in the United States of America

*To my mother, Patricia Williams,*
*who made it possible,*
*and to my father, Gerald Williams,*
*who would have been proud.*

## Acknowledgments

It would not have been possible to get this edition to press on time without my sister, Shannon Williams. I thank you so much, Shannon, for all you do for me. *I love you.*

And so many thanks to Carole Quandt for proofreading the book under such pressure!

We are confronted
with insurmountable
opportunities.
*Pogo*
*— Walt Kelly*

# CONTENTS

**Read Me First** . . . . . . . . . . . . . . . . . . . . . . . . . . . . . . . . . . . . . . . . . . . . . **7**
The Concept; My Suggestion

## Part the First                                          THE BASICS

**1  Ks, Megs, and Disks** . . . . . . . . . . . . . . . . . . . . . . . . . . . . . . . **11**
Technical Magic; Bits; Bytes; Kilobytes; Floppy Disks; Disk Capacity;
Caring for Floppy Disks; Initializing a New Disk; Locking a Disk; Hard
Disks; Megabytes; Backup Disks; Rule #3; Labeling Your Disks

**2  Starting Up** . . . . . . . . . . . . . . . . . . . . . . . . . . . . . . . . . . . . . . . **17**
Turning It On; System Folder; The System and the Finder; Inserting
a Disk; Installing New Software; System and Software Versions; Only
One System per Computer!; Power User

**3  The Desktop and Finder** . . . . . . . . . . . . . . . . . . . . . . . . . . . **23**
The Desktop or Finder; Hierarchy and the Desktop Level; The Desktop
as Home Base; Organizing Your Desktop; Clean Up the Desktop

**4  The Mouse** . . . . . . . . . . . . . . . . . . . . . . . . . . . . . . . . . . . . . . . **27**
The Mouse; Single Click; Double Click; Press; Press-and-Drag; The
Pointer; Trackballs, PowerBooks; Connecting the Mouse; Mousepads;
Moving the Mouse; Did You Ask Why?; Cleaning the Mouse

**5  Menus** . . . . . . . . . . . . . . . . . . . . . . . . . . . . . . . . . . . . . . . . . . . **31**
Pull-Down Menus; Choosing a Menu Item; Pop-Out Menus; Gray vs.
Black Commands; Keyboard Command Shortcuts; Ellipses and Dialog
Boxes; Other Menus; Watch for Shadows; Sideways Arrows and Edit
Boxes; Downward Arrows

**6  Important Keys** . . . . . . . . . . . . . . . . . . . . . . . . . . . . . . . . . . . **35**
The Keyboard; Modifier Keys; Any Key; Caps Lock; Command Key;
Control Key; Delete Key/Backspace Key; Enter Key; Escape Key;
Option Key; Return Key; Spacebar; Shift Key; Tilde Key; Asterisk;
Forward Slash; Fkeys; Tab Key; Arrow Keys; Numeric Keypad; Edit
Keys; Power-On Key

**7    All Windows** . . . . . . . . . . . . . . . . **41**
Windows; Title Bar; Moving the Window; Active Window; To Make
the Window Active; Size Box; Zoom Box; Scroll Bars; Gray Scroll Bar;
White Scroll Bar; Scroll Arrows; Scroll Box; Press-and-Drag the Scroll
Box; Clicking in the Scroll Bar; Close Box; Information Bar

**8    Desktop Windows** . . . . . . . . . . . . . . **45**
Desktop Windows; Views of the Window; List Views; Customize
the Window View; Clean Up Window; Gray Icons; Close all the
Windows; Hierarchy of a Window; Minor Differences; Other Cool
Tricks; Print the Window; Print the Screen; Print Other Windows
or the Screen; Outline View

**9    Icons** . . . . . . . . . . . . . . . . . . **57**
Icons; Disk; Folder; Application; Document; Blank Document; System;
Highlighted (Dark); Open (Gray); Moving Icons; Renaming Icons;
Undo Icon Name Change; If You Can't Change the Name; Color Your
Icons; Create Your Own Icons; Screen Shot; Get Info; Locking the File;
Stationery Pads; Putting Away

**10    Folders** . . . . . . . . . . . . . . . . . **69**
Folders; Creating a New Folder; Naming the New Folder; Changing
the Name; Putting Something Inside; Opening; Removing Something;
Organizing Your Disk Using Folders; Outline Mode; Creating Project-
Specific Folders

**11    Copying and Selecting** . . . . . . . . . . . . **75**
Why Copy?; Copying; Duplicate/Copy File on Same Disk; Copy From
Floppy to Floppy with Only One Floppy Drive; Copying More Than
One File at a Time; Selecting More Than One File at a Time; Shift-
Clicking to Select More Than One File; Shift-Clicking to Deselect;
Selection Shortcuts; Selecting from Expanded Views; Using Find File

**12    Trash Can** . . . . . . . . . . . . . . . . **83**
The Trash Can; Emptying the Trash; Disable the Warning Box

**13    Opening Applications or Documents** . . . . . . **85**
What is an Application?; Opening an Application; Opening a
Document from the Desktop; Drag-and-Drop to Open a Document;
New vs. Open; An "Open" Dialog Box

**14    Typing** . . . . . . . . . . . . . . . . . **89**
Typing; I-Beam; Insertion Point; Delete/Backspace; Highlighting
Text; When to Use the Return Key (Word Wrap; Hard Returns;
Double Spaces; Removing a Return); Blank Spaces; Centering Text;
Changing Fonts (Typefaces); Rule #2; Changing Style; Changing Styles

Mid-Sentence—Without Using the Menu; Changing Type Size; Alignment; Cut, Copy, and the Clipboard; Cut; Copy; Paste; Delete or Clear and the Clipboard; Undo; Command Z, X, C, V; Accessing Special Characters (Key Caps); List of Special Characters; Using Accent Marks; List of Accent Marks; One Space After Periods

**15  Saving** . . . . . . . . . . . . . . . . . . . . . . . . . . . . . . . . . . . . . . . . . . . . . . . **101**

Save the Document; RAM: Random Access Memory; Danger!; Rule #1: Save Often!; Save As… vs. Save; Making Several Versions; Revert to Save; "Save As…" Dialog Box; Visual Clues; Navigating

**16  Printing** . . . . . . . . . . . . . . . . . . . . . . . . . . . . . . . . . . . . . . . . . . . . . . **107**

Printing; Printers; Chooser; Let's Print!; Print From the Desktop; Print the Window; Print the Desktop; Save Laser Printer Toner & Paper; PrintMonitor; Align ImageWriter Pin-Fed Paper

**17  Closing and Quitting** . . . . . . . . . . . . . . . . . . . . . . . . . . . . . **117**

Closing a Document; Quitting an Application; Shutting Down

**18  Ejecting Disks** . . . . . . . . . . . . . . . . . . . . . . . . . . . . . . . . . . . . . **119**

Ejecting; Shutting Down; From the Menu or the Keyboard Shortcut; Through the Trash; Through Dialog Boxes; More Keyboard Shortcuts; Mouse Trick; Paper Clip Trick; Mounting and Dismounting

**19  Shutting Down** . . . . . . . . . . . . . . . . . . . . . . . . . . . . . . . . . . . . **123**

Shutting Down; Good Housekeeping; Quit All Programs; Shut Down

**Part the Second**                    BEYOND THE BASICS

**20  System Folder** . . . . . . . . . . . . . . . . . . . . . . . . . . . . . . . . . . . . **127**

What is the System Folder?; System File; Finder; Clipboard and Scrapbook File; Note Pad File; Control Panels; Apple Menu Items Folder; Startup Items Folder; Extensions Folder; Preferences Folder; Installing Files into the System Folder

**21  Fonts** . . . . . . . . . . . . . . . . . . . . . . . . . . . . . . . . . . . . . . . . . . . . . . . **133**

Fonts; Printers: PostScript and QuickDraw; PostScript Fonts; What Do You Get on a Font Disk?; TrueType Fonts; Adobe Type Manager (ATM); Which Font Technology For You?; How to Install Fonts; Resident Fonts; Fonts of the Same Name; City-Named Fonts; Substitute Fonts; Is It TrueType or PostScript; Why Do You See Both Icons?; You Can See What Any Font Looks Like; Font Sizes

**22  Desk Accessories** . . . . . . . . . . . . . . . . . . . . . . . . . . . . . . . . **147**

Desk Accessories; Alarm Clock; Calculator; Chooser; Key Caps; Note Pad; Scrapbook; Puzzle

**23  Apple Menu** . . . . . . . . . . . . . . . . . **155**
The Apple Menu; Aliases; Installing Apple Menu Items; Alphabetized
Apple Menu; Suggestions for Customizing Your Menu; Hey—Let's Get
Really Fancy

**24  Control Panels** . . . . . . . . . . . . . . . **159**
Control Panels; General Controls; Brightness; Date & Time; Keyboard;
Labels; Color Your Icons; Launcher; Memory; Monitors; Mouse;
Numbers; Sound; Startup Disk; Networking Control Panels; Views

**25  Aliases** . . . . . . . . . . . . . . . . . . . . . **169**
Aliases; Making Aliases; Fine Points; Using Aliases; Finding the Original File

**26  Find File** . . . . . . . . . . . . . . . . . . . . **175**
Find File; You Can Find:; Simple Finding; More Complex Finding; All
At Once; Restricting Searches; Back to Simple Finding; Search Within
a Search; Other Search Ideas

**27  Simple Networking and Sharing** . . . . . . . **181**
Sharing Files, Networking; File Sharing Software; AppleTalk and
LocalTalk; Network Control Panel; Step 1: Connect the Computers;
Step 2: Name the Mac; Step 3: Make a Folder to Share; Step 4: Connect
the Other Mac to Yours; Step 5: Share Files; Disconnecting; Reconnect-
ing; Office-on-a Disk; Just the Tip

**28  Other Features** . . . . . . . . . . . . . . . . . **191**
Balloon Help; Publish and Subscribe

**Part the Third**                        IMPORTANT INFORMATION

**29  Navigating** . . . . . . . . . . . . . . . . . . . **195**
Where is Your File?; Different Ways of Looking at the Same Thing;
Where Does the Document Go?; For Instance; Which Folder?;
Keyboard Shortcuts for Navigating; Why Is It?;

**30  Very Important Information** . . . . . . . . . . **205**
Very Important Information; Hard Disk vs. Memory; Suggestions; Save
Regularly; Check the Applications Heap; Use a Font Management
Utility; Virtual Memory; The Upshot

**31  Visual Clues** . . . . . . . . . . . . . . . . . . **213**
What is a Visual Clue? Ellipsis in the Menu; Default Button; Highlighted
Text; Checkboxes vs. Radio Buttons; Mini-Menus Above a List;
Matching Icons; Changing Files Names; Gray Icons; View Clue;
Number of Items; Scroll Bars; Scroll Box; Menu Checkmark or Lack

of Checkmark; The Boot Disk; Are You Using System 7?; Diamond in the Application Menu; Look for Clues

**32   A Few Extra Tips** . . . . . . . . . . . . . . . . . . . . . . . . . . . . . . . . . **221**
Compendium of Tips; Application Menu; Tab to Select; Brightness Control; Screen Savers; One Space; Real Quotation Marks!; StartupScreen; Startup Movie; Rebuilding Your Desktop; Write Your Tips Here!; How Much RAM?; Checking Your Fonts at the Desktop; Disable All Extensions

**33   Aack!!! Help!** . . . . . . . . . . . . . . . . . . . . . . . . . . . . . . . . . . **231**
What To Do If: The Computer Doesn't Turn On; You Get the Question Mark, the Flashing X, or a Sad Mac on Startup; The Screen Freezes; Can't Find Your Document; Can't Open a File; Viewing Clipart Files; System Bombs; "Not Enough Memory"; Text Formatting Unexpectedly Changed; Printing Doesn't Work; Can't Form- or Line-Feed the ImageWriter Paper; There's Garbage Hanging Around Outside the Trash Can; Gray Disk Icon is Left on Screen; Lost Your Application?; Other Windows Popped Up in Front of Your Face?; Desktop Windows Open Very Slowly; Erratic Typing or Mouse Movement; The Documents Folder; Reset Switch

## Part the Fourth                    PERFORMA AND AT EASE

**34   The Performa** . . . . . . . . . . . . . . . . . . . . . . . . . . . . . . . . . **243**
The Macintosh Performa; The Launcher; Launcher Items are Buttons; The Documents Folder; Sanity Protection; Remove Items From the Launcher; Add Items to the Launcher; Make Backups of Your Files; Removing the Launcher

**35   At Ease** . . . . . . . . . . . . . . . . . . . . . . . . . . . . . . . . . . . . . . . **253**
What Is At Ease?; Limitations; Menu Bar; Customizing; Using At Ease; Turning Pages of the Panels; Opening Other Documents; Opening Other Applications; Opening More Than One Application; Saving a Document; Ejecting a Disk; Switching Between At Ease and Open Applications; Getting to the Finder; Turning At Ease Off; Bypassing At Ease When You Start Up; Customizing At Ease; Change the Password; If You Forget the Password; Permanently Removing At Ease; Mouse Practice

## Part the Fifth                    WHAT DOES IT ALL MEAN?

**36   Jargon** . . . . . . . . . . . . . . . . . . . . . . . . . . . . . . . . . . . . . . . **271**

## Part the Sixth — WHERE DO I BEGIN?

**37   Tutorial** . . . . . . . . . . . . . . . . . . . . . . . . . . . . . . . . . . . . . . . . . . . . . . **301**
At Ease; Performa; Start Here; Read a few things first; Using the mouse;
Menus and commands; Using the desk accessories; Viewing windows;
Icons; Manipulating windows; Keyboard commands; Folders, backing
up, and the trash; Word processing (including cut, copy, paste, and
the Clipboard; Scrapbook; Saving; Printing; Quitting) Other Very
Important Features; p.s.

## Part the Seventh — WHERE IS IT?

**Index** . . . . . . . . . . . . . . . . . . . . . . . . . . . . . . . . . . . . . . . . . . . . . . **313**
A Very Important Part

## Charts — VERY HANDY

**Typeface Samples** . . . . . . . . . . . . . . . . . . . . . . . . . . . . . . . . **328**

**Zapf Dingbats Chart** . . . . . . . . . . . . . . . . . . . . . . . . . . . . . . **329**

**Special Characters Chart** . . . . . . . . . . . . . . . . . . . . . . . . . **330**

# READ ME FIRST

I hope you were warned, before you ever invested in a Macintosh, that this little computer is addictive. It pulls you in. It has you inventing work for yourself just so you can use it. It creates an attitude that makes you feel like you're having fun while being productive—what a concept.

**The Concept**

This book is just a direct path to the essentials of operating the computer so you can get straight to the fun, I mean *work,* without wasting too much time diddling around trying to figure it out. There's not much technical information here because most of us don't need it or want it; you don't have to know how to fly the plane to take a vacation in Rio.

This book used to be very little. It's gotten bigger because the Macintosh has gotten more complex. The Mac is still the easiest and most empowering computer to use, but it is a fact that there are some things that are now a little more confusing than they used to be. And in these days of everyone always in a rush and no one having time to do anything luxurious like spend time learning how to use a new computer, these confusing features can be very frustrating. I know—you want to get straight to work.

Wanna know my recommendation? I suggest you start this book with the Tutorial, Chapter 37. It will walk you through just what you need to know to get up and running and on your way, telling you specifically which parts of the book to read. The rest of the book you can read another time—pick up the book while you're

**My Suggestion**

waiting for a document to come out the printer, open it when you realize there is something specific you don't quite understand, browse through it while waiting for the coffee to drip. You see, if you read this book all the way through, many of the tidbits of information won't get absorbed the first time around. I've found that we need to let a certain amount of information sink in before we can absorb other bits.

And skip over anything that doesn't make sense right away. That's one of the most wonderful things about the Mac—we can bumble along for a long time on a surprisingly small amount of information. When your brain is ready to absorb more, come back to the parts that didn't make sense the first time around. The information will still be there.

**!!!** **Whenever you come across a term you are not familiar with, check the index.** It will refer you to the page where that term is defined. Really—I spent an inordinate amount of time on the index so you would be able to find an explanation for every term in this book.

After all, I do want you to have fun and take advantage of this new concept in productivity as you, too, become addicted.

[?]

*If you see this symbol in your menu bar, you are using (often called "running") System 7.*

*p.s. In this edition of the book I assume you are using System 7. (If you see the little question mark in a balloon in the upper right corner of your menu bar, you are using System 7.) If you are still using System 6, you may want to check with Peachpit Press for a copy of the second edition of* The Little Mac Book, *which includes information on both System 6 and System 7.*

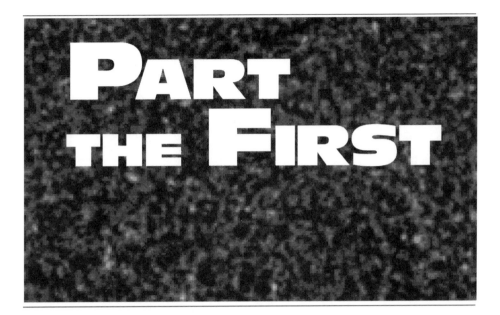

# PART THE FIRST

This section describes the things you need to know to get up and running on your Macintosh, from starting up to shutting down. This section actually tells you more than you *need* to know—there are lots of little tips and tricks embedded in these chapters, tips and tricks that may even impress your power user friends.

Remember, though, if you are in a hurry, you might want to start with the Tutorial (page 299). The Tutorial tells you exactly which pages to read and what to practice so you can get right to work. Then you can come back later and read all the parts you missed.

If you find terms you don't understand, look them up in the index!

*There is no substitute for paying attention.*
*—Diane Sawyer*

# CHAPTER ONE

# Ks, Megs, and Disks

People who've been working with the Mac for a while start tossing around jargon like, "It won't fit cuz it's a 900K document," or "Hey, *my* Mac has a 240 meg hard disk," and people who are not familiar with the Mac feel dumb because it all sounds so esoteric and we're sure we'll never be able to understand all this sophisticated computer stuff and besides we don't want to know all that technical stuff anyway, we just want to learn how to run the darn thing. Well, as far as technical stuff goes, all most of us need to know is the machine is magic. Pure, simple, magic. Like an airplane.

Knowing the difference between a bit and a byte and a K and a meg, though, can help organize things in your brain a little bit so what you are working with will make more sense. This is how it goes:

Actually, the computer isn't that smart; it can only count to one. Remember in school when we learned the binary system, which we have now completely forgotten about, except that for some reason we could only count from zero to one and we had to use exponential notation? Well, the Mac uses a binary system: it counts zero and one—zero means Off and one means On. It sends these little electronic messages, each a series of Off and On. And each one of those little messages is a **bit**.

## Technical Magic

## Bits

**0 1**

*Each one of these electronic messages is one bit.*

**Bytes**

**01000001**
*This byte represents the letter A.*

Now, one little bit doesn't tell the computer a whole lot, so it strings together a bunch of bits to create a more important message: eight bits, such as **01000001**, makes one **byte**. As you can see in the column to the left, one byte of information is still rather limited—it takes a lot of bytes to create any sort of document.

**Kilobytes**

*Approximately 1000 Bytes equals 1 Kilobyte.*

So a bunch of bytes is grouped together and called a **kilobyte**. You would think that a kilobyte would be a thousand bytes, yes? No. Since the computer can only count to one, the closest it can get to 1000 in its binary system with exponential notation is 1024. But we generally round it off and say there are about 1000 bytes in a kilobyte. And kilobytes are the **K**s everyone talks about.

How do Ks figure in real life? Kilobytes are what disk space and file/document size are measured in; the larger and more sophisticated the document or the software program, the greater the number of K it will occupy on the disk.

**Floppy Disks**

You've probably seen the nice little 3.5" **floppy disks** that the Mac uses. A disk can store information for running the computer, for operating the programs, for saving the documents you create. Originally the Mac could only deal with a single-sided disk (one that took information on only one side of itself), but unless you have a very old machine with only a single-sided drive, you won't be using single-sided disks.

**Disk Capacity**

A **double-sided disk** holds about **800K** (kilobytes) of data. Four pages of double-spaced typewritten text takes about 6K of disk space; therefore, you can get about *500 pages* of textual information on one disk (leaving some room for the messages the disk has to send to the computer). Spreadsheets, graphics, and other complex info take up a lot more space, of course.

A **high-density double-sided disk** holds about **1.4MB** (megabytes, which are bigger than kilobytes, see pages 12 and 15) of data. These disks look just like normal disks, except they usually have the letters HD somewhere on them, and they have an extra hole with no tab to close it. That extra hole tells the Macintosh that the disk is high-density. Only Macs with an "FD-HD" drive (floppy disk, high density), also known as a "SuperDrive" (which includes any Mac since the SE30, including Classics and Performas) can read these high-density disks. Some people may suggest putting a piece of tape over the extra hole to trick older Macs into reading the disk, but that almost always eventually ends in a disk failure. Don't risk your valuable work.

*High-density disks have an extra hole on the right side of the disk.*

## Caring for Floppy Disks

Why is the disk called a floppy disk when it's not floppy? Actually, it *is* floppy. If you slide over that metal end you'll see the floppy disk inside. Don't touch it! It's full of tiny messages that your oily fingers or sharp nails can destroy. Keep your disks away from heat: they'll warp just like a record album when left in your hot car. And keep them away from magnets—a magnet will destroy all the data on the disk. So don't attach them to your refrigerator; don't store them near your telephone or stereo or any other electronic device; and don't pile them on top of your magnetic paper clip holder.

I also recommend you don't keep disks in those little plastic bags they often come in; the plastic can build up static electricity which has the potential to destroy your precious data.

## Initializing a New Disk

When you buy your floppy disks, they aren't *formatted* and so they must be **initialized**. They come unformatted because other computers are now using these handy little things, and they can be initialized for several types. So when you first insert an uninitialized disk, the Mac asks you several questions. You need to name the disk and you need to choose to initialize it single-sided or double-sided. Obviously, if it's a double-sided disk you'll choose double-sided. The system may warn you that you are going to erase all the information on the disk, but since it's blank, so what. When you finally click OK, the Mac will lay down the formatting it needs to store all the valuable info you will be giving it.

### Locking a Disk

It is possible to **lock** a disk. When a disk is locked, whoever is using it cannot change anything on it, nor can other files be saved onto it. To lock a disk, find the little black tab in the corner. You'll notice you can slide it up or down.

*This disk is unlocked.*

▼ When the tab covers the hole, the disk is unlocked.

▼ When you can see through the hole, the disk is locked.

Some disks have two holes, but only one has a tab that can be moved. The second hole indicates that the disk is a high-density disk (see the following page) and has nothing to do with locking.

### Hard Disks

A **hard disk** is actually a large, *hard disk,* rather than a floppy piece of film. In principle it works the same as a floppy disk, but it can hold a great deal more data. The hard disk itself may be installed inside your Mac, or it may be a separate unit encased in a sturdy plastic box. There are also hard disks on cartridges that you can insert into a removable disk drive, sort of like how you insert a video into your VCR, so you can have a collection of cartridge hard disks.

In any form, a hard disk is a storage container, like a filing cabinet, that holds all your software programs and documents, and holds the *System Folder* that is essential to starting your machine (see page 18 for general info on the System Folder, and Chapter 20 for details). Hard disks allow you to store your files all on one disk instead of on a lot of separate floppies, which makes it *much* easier and faster to work. It is essential now to have a hard disk, as programs and documents are rapidly out-growing even the double-sided disks.

In fact, a hard disk holds so much data that it's not even measured in kilobytes; it's measured in **megabytes**, also known as **megs** or **MB**. You've already figured out that one megabyte is 1024 kilobytes, right? Right.

Now, 1024 kilobytes (one megabyte) is more than what *one* normal floppy disk can hold. Hard disks come in various sizes, able to store from 20 megs to 30 to 80 to 160 megs of information, and they're getting bigger all the time. So on a small hard disk then, say 20 megs, you have as much storage space as on *more than 25 floppy disks!* You can load all kinds of applications onto your hard disk and create all kinds of documents without having to fiddle with putting floppies in and out. As the software applications get more and more sophisticated, they take up more and more space, and already there are applications that just can't be used without a hard disk.

Always **back up** your software applications. As soon as you buy a new application, make a copy of all the disks (see pages 75-80) and **use the copy** (the *copy* is your back up); keep the original disks safe in a clean, dust-free place. That way if a catastrophe happens to befall your application that you paid so much money for, you always have an extra copy. Software companies, you know, won't give you a new copy if you destroy yours.

Also and even more important, always make sure you have a current back up copy of *everything* on your hard disk—all your documents you have so laboriously created. A hard disk can "crash" and leave no survivors. Now, I know that in everything you ever read about the Mac you will be warned to back up regularly, but you won't really do it until you have experienced your own

## Megabytes

*Approximately 1000K equals one megabyte.*

## Make Backup Disks

*Back up any document that is important to you*

catastrophe of considerable dimension. As it has been so truly stated, "Experience is what you get when you don't get what you want," and "Experience teaches us to recognize a mistake when we've made it again."

At the end of each working day, *or more often if it is really important,* make copies (page 75) onto disks of everything you created or modified that day. Then label those disks! Never work longer without backing up than you could stand to re-do the work. That is, if you're working on a catalog and the last time you created a backup copy was three hours ago, would you mind re-creating those three hours? Then back it up.

A hard disk comes with a back up application—be sure to check it out. If you are in a situation where there are massive amounts of information to back up regularly, check into those applications designed specifically for large-scale, automatic backing up.

**Rule Number 3**   **Back Up Often.** Like everyday. *(No, you didn't miss Rules 1 and 2—Rule 1 is on page 102; Rule 2 is on page 93.)*

**Labeling Your Disks**   Below is a diagram for putting the **label on your disk** At first it may seem as if this diagram is telling you to write the information upside down, but once you start storing disks in a box of some sort, you will realize that writing on them as shown below makes the words upside right when they are stored.

*If your label has a colored tab, fold that tab over the top of the disk. You can use the tabs to color-code your filing system (ha—do your organizational skills really go beyond good intentions?). Write the most important information across the top where you will see it easily when the disks are stored in a box. Write the name of every file on this disk! Always date each file. Really. This will save you much time and occasionally grief.*

# CHAPTER TWO

# STARTING UP

Depending on what kind of Macintosh you have, the on switch is located in various places. The smaller Macs turn on with a little switch on the back left of the machine (*back,* yes, as in behind the monitor)—admittedly a very inconvenient place. Most of the larger, modular Macs are turned on with the big key with the triangle on it at the top of the standard keyboard (that key that is useless for everybody else), or the key on the top far right on the extended keyboard. On some models, like the LC, you may have to press on two buttons on the back of the monitor. Don't let all this confuse you, though. Even though you'll forget half the other stuff in this book, once you figure out how to turn on your computer you probably won't forget it.

**Turning It On**

If you have an *internal hard disk* for your machine (which you most surely do if you bought a new Macintosh in the past three years), as soon as you turn it on it will **boot up** from the System on the hard disk. (The term "boot up" or "boot" comes from the idea of pulling itself up by its bootstraps, as the Mac is going into its own System and turning itself on.)

*Internal Hard Disk*

If you have an *external hard disk,* that piece of hardware should be turned on first, and then turn on your Mac.

*External Hard Disk*

If your computer has *any other switches* for turning it on, either on top of the monitor or on the keyboard, the switch on the back of the Macintosh must always be turned on as well.

*Other Switches*

### System Folder

**System Folder**

You must have a **System Folder** on your hard disk. The System Folder must have at least two icons in it: the System icon and the Finder icon (shown below, left). Without those two items in the machine, the Mac can't start itself up; it will spit out any other disks you try to insert and will give you the sad–Mac face. The System Folder is an extremely important item, so important that there is an entire chapter dedicated to it (Chapter 20, page 127). Although you *can* rename the folder, I strongly suggest you don't, just to keep the concept clear.

### The System and the Finder

**System  Finder**

The **System** and the **Finder** are sort of like this: You are going on a trip. Your car is full of gas. You have the keys. You put a key in the ignition and start the car; the engine hums. But you can't get to where you're going yet— your car will sit in the driveway all day humming away until what? (Go ahead—think a minute.) Until you *put it in gear*. And that's sort of like what the Mac does: Your machine's plugged in. You turn it on. The screen gets bright and a little picture may be flashing. But you're not going to get anywhere until you *put it in gear* by inserting a System and a Finder (the Finder runs the *Desktop,* which is the first thing you see when you boot your Mac; see the next chapter).

### Start up disk

The disk icon that appears on your Desktop in the upper right corner is the *start up* disk, the disk that holds the System Folder that booted (started) the Mac.

### Inserting a Disk into a Floppy Drive

The term **internal floppy drive** refers to the little slot on the front of your machine where you **insert a floppy disk**. Disks go in the slot with the label-side up (the side that does *not* have the *round* metal piece on it), and the metal end goes in first. (If the box portion of your computer is on its side, then "up" refers to what *would* be up if the box was not sideways. The Macintosh logo on the front gives you a clue as to which side should be up.)

You might have two internal drives, and you might also have an **external drive** (usually a little box that sits on the side of the computer). You can have a floppy disk in each of these floppy drives, and you can save data onto any disk in any drive.

You may have had your software installed before you brought your computer home, in which case it is already on your hard disk waiting for you. But if not, or if you bought some new software, you may need to **install it yourself**. Piece o' cake. These instructions here, though, are very generic and thus very limited. I can't cover every piece of software, so really the best advice is: **RTFM**. That stands for "Read The Manual." Always make sure the software disk is locked before you insert it so you can't change anything.

If your software arrived on **one disk** and there are only one or two normal-looking icons on it, you can create a new folder on your hard disk (see page 69) and just copy those files into the new folder (see page 76). What do I mean by "normal-looking"? Well, that's hard to say, isn't it. If the icon is kind of pretty and a little fancy, it is probably normal. If it looks like a monkey wrench or like exploding arrows or if it has an abbreviation after the name like "sea" or "sit" (see below) then the program has probably been *compressed* so it could fit onto one disk.

If you have any clue that the software has been **compressed**, then you need to first copy that compressed file into a new folder on your hard disk (see page 69; the new folder actually has nothing to do with it except to provide a contained place for the related files). Once the compressed file is on your hard disk, double-click on it. It will usually open itself up and put files where they belong. After you uncompress the software, you can throw away the compressed file, if it still exists. You have the original still on the disk.

## Installing Your New Software

### One-disk software

DeskPaint®

*This is a normal-looking, kind of pretty, and a little fancy application icon.*

### Compressed software

MAD　　PlayBall.sea

*These are commonly seen compressed files. These particular files are the kind you can double-click on to uncompress, called "self extracting archives."*

**Multi-disk software**

If your software arrived on **more than one disk**, the disks are probably labeled and one of the labels says something like "Program disk" or "Installer disk" or "Disk 1." Find the one that looks like the first in the series and insert it into the internal floppy drive. There is probably an icon called "Installer." Double-click that icon and it will install the program for you. It will spit out the disks when ready and tell you which one to put in next. If there is an installer, *use it.* Many installers put various files in various folders in and around the System Folder, besides the main program where you can see it. If there is an installer, chances are great that the program won't even work if you try to just copy the files onto your disk.

**Read Me files**

ReadMe

*Sometimes this file may be called "Read Me First."*

You will often see a file called **ReadMe** on new software disks. Guess what you should do with that file? Yes, you should read it. Just double-click on the icon. The word processing utility called TeachText is often on the disk also, and the ReadMe file opens in TeachText. If you have no version at all of TeachText (which would be very surprising), you can open ReadMe files in almost any other word processor. This file contains important information that was discovered too late to put into the manual. Yes, you should also read the manual.

**Installing new fonts**

Installing new fonts (typefaces) is different than installing a software application. Please see the chapter on Fonts, page 133.

**System and Software Versions**

All computer software is constantly being upgraded and updated, making it more efficient, powerful, magical. And sometimes they update software just to fix a *bug* (which is a minor problem that is not supposed to be there but supposedly they didn't know it was there when they sent it to you). The developers let you know which upgrade you have by labeling it with a **version number**.

There is usually a period in the version number, which is pronounced "point." Thus the version 4.2 is pronounced "four point two." The version 5.0 is pronounced "five point oh," and 5.01 is "five point oh one." And 6.0.7 is "six point oh point seven."

*But* when a file name for a *document* includes a period, the period is pronounced "dot." For instance, a compressed file may be labeled "Brochure.sit" (the "sit" is a common file name *extension* that gives you a clue that the file is compressed). This is pronounced "brochure dot sit."

As the System upgrades, the software programs are created to work with the particular nuances of the newer System, so it's a good idea to keep up on both System upgrades and software application upgrades. Although you don't *have* to use the newest System, it's usually free, so why not take advantage of it? (Software program updates, though, are rarely free.) And if you never upgrade the System, eventually you will be severely limited as to the software you can use with your Mac.

You should never have more than one System in the computer. This will invariably end in a bomb (see page 235). It's not as easy to have more than one system anymore, because the System itself is so big. But until recently many programs and especially game disks arrived on your desk with a System Folder also on the disk. Many people (not you, of course) copied the entire disk onto their hard disk, which means they copied the extra System Folder also. It is still possible to do this.

If you have any suspicion at all that there may be more than one System in your computer, use Find File (Chapter 26) to find it. Remove any extra Systems besides the one that is running your machine (don't worry—you won't be able to trash the one that is running your machine). You should, in fact, remove any extra System Folders, not just the System file itself. You may want to have your power user friend help you do this.

**Power User**

What is a **power user**? A power user is a person who knows more than you. Well, real power users know a lot. They can throw around terms like "32–bit addressing" and "clean ROMs" and "CPU" and actually have a clue as to what they mean. Power users use all the keyboard shortcuts instead of the mouse, and they load up their computers with all the INITs and cdevs they can find. They get a thrill out of the speed of the SCSI-2 port and debate the advantages of RISC *vs.* CISC. A real power user even uses ResEdit without quivering. Everyone should have a power user as a friend.

# CHAPTER THREE

# THE DESKTOP AND FINDER

## The Desktop

The **Desktop** is what you see on the screen when you first start up your Macintosh. Consistent with the Mac environment that analogizes everything to parts of our real lives, this Desktop works much the same as your desktop at home or in your office: You have desk accessories (under the Apple menu) such as a calculator, a clock, and a note pad. You have a filing cabinet (the disk) that stores all your folders full of information. You have as many file folders as you could possibly want to organize it all. You can put folders inside of folders inside of folders almost *ad infinitum* just like you would organize your hanging files. You even have a trash can.

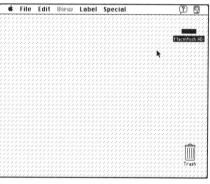

*The Desktop;*
*also known as the Finder.*

## The Finder

The **Finder** is the system software that manages the Desktop. The Finder keeps track of all the files you have stored on your Desktop, as well as where you keep your applications and which disk you have stuck in the floppy drive, among other tasks. When you upgrade to a higher System (such as from System 6.0.5 to 6.0.7), you also get a new, upgraded Finder. It appears, with the advent of System 7.0, that the Finder version number will now match the System version number; that is, if you are running System version 7, the Finder is also version 7.

*(Well, that's logical, you say. But, you see, the numbers have never before matched. I'm so happy now that I just had to mention it.)*

Finder

*You'll see this icon*
*in your System Folder.*

**Well, What's It Called—the Desktop or the Finder?**

The **Desktop** is the actual place you see, and the **Finder** is what controls and keeps track of the Desktop. But because the two are so closely related and you can't have one without the other, you will hear people interchange the terms as if they were the same thing. That's okay (it has to be okay cuz that's the way it is). When you hear someone say, "Are you at the Finder?" you will understand that they mean, "Are you at the Desktop?" and vice versa.

**Hierarchy and the Desktop Level**

In the **hierarchy** of things, the **Desktop is the top level**. You can store files and folders right on the Desktop. From there, your hard disk is the next level, and of course you can store files and folders there. Then each folder is a level, and if a folder is within a folder, that is down one more level. The Finder keeps track of all this. When you hear people talk about the "hierarchical filing system" or a "hierarchical menu," it refers to this folders-within-folders filing system within the hard disk which is on the Desktop.

In the example below, you can see the hierarchy of a folder. This is an example from the "Save as" dialog box, the box you see when you give a new document a name.

🗁 **Memory Analogy**
🗁 **MacHomeJournal**
🗁 **Publications**
🗀 **Hard Disk**
▦ **Desktop**

*The first name in this list tells me what level I am at right now—the folder named "Memory Analogy."*

*This also tells me the folder "Memory Analogy" is in the folder "MacHome Journal," which is in the folder "Publications," which is on the Hard Disk, which is on the Desktop.*

*This is the top level of the hierarchy. I know it's at the bottom of the list, but it's the top of the hierarchy. If you come from a DOS computer background, you can consider the Desktop to be the root directory.*

*If I were to slide down this menu and choose any other level, I would be shown a list of the items held in that level—in that folder, or in the hard disk, or at the Desktop. If I view the Desktop level, I would see a list of all the files that are on the Desktop at the moment, including the names of any floppy disks that are in any of the floppy drives.*

Whenever you Quit working in an application, the Mac automatically takes you back to the **Desktop level**, which is kind of like home base. If you don't see "Special" in the menu, *then you are not at the Desktop*—perhaps you didn't actually "Quit," but just "closed" and you are still in the application, or perhaps you're in some other application that is still open. To actually get to your Desktop/Finder, click once on what you see of the Desktop. As soon as you click, you'll notice that your menu will have "Special" in it. If this does not make complete sense to you (this is a test), then you really, really should read the chapter called "Very Important Information." It will make you a happier, more powerful person.

It's a good idea to keep your Mac **Desktop organized**, just like you would your office desktop. Create new folders (from the File menu; also see page 69) for each category of information, and store all applicable files in it. If you create a new folder on the hard disk before you begin work in an application, then you can put your new document right into that folder when you *Save* (see page 104). This way, when you come back to the Desktop after working, everything is organized and in its folder so nothing gets misplaced.

**The Desktop as Home Base**

**Organizing Your Desktop**

*This is an example of a neatly organized hard disk window, utilizing the* hierarchical filing system *(HFS), which is a fancy way of saying folders-inside-of-folders. Each category of software or documentation has its own place, and inside these folders may be other folders, each compartmentalizing specific data. It's much easier to keep things organized on a Macintosh Desktop than it is on an oak desktop.*

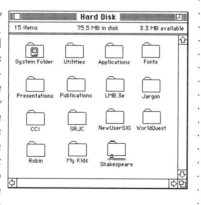

## Clean Up the Desktop

| Special |
|---|
| **Clean Up Desktop** |
| Empty Trash |
| Eject Disk ⌘E |
| Erase Disk... |
| **Restart** |
| **Shut Down** |

*When the Desktop level is selected, the Special menu displays "Clean Up Desktop."*

You can store files on the Desktop level, outside any window. Really. Just drag 'em outside the window and stick 'em on the patterned background. When you're working in an application, you can choose to save a document onto the Desktop level. Sometimes, though, with all the stuff hanging around the Desktop, like the disks and maybe a few aliases and a document or two and some e-mail, the place starts looking a little messy. It's easy to **clean up the Desktop**, though.

▼ Click once on any icon on the Desktop, like your hard disk icon or on the trash can. (If you see "Special" in the menu and a window is active, showing the lines in its title bar, then you can also press Command UpArrow to select the Desktop.)

▼ Press on the Special menu. The first item is now "Clean Up Desktop." This will make all the *icons* (not open *windows*) snap to the nearest spot on an underlying invisible grid.

▼ If you press the Shift key before you choose "Clean Up Desktop," then only the items you *selected* will snap to the grid.

▼ If you press the Option key before you choose "Clean Up Desktop," then all the icons on the Desktop will snap over to the far right and will line up in alphabetical order (but the disk that is running your computer, sometimes called the "startup disk" is always first and the trash can is always last).

▼ If you're interested, see page 49 for what happens when you hold the Command key down and move an icon on the Desktop.

# CHAPTER FOUR

# THE MOUSE

The **mouse**, of course, is that handy little piece of hard-ware that controls the movement of the cursor on the screen. As you move the mouse across the desk, the cursor moves across the screen in the same direction. In most Macintosh applications, you cannot fully utilize the program without the mouse. A few programs give you the option of doing absolutely everything from the keyboard if you choose; but why learn 450 keyboard commands—isn't that just what we're trying to avoid? You'll use the mouse in several different ways:

A **single click** is a quick, light touch on the button of the mouse, with the cursor (a pointer, an I-beam [page 89] or other shape) located at the spot of your choice on the screen.

> Single-click with the *arrow* on an icon at your Desktop to *select* the icon; single click with the *I-beam* to *set down an insertion point.*

A **double click** is a quick click-click on the button, again with the cursor located at the appropriate spot on the screen. A double click has to be quick and the mouse must be still, or it will be interpreted as two single clicks.

> Double-click on a file to *open* that file; double-click on a word to *select* that word for editing.

A **press** is simply pointing to something and *holding* the mouse button down.

> Press with the pointer on the *menu* to see the commands under that item; press on the arrows in a scroll bar to *scroll* through that window.

## The Mouse

## Single Click

## Double Click

## Press

*This is often misleadingly referred to as "click." You may see directions that tell you to "click" on the menu. They really mean "press" on the menu.*

**Press-and-Drag**

*(also known, misleadingly, as click-and-drag)*

**Press-and-drag** means to point to the object or the area of your choice, *hold/press the mouse button down,* and *drag* across, then *let go* when you reach your goal.

> Press-and-drag to *choose menu commands;*
> press-and-drag *to move icons* across the screen;
> press-and-drag to *select text.*

**The Pointer**

When you're using the **pointer**, remember that the only part of the pointer that does the trick is the *very* tip, called the "hot spot." So be sure that the extreme point of the arrow is in the area you want to affect.

*The hot spot* . . . . . .

*The tip of the pointer does the trick.*

**Trackballs, PowerBooks**

Some people prefer to use a different "pointing device," such as a joy stick or a **trackball**. The Macintosh **PowerBooks**, the beautiful little laptop Macs, use a trackball. A trackball is like an upside-down mouse— instead of moving the little mouse box around to make the ball roll underneath, you use your fingers to roll the little ball on top around as it sits in the box. Trackballs have buttons to press that act like the button on the mouse. Depending on what kind of trackball you have, you may click the button with a finger or, as seems to be easier on the PowerBook, with your thumb.

Trackballs are particularly convenient for those people who have to use the mouse backwards. Yes, I have personally met several people who have to turn the mouse with the tail facing themselves. When they push the mouse to the right, the pointer on the screen moves to the left. If more than one person uses this computer, each person has to turn the mouse around. With a trackball, your idiosyncrasies don't matter.

The mouse can be **plugged** into any of the plugs (ports) that they fit into, which are all called ADB ports (ADB for Apple Desktop Bus). You'll find a port on the back of the computer (you can't miss it—it's the only one that fits) with a funny little symbol on it (shown to the right). There is also an ADB port on either side of your keyboard. If your computer is too far from your mouse pad, you might want to plug the mouse into the keyboard. The keyboard cable itself can be connected into either side, so if you are left handed, plug the mouse into the port on the left-hand side of the keyboard.

> Before plugging and unplugging *anything* from your computer, including the mouse or the keyboard, always shut down completely and turn off the power.

### Connecting the Mouse

*Left-handed mousing*

You've probably seen a **mousepad**, a small pad to put on your desk to roll the mouse across. The pad has nothing to do with the operation of the mouse, really—the mouse will work just fine without a pad. The purpose of a mouse pad is simply to provide better traction and a clear spot on your desk for the mouse. You can use a book, illustration board, or even a piece of smooth paper.

### Mousepads

Sometimes you may be **moving the mouse** across the mouse pad or the desk and **run out of space** before the pointer or the I-beam gets where you want it to go. Just do this: Keep your finger on the mouse button, pressing it down. Pick up the mouse, keeping the button down, and move the mouse over to where you have more room. Then just continue on your path.

### Moving the Mouse
*when you've run out of space*

**Why is it called a mouse?** Well, if you grab the cord about four inches from the mouse and hold it at arm's length, squint your eyes and wrinkle your nose, the device looks like a dead mouse.

### Did You Ask Why?

**Cleaning the Mouse**

It's important and easy to **keep your mouse clean**. As you're rolling it around you can feel if any cat hairs or dustballs have gotten inside. Take it apart regularly and clean it, following these steps:

1. Take the mouse in your hand and turn it upside-down.

2. With your thumbs, slide the round wheel to the left until the little marker on the wheel points straight up to the "O" (those little symbols on the back of the mouse actually are an "O" and an "L" for Open and Lock). This will open the lid.

3. Turn it back over into your left hand so the lid and the ball fall out into your palm.

4. You can clean the ball with a soft, dry cloth; clean the rollers inside with a cotton swab dipped in rubbing alcohol.

5. When clean, put the ball in your left hand; with your right hand place the mouse on top of the ball and flop your hands over. This places the ball safely into its little cubby.

6. Put the lid back on and twist it to the right, lining up the marker with the "L" for Lock. That's it!

# CHAPTER FIVE

Almost every program you'll ever use on the Mac has a **menu** across the top of the screen. This is called a **pull-down menu**, because when you point to a menu item and *press* the mouse button down, a list of menu commands drops down.

## Pull-Down Menus

| | | | | | | | |
|---|---|---|---|---|---|---|---|
| 🍎 | **File** | **Edit** | **View** | **Label** | **Special** | ⑦ | ▣ |

*The Desktop, or Finder, Menu*

To **choose** an item in the menu, simply keep the mouse button pressed and slide the pointer down; you'll notice that certain commands become selected, or *highlighted,* as you pass over them. When the command you want is highlighted, *just* **let go** *of the mouse button—don't click!*

## Choosing a Menu Item

*The command "Close" is highlighted—just let go to choose it!*

In some programs the pull-down menu itself contains a **pop-out menu** where you not only slide *down,* but also *out to the side,* usually (but not always!) in the direction of the arrow. These are also known as **hierarchical menus,** or **h-menus**

You will also find *pop-up* menus, where you press on an item toward the bottom of the screen and the list pops upward.

## Pop-Out Menus

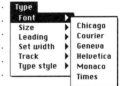

*Pop-out menus don't always pop out in the direction of the arrow!*

## Gray vs. Black Commands

**File**
New Folder
Open
Close
Get Info
Eject

*Some commands are gray; some are black.*

In the list of menu commands, you can see that some **commands** are in **black** letters and some commands are in **gray**. When a command is gray, it means that particular command is not available at that moment.

The most common reason that a command is unavailable is that you did not *select* something before you went to the menu. For instance, you cannot choose "Open" from the File menu if you haven't first selected a disk or file as the item to be opened. You cannot "Copy" text unless you have first selected the text you want to copy. To select an object, click *once* on it; to select text, press-and-drag over it.

## Keyboard Command Shortcuts

**File**
New Folder ⌘N
Open ⌘O
Get Info ⌘I
Eject ⌘E

*Sometimes the keyboard shorcut on the right of the menu will include other symbols; see the following chapter.*

To the right of the commands in the pull-down menus you often see a little code, such as ⌘N. This is a **keyboard shortcut** you can use *instead* of using the menu. Memorize it from the menu, then use it instead of picking up your mouse.

**To use a keyboard shortcut**, hold down the Command key (the one with the apple and the cloverleaf symbol on it: ⌘). While this key is down, type the letter associated with it. The computer reacts just as if you had chosen that command from the menu. For instance, if you click once on a file to select it and then press ⌘O, the selected file will open just as if you had chosen that command from the File menu with the mouse. Thoughtfully, most of the keyboard shortcuts are alliterative: **⌘O O**pens files; **⌘P P**rints; **⌘E E**jects; **⌘W** closes **W**indows; etc.

In written documentation you will see keyboard shortcuts spelled out with a hyphen, a plus sign, or perhaps a comma between the keys. *Don't type the hyphen, the plus sign, or the comma!* Just press the keys! For instance, if you see a shortcut spelled out as "Command + Shift + B" ignore the plus signs—just hold down the Command and Shift keys, then tap the letter B. I wish they wouldn't write them like that.

Anytime you see an **ellipsis** (the three dots: **…**) after a menu command (as in "Open…" or "Save as…"), it means you will get a **dialog box**. There are different varieties of dialog boxes, such as alert boxes or message boxes, but basically they all are meant to communicate with you.

Dialog boxes always give you an option to **Cancel**, so it is quite safe to go exploring menu commands this way. Just choose a command that is followed by an ellipsis, check out the dialog box, then click Cancel. Even if you click around on buttons or type in the dialog box, clicking the Cancel button will make sure none of your changes are put into effect.

*A "Save as…" dialog box; notice you can click the button to Cancel. You can also click the Eject button to eject a floppy disk if you need to remove or swap disks.*

You'll find other menus in all kinds of odd places. Well, they won't seem so odd once you become accustomed to the visual clue that indicates a menu is hiding. In the dialog box below, can you guess which boxes have menus hiding beneath them? (See the next page.) Also, what do you think will happen if you click on either the button "Rules…" or "Spacing…"?

*Both the "Rules…" and the "Spacing…" buttons have ellipses, indicating that if you click either button you will get another dialog box.*

## Ellipses… & Dialog Boxes

*Take advantage of those ellipses to snoop around!*

## Other Menus

**Watch for Shadows**    Notice that the boxes for "Alignment" and "Dictionary" have a little **shadow** behind them. That little shadow tells you that if you press on the word, you will get a pop-up menu. Look for that shadow!

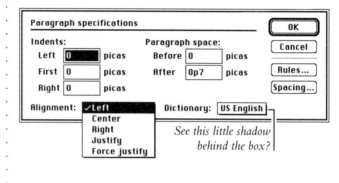

**Sideways Arrows and Edit Boxes**    Here is a closer look—in the example below, the **edit box** for "Bottom" has no shadow behind it; "Grid size" has a shadow, plus it has an **arrow**, which is another visual clue indicating a hidden menu.

Bottom:  `2`  picas

Grid size: `0`  points   *When you see a sideways arrow in its own box (as in "Grid size"), you can press on the arrow to get the menu, **or** you can type right in the edit box to change the information.*

*You can type in an **edit box** to make changes.*

| |
|---|
| 6 |
| 8 |
| 9 |
| 10 |
| 12 |
| 14 |
| 18 |

**Downward Arrows**    When you see a **downward-pointing arrow**, generally above a list box, you can press anywhere in that label to view and choose from the menu.

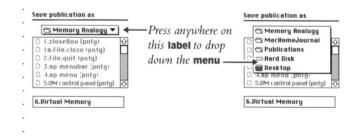

*Press anywhere on this **label** to drop down the **menu***

# CHAPTER SIX

# IMPORTANT KEYS

There are several keys on the Macintosh **keyboard** that are particularly important and useful. They come in handy for shortcuts, manipulating images, accessing alternate characters, and any number of things in specific applications.

Speaking of keyboards, there are basically two kinds for the Mac. There is the *standard* keyboard with the keypad at the end (like a ten-key adding machine)—one version for the Mac Plus and older models, and one for SEs, Classics, and similar models. And there is the *extended* keyboard that has all the function keys and other little arcane sets of keys. Often people think the *standard* keyboard is the *extended* one because it has the numeric keypad (that calculator pad on the right) that we didn't have on our typewriters. It isn't. Both keyboards have standard characters, although they may be in different placements on different models. No matter where they are placed, though, all the keys perform the same function (although the function of some keys varies from program to program).

The symbols shown in the outer column under each of the following headings are the symbols that will appear in menus to indicate pressing that key. Most of these keys are called **modifier keys** because they usually don't do anything all by themselves, but they are used in combination with regular keys to make something happen, like keyboard shortcuts (see "Keyboard Command Shortcuts" on page 32). The Shift key, for instance, is a modifier key

## The Keyboard

## Modifier Keys

you are already familiar with. The Shift key doesn't do anything all by itself, but if you hold it down while you type an alphabetic character, you get a capital letter instead of a lowercase.

Sometimes the keyboard shortcut uses more than one modifier. Always hold down all the modifier keys together (Command, Shift, Option, etc.) while you give a quick tap on the associated letter key. For instance, to *paste* an item the shortcut is ⌘ **V**: hold down the Command key and type a quick V. If you *hold* the character key down, you will often end up repeating the command.

**Any Key**

There really is no **Any key**. When a direction tells you to "PRESS ANY KEY," it means to press any key you want on the whole keyboard.

**Caps Lock**

The **Caps Lock key** does *not* act just like the Shift Lock on a typewriter. In Caps Lock you get capital letters, yes, but you do *not* get the characters above the numbers or above the punctuation. If you want the Shift-characters you must still press the Shift key to get them. Some keyboard shortcuts will not work if the Caps Lock key is down, so check its position if you're having problems.

**Command Key**

⌘

*In the Chicago font, press Control Q to produce ⌘.*

The **Command key** is on the bottom row, the key with the California freeway cloverleaf symbol on it: ⌘. On most keyboards it also has an apple on it, and you may hear it referred to as the "Apple key" or "Open Apple." Most keyboard shortcuts you see listed in the menus use the Command key.

**Control Key**

**ctrl**

∧

The **Control key**, found only on the bigger, "extended" keyboards, doesn't do much yet in many applications. Often it's just a dead key, although more programs are using it in keyboard shortcuts and commands. And it's important for people who are running DOS programs on the Macintosh.

The **Delete key** (labeled the **Backspace key** on older keyboards), is located on the upper right. The name was changed to Delete because that's really what it does—whatever is *selected* will be removed when the Delete key is hit; whatever letter is to the *left* of the insertion point will be deleted as it is backspaced over.

**Delete Key/ Backspace Key**

The **Enter key** on the numeric keypad will also activate buttons with the double border, just the same as the Return key as noted below, and it will usually start a new paragraph as well. Different programs use the Enter key in many different ways.

**Enter Key**

⌃

The **Escape key** on the upper left of the larger keyboards is another key that we will grow into. It's used in a few programs (like SuperPaint, to undo the latest action), but at the moment not too many programs make use of it. If your screen freezes (when neither the keyboard nor the mouse have any effect), you can try holding down Command Option and then pressing the Escape key. This will often, but not always, unfreeze the screen.

**Escape Key**

esc

*This is a "force Quit." See page 233.*

Next to the Command Key is the **Option key**. It's often used in combination with the Command key and/or the Shift key. It's through the Option key that you access the special characters, such as ¢ and ®, as well as accent marks, as in résumé and piñata (see page 99).

**Option Key**

⌥ or ⌥

The **Return key** is often used for other procedures than simply starting a new paragraph. For instance, any button in any dialog box that has the double border around it can be activated with the Return key instead of the mouse. Different programs use it in different ways.

**Return Key**

¶

The **Spacebar** is represented in menus by the symbol shown to the right *or as a blank space*. That blank space will really throw you. How long does it take to figure out that "⇧⌘ " means to press the Shift key, the Command key, and the Spacebar?

**Spacebar**

␣

**Shift Key**
⇧

The **Shift key** is one of the most common keys used in keyboard shortcuts, symbolized by an upward arrow.

**Tilde Key**
~

The **Tilde key** (~) is located on the upper left of some keyboards and next to the Spacebar on others. It's often called the Undo Key, because in certain applications it will undo the action immediately preceding (such as in SuperPaint or HyperCard). Although on some keyboards the upper left key now says **esc** (*escape*) and the Tilde has been placed next to the Spacebar, in many applications *esc* can still be considered the Undo key because it usually does the same thing.

**Asterisk**
⋆
**(star)**

The **asterisk** (⋆) is used as a multiplication symbol in calculators, spreadsheets, databases, etc. You can use the asterisk on the numeric keypad or you can press Shift 8 to get the asterisk above the number 8 on the keyboard. This symbol is also known as the **star** key (I think it's become known as the star key because so few people can spell or pronounce "asterisk.")

**Forward slash**
/

The **forward slash** (/) is used as a division symbol, in calculators, spreadsheets, databases, etc. You can use the slash on the numeric keypad or the one on the regular keyboard. Don't use the straight slash ( | ) or the backward slash ( \ ) when you mean to divide.

**Fkeys**

The **Fkeys** are at the top of the *extended* keyboards, that row of keys labeled F1, F2, F3, etc. If you don't see Fkeys, you don't have an extended keyboard, (that's okay if you don't—you can live without it). But those Fkeys are handy for shortcuts. In most programs you can press F1 to *undo* your last action; you can press F2 to *cut* an item, F3 to *copy,* and F4 to *paste* (see pages 95-96 for information on what it means to cut, copy, and paste). Some programs use the other Fkeys in other ways, and you can even program the extra ones yourself.

The **Tab key** (upper left) acts like a Tab key on a type-writer in that when you press the Tab key you'll start typing at the next tab stop you have set. In most word processing programs, you simply click in the ruler you see across the top of the screen to create a tab stop (press-and-drag the tab down off the ruler to remove it).

An aside: Electronic tabs in word processing and page layout can be tricky to work with until you understand their electronic logic (yes, there is logic). Keep in mind, as you scream and yell at tabs and indents, that tabs and indents are extremely consistent and dependable and *they do exactly what you tell them.* But *you* need to know what you are telling them.

In spreadsheet and database programs, the Tab key will move the selection to the next cell or field *to the right,* just as it would move your typing to the right (the Return key will move the selection to the next cell or field *down*). You can usually hold the Shift key down as you press Tab to move the selection backwards to the left (or Shift Return to move up).

Depending on your keyboard, you may have **arrow keys** (keys with nothing but an arrow on them) tucked in with your letter keys, or you may have a separate little set of four arrow keys. Arrow keys are used in different ways in different programs. In word processing programs you can use the arrow keys to move the insertion point.

> Usually if you hold down the Shift key as you hit the arrow key, the text will be selected as the insertion point moves along. Try it.

Other programs, such as page layout or graphics programs, may use the arrow keys to nudge graphic images around on the screen. In spreadsheets and databases, they might be used to move the insertion point or they might be used to select other cells or fields.

*—arrow keys continued*

## Tab Key

➡|

*The Tab key is not usually used in conjunction with other keys. You may see this symbol in word processing to indicate that a Tab has been pressed.*

## Arrow Keys

→ ↔ ↕ ↕

**RightArrow**
**LeftArrow**
**UpArrow**
**DownArrow**

In the documentation I write I use what might seem like an odd convention for naming the **arrow keys**, as shown in the left column. I do this because I have seen beginners follow a command such as "Press Command + right arrow" by pressing the Command key and then looking for the key that says "right," plus an arrow key. (And many new users also try to press the + key.) So it seems to me that even though it may seem odd at first, combining the two words at least makes it clearer that there is just one key.

**Numeric Keypad**

On the far right of the keyboard is a **numeric keypad** that looks like calculator keys. These keys will sometimes type numbers and  sometimes move the insertion point. Sometimes they do both, depending on whether you have pressed the "Clear" key (sometimes called "Num Lock" because it locks the keypad into typing numbers). In the Calculator desk accessory, these keys can operate the calculator. The asterisk (∗) is the multiplication key, and the slash (/) is the division key.

**Edit Keys**
**Help**
**Home**
**End**
**PageUp**
**PageDown**
**Del**
**Ins**

If you have an extended keyboard, you have an extra little set of keys between the alphabet keyboard and the numeric keypad called the **edit keys**. These keys are primarily there to make the Macintosh compatible with IBM PC programs. Not many Mac programs use these keys, although if you read your manual you may be surprised. Try them in your word processor. Or select a file in a Desktop window and try the PageUp and Down keys, as well as Home and End.

**Power-On Key**

The **Power-On key** is the big key embossed with a left-pointing triangle, found at the top of some keyboards and at the upper right in others. This key turns on some models of Macintosh. On the other models, it's a useless key. The Power On key makes it very easy for your cat or your small child to turn on your Mac when you least expect it. Thank goodness this key does not turn the machine off.

# CHAPTER SEVEN

# ALL WINDOWS

A **window**, as shown below, is a basic, fundamental element of the Macintosh. The first windows you'll use on the Mac will be those at the Desktop (or *Finder*). In this chapter I explain the details you will find in just about *every* window on the Mac, whether it is in your word processor, spreadsheet, database, or whatever application you love to work with, *as well as* the windows at the Desktop. But because Desktop windows have many more features than the windows you will use in your applications, I've devoted the entire Chapter 8 exclusively to the features of Desktop windows.

You will find each of the items labeled below in just about every window on the Mac *(icons are only found at the Desktop)*.

**Windows**

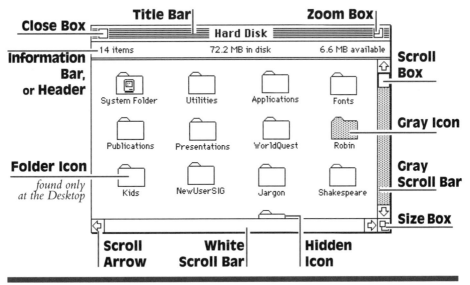

**Title Bar**

The **title bar** is the area at the top of the window in which, logically, the title appears. This title is the name of the disk, folder, or document you have opened.

**Moving the Window**

If you position the pointer in the title bar, then press-and-drag, you can **move** any window around the screen. As you drag, you will see the *outline* of the window. Just let go when you have the outline placed where you want, and the window will appear in that position.

**Active Window**

If you have more than one window open, only one will have lines in its title bar; this means it's the **active window**. If the windows are overlapping, the active window is the one that is foremost.

The active window is the window that the commands from the keyboard or the menu will affect. For instance, if you go to the File menu and choose "Close," it will close the active window. If you choose to "Paste," the item will be pasted into the active window.

**To Make the Window Active**

To make a window **active**, simply click on any visible part of it; this will also bring that window to the front of any others. You may have to move other windows around in order to see the window you want to make active.

> To move a window *without* making it active, hold down the Command key while you press-and-drag in its title bar.

**Size Box**

On the bottom right corner is the **size box**. If you press-and-drag in the size box, you will make the window larger or smaller. This is great—if you have several windows open, you can resize and rearrange them so they all fit on your screen without overlapping. You can have two word processing documents on the screen, or perhaps a database file and a spreadsheet worksheet and a word processing letter, and view them all at the same time.

On the upper right corner is the **zoom box**. If you click in the zoom box it will enlarge to fill almost the entire Desktop. If you click in it when it's large, the window will zoom back down to the size it was *just before* you zoomed it larger.

**Zoom Box**

Along the right and bottom edges of the window are the **scroll bars**. The scroll bars allow you to view everything in the window, even if it cannot all fit on the screen at once or if the window is sized too small. You'll notice in the example on page 41 that the scroll bar along the right side is gray, while the one on the bottom is white.

**Scroll Bars**

When a **scroll bar is gray**, it indicates that there are other items in the window you can't see. In the example on page 41, you can see a folder along the bottom edge that is barely visible, so the scroll bar is gray, telling you something more is beyond its borders. When you see a gray scroll bar in a list of items, such as in an "Open" dialog box, it means there are more items in the list than can be displayed. You need to scroll to see the others.

**Gray Scroll Bar**

When the **scroll bar is white**, it indicates there is nothing more in the direction of the arrows (the horizontal direction in the example) than what you can see.

**White Scroll Bar**

At either end of the scroll bars are the **scroll arrows**. When the scroll bar is *gray* you can press on a scroll arrow, making the contents of the window glide past you, like the scenery outside a train window.

**Scroll Arrows**

Notice the little **scroll box** in the gray scroll bar (you will *only* see a scroll box if the scroll bar is gray). As you press on the arrows, this box moves so you can tell what portion of the window you are viewing. When the scroll box is all the way at one end, that's the end of the list or of the window. Some people call the scroll box an *elevator* because it goes up and down like one.

**Scroll Box**

*Scroll Box*

## Press-and-Drag the Scroll Box

*Press-and-drag this scroll box*

Another useful technique using the scroll box is this: if you **press-and-drag the scroll box**, you can move it to any position on the scroll bar, let go, and the window will immediately jump to that particular place rather than scroll through everything. This is very handy inside an application like a word processor where you have a long document and scrolling with the arrows would take too long. In some applications a number appears within the scroll box to indicate what page you're on.

## Click in the Scroll Bar

There's yet another way to use the scroll bars: if you simply **click** the pointer in any *gray* area of the bar, the window will move up, down, or across, usually a full window view—what was at the bottom of the view will then be at the top or vice-versa.

## Close Box

And, of course, in the upper left is the **close box**. Click once in that little box to close the window, which sends the document it was displaying back to the disk or folder it came from. Many programs use the keyboard shortcut Command W to close the *active window*. That is, instead of clicking in the close box, you can press Command W to put the window away.

## Information Bar, or Header

| 4 items | 596K in disk | 175K available |

The example on page 41 shows an **information bar**, or **header**, that provides information about the window and the disk. You will only see this kind of information bar when you're looking at windows at the Desktop/Finder (see page 49 for details). Within programs, this area in the window may vary. For instance, in a word processing program, you'll see a ruler at the top of the window instead of this information bar.

# CHAPTER EIGHT

The Macintosh allows you a great deal of control over the look and the feel and the options available so you can arrange your work in a way that is most effective for *you*. The **Desktop windows** are a good example—you can choose to see what's in your window in a variety of ways, all appropriate for different purposes or styles; you can organize them any way you like, you can create new icons for the files. The techniques in this chapter apply only to the windows on the Desktop level (also called the Finder).

## Desktop Windows

You can change how you **view** the items in a Desktop window. These different views are found, of course, in the View menu when you're at your Desktop. First click anywhere in the window to make it *active,* because when you choose a view it applies to the *active window* (the one that has the lines in its title bar). The window will stay in that display until you change it.

## Views of the Window

The options you see in the Views menu depend on what you have chosen in the Views Control Panel. So if one of these views interests you but you don't see it in your menu, read the details on page 48 for customizing your window and menu.

*This is the View menu. Yours may not look exactly like this because your Views Control Panel has different options checked.*

**View by Small Icon** retains that feeling of looking at pictures, if that's what you prefer, but the icons are tiny so you can fit more in the window. The icons are not arranged in any specific order.

### View by Small Icon

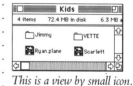

*This is a view by small icon.*

**45**

**View by Icon**

**View by Icon** is what you typically see—icons are the pictures representing the files. Visually-oriented people (like me) tend to prefer to view by icon. The files are in no specific order, although there is a little trick by which you can organize the icons by name or size or date, etc. See page 50.

**The List Views**

The rest of the view options do not show icons—the files are arranged in a **list**. When you view the files as a list, you can still manipulate any item in the list just as if it was an icon; that is, you can pick it up and put it in the trash or in another folder, rename it, copy it, open it, etc. (see Chapter 9 on Icons). For information on what those little triangles are doing in your window, see Chapter 10 on Folders.

If you are viewing the window by one of the lists (Name, Size, Label, etc.), you can switch views simply by clicking once on another column header in the information bar, instead of having to choose it from the menu. You'll see an underline below the header that indicates how the list is currently organized.

*Click on one of these column headers to switch to that view.*

| Hard Disk | | | | |
|---|---|---|---|---|
| Name | Size | Kind | Label | Last Modified |
| ▷ ☐ Applications | — | folder | — | Fri, Oct 16, 1992, 7:55 PM |
| ▷ ☐ Fonts | — | folder | — | Wed, Oct 14, 1992, 12:28 PM |

**View by Name**

**View by Name** turns the icons into text for those who prefer looking at words rather than pictures. A tiny little generic icon is still present so you can see what sort of file it is. They're listed in alphabetical order by name.

If you would like to view your list by name yet still see the individual icons that belong to the files, use the Views Control Panel to make the icon bigger. See page 50, "List View Icons."

**View by Size** lists the files in order of size, beginning with the largest. It tells you how much space, in K (kilobytes), that particular file is taking up on your disk. This is handy if you need to remove something to make more room on a disk; you can see which files you would need to remove to clear enough space. Or organize a window full of graphic files by size so you can keep tabs on reality.

*View by Size*

Unfortunately, View by Size won't show the size of folders; to find their size you need to select the folder and choose "Get Info" from the File menu (see page 66). *Or* you can customize the view so it *will* display the sizes of folders (see the Views Control Panel, page 48), but then it takes too long to display the list.

**View by Kind** lists the files in groups of applications, documents, or folders. This is handy if you want to see a list of all your applications, or all the documents you've stored in your budget folder, etc.

*View by Kind*

> View by Kind is particularly useful for a folder that holds an application and all its accessories— dictionaries, tutorials, technical files, samples, etc. This view will always put the application itself at the *top* of the list so it's easy to find.

**View by Label** groups the files according to their label. A label is something you make up and apply to a file. For instance, you can create a label called Love Letters and apply it appropriately. Then when you View by Label, all the love letters in that window will be grouped together. For details on labeling, see page 162, Labels Control Panel.

*View by Label*

**View by Date** lists the files in chronological order backwards from the date they were last *modified,* not the date they were originally created. This is handy when you have, for instance, several budget documents and you want to see the most recent edition.

*View by Date*

**View by Version** · **View by Version** lists the files in alphabetical order, with
· applications being listed first. Each application has its
· version number displayed. Have you ever noticed how
· many copies of TeachText you have in your computer?
· Well, you can use Find File (Chapter 26) to find and
· gather them all into one folder, then view that folder By
· Version. Throw out all but the newest version, the one
· with the highest number.

**View by**  · **View by Comments** will display in the window the first
**Comments** · 31 characters of the text you typed into the Comments
· box in the Get Info window (see page 66).

**Customize the** · You can **customize** the information displayed in these
**Window View** · lists; that is, you can choose to show just the labels, or
· just the dates they were last modified, etc. You can also
· customize the size of the icon that shows in a list view, as
· well as the typeface, and also how you want the icons to
· align. To get the **Views Control Panel**, choose "Control
· Panels" from the Apple menu. Double-click on "Views."

*Press on this box to
get a menu listing
all the fonts you
have installed. The
one you choose is
the one that will be
used in your
Desktop windows.*

*Press this arrow to get a list of font sizes.
Choose one, or type in a number.*

*If you check this,
your icons will
always snap to the
nearest empty spot
in the underlying
invisible grid.*

**Views**

Font for views: **Geneva**  ▼  **9** ▼

Icon Views
⦿ Straight grid
○ Staggered grid
☐ Always snap to grid

*You can choose
whether the invisible
grid that icons will
snap to is straight
across or staggered
(staggered gives more
room for long names).*

List Views
⦿  ○  ○

☒ Show size
☒ Show kind
☒ Show label
☒ Show date
☒ Show version
☒ Show comments

☐ Calculate folder sizes
☒ Show disk info in header

*You can choose to
have the size of
folders displayed in
a list, but keep in
mind that it then
takes much longer
to open windows.*

*Choose this to have two lines
of information in the window
header—disk information and view
information. See the following page.*

*Click any number
of these to determine
what information you
want displayed in
your window when
you view as a list.
The ones you choose
here will also appear
in the View menu
at the Desktop.*

Keep in mind when you choose a font for your windows that fonts with city names are easier to read on the screen (fonts like Geneva, New York, Boston, etc.). Also, when you choose a size, the size number that is in outline style will be easier to read on the screen also (see the note ☞).

*Now, I do hope no one is ever so mean to you as to sneak into your Views Control Panel when you aren't looking and change the font to something like Zapf Dingbats or Symbol, and perhaps the size to 24. Won't they be embarrassed when you catch them, tell them to change it back, but they can't find the Views Control Panel again because it now looks like this: ✳❈❊▶▲. Well, don't worry, you'll show them—from the Apple menu, choose "Control Panels." Type the letter **v** to select "Views." Press Command O to open the control panel, and you can correct the font.*

### Font and font size

*Not only in your windows, but everywhere on the Mac you will notice that the size that is displayed in the menu in the outline style (9 and 12 in this example) will look clearer on the screen.*

When you choose **Staggered grid**, the icons will align in a staggered format, which gives you a little more room for those files with long names.

Whether you choose staggered or straight, the **Snap to grid** button will make all icons snap to either the straight or the staggered grid. You already knew this, but what I really want to tell you is that you can hold the Command key down as you move icons and it will override whether that box is checked or not. That is, if the box is *not* checked, when you hold the Command key and move an icon, that icon will snap into a cubby on the grid. If the box *is* checked, when you hold the Command key and move an icon, it will *not* snap into a spot on the invisible grid and you can put it wherever you want.

### Staggered grid and Snap to grid

*A staggered grid leaves more room for long file names, which is especially handy if you have enlarged the font size.*

Just under the title bar there is very useful **information**. *If your window is showing icons,* you'll see how many items are in that window, how much space is being used and how much space is left on the disk. *If your window is not showing icons,* then the information bar indicates how your files are currently being organized, but not how much space is on your hard disk. You can customize the bar so you can see *both* lines of information, as shown in the example to the right. Click "Show disk info in header" in the Views Control Panel.

### Information Bar, or Header

*In the information bar above I see both rows of information.*

**List view icons**

*Click the largest icon to view your window as shown to the right.*

When you choose a **list view**, you no longer have the advantage of seeing the **icons** which give you so many visual clues about their function—all you see are generic little icons that give you a hint that the file is a folder or a generic document or application. But if you click one of the larger icon sizes in the Views Control Panel, as shown to the left, you can have the best of both worlds—you can view the contents as a list, but still see the specific icon for the file.

**Clean Up Window**

*This is the button I want in my house—the dishes jump onto their shelves, the laundry puts itself away in the drawers, and all the toys go back in the toybox.*

When you're viewing *icons* in your window, they often get all scrambled up and the place looks like a mess. To align all your icons nicely, simply choose **Clean Up Window** from the Special menu—all the icons will fly to the nearest little cubby available on the underlying invisible grid. If the name of an icon is too long, though, there will be an empty spot next to that icon so its name doesn't bump into the next icon. That's a good reason to give your files short names, and to never use all capitals letters because they take up twice as much room (besides being more difficult to read).

▼ If you want to **force an icon** into one of those empty spaces, hold the Command key down while you drag the icon near the space. The Mac will pull it in and tuck it right into the invisible cubby.

▼ To **organize the icons**, here's a good trick: If you hold the Option key down before you choose "Clean up Window," the Mac will arrange the icons according to the last list view you chose! For instance, choose "By Size" and you will get a list in order of largest to smallest. Then choose "By Icon" again. Now hold the Option key down while you press on the Special menu, and you'll notice the menu command has changed to "Clean up by Size." Cool.

▼ **To clean up selected icons**, press the Shift key as you choose "Clean Up" from the Special menu. Selected icons will snap to the nearest available spot on the invisible grid.

▼ If you click on one of the items on your Desktop, such as your hard disk icon or the trash can (or if you press Command UpArrow), then the Special menu will show **Clean Up Desktop**. Choosing this command will make all the icons (not the open windows) on your Desktop snap to the nearest spot on the underlying invisible grid. If you press the Shift key first, then only the selected items will snap to the grid.

▼ If you press the Option key before you choose "Clean Up Desktop," then all the icons on the Desktop will snap over to the far right and will line up in alphabetical order (your hard disk always being first and the trash can always being last, though).

▼ No matter where you are or what is selected, if you hold the Command key down while you move an icon or group of icons, they will jump neatly to the nearest little cubby in the underlying invisible grid. (This is actually just overriding your choice of "Snap to grid" in the Views Control Panel [previous page]. If you choose *yes* to "Snap to grid," then the Command key works the opposite—instead of snapping to the grid, you can place the icon wherever you like.)

Also check out the information on the Views Control Panel (page 48) for even more ways to customize how you can clean up your windows.

Sometimes you can't see the window itself but you *can* see the **gray icon** of a folder or disk, which indicates the window is open somewhere, you just can't see it. In that case, double-click on the gray icon to bring its window forward and thus make it active. (Also see pages 61 and 119 regarding gray icons.)

*Clean up Desktop*

**Gray Icons**

## Close all the Windows

!

To simultaneously **close every window** that is open on your Desktop, hold down the Option key while you click in the active window's close box; all the windows will go away one after another!

▼ You'll notice in the File menu a keyboard command for closing the active window: Command W. If you want to close all the windows at once, press Command Option W and *all* the windows will fly home.

▼ Another fancy trick to close all the windows is to hold down the Option key when you choose "Quit" from any application. *Keep holding the Option key down until you see your Desktop.* When you arrive, there won't be a single window open. If you use this trick you can legitimately call yourself a Power User.

▼ Often the file you want to open is buried within several folders. Hold the Option key down while you double-click to open those folders. They'll close up behind you as you go along.

▼ When you eject a disk or turn off the computer, the Macintosh remembers which windows were open when you left. When you insert the same disk or when you turn the computer back on, those windows will re-open in the position you had left them in. You can take advantage of this fact, or you might find it irritating sometimes to open a disk and have windows pop up all over the place. But if you hold down the Option key when you insert a disk or start the computer, any windows that had been left open will be closed when you get to the Desktop.

## Hierarchy of a Window

!

To **view the hierarchy of a nested folder** (that means to see the folders that this particular folder is contained within), hold the Command key down and press on the title of the window (not the stripes in the title bar, but on the actual title itself). This displays a pull-down menu, as shown to the left. You can choose any other folder in that menu to open its window and bring it to the front. If you choose the bottom level of the hierarchy, which would be the disk, it will open and display the window for the disk.

The following three items are notes on how several of the common features of windows act a little **differently on the Desktop** than they do in applications.

### Minor Differences

▼ When you click in the **zoom box** (upper right of the window, see page 43), the window will only zoom open as large as it needs to be to display all the files. If you want to open the window as large as possible (yet still see the trash can), hold the Option key down as you click in the zoom box.

*Zoom box*

▼ The window will **scroll** as you drag an icon within it. When you let go of the mouse button, the icon will pop into the nearest space in the window. You can also press the arrow keys to select icons, which will in turn scroll the window as well. Or in a list view, you can press in a blank area and drag the mouse up or down to scroll. Also see the chapter on Selecting (page 75), because selecting icons can make the window scroll, plus there are some great tricks.

*Drag an icon to scroll*

▼ When you click on a window, that **window** becomes **active** and comes to the front, obscuring the other windows. Sometimes you don't want it to do that. Remember, you can *move* a window without making it active by holding down the Command key and dragging its title bar. Also, keep in mind that when you click on an item in a window that is *not* active, the window doesn't become active until you *release* the mouse button while the pointer's still in the window. This subtle bit of information makes it easier to move and copy items that are in different windows; that is, you can grab a file from an inactive window and drag it into another window without

*Active windows*

the first window popping up to the top. (Make sure you press on an icon or a file name, though; if you just click in any *blank* space in the window, that window will immediately become active and pop to the top.)

**Other Cool Tricks** There are a great number of **cool tricks** you can use to manipulate the windows at the Desktop (Finder). In fact, there are so many that Apple has provided several Help screens describing them. All of these shortcuts are embedded somewhere in this book in their appropriate places, but using the "Finder Shortcuts" information is probably handier than having to look them up, or worse yet, having to memorize them. But, y'know, if you *do* memorize and use them, you will really impress people.

To view these Help screens, press on the Help menu (the question mark in the far right of the menu bar). Choose "Finder Shortcuts."

If you don't see the "Finder Shortcuts" command, it is because you are not at the Finder (Desktop). To get to the Finder, press on the icon in the top far right of the menu bar, next to the question mark, and choose "Finder." Or, if your trash can is showing, click once on it.

Here's an **example** of a Finder (Desktop) shortcut:

| | |
|---|---|
| To make the desktop active | ⌘-Shift-Up Arrow |

This means that if you are looking at windows on the Desktop where there is probably an active window, and you want to make the *Desktop level active* (perhaps you want to make a new folder on the Desktop itself, not in a window, or you want to clean up the Desktop), then you can press Command Shift UpArrow. (You could also click on any icon on the Desktop, but this shortcut lets you do it without having to pick up the mouse.)

Occasionally you may have a need to **print** the information you find in a particular **window**. For instance, you might want to make a list of all the documents that are on that floppy disk, or all the dated budget files that are in the Budget folder. *This only works on the windows on the Desktop.* If you want to print a window or a screen within an application, or any dialog box, see the next page, "Print Other Windows."

To print the info in the active window:

▾ Turn on your printer.

▾ Make sure the window that contains the data you want is the active window (click once on it).

▾ From the File menu, choose **Print window...** (it's the very last item).

▾ In the Print dialog box, change any of the options to suit your fancy, then click OK (or hit the Return key).

The above procedure prints only the *visible* contents of the *active window*. While you are at the *Desktop* (this will only work at the Desktop level), if you want to **print everything on the screen**, the whole screen and nothing but the screen, then follow these steps:

▾ Turn on your printer.

▾ Make sure the Desktop is active (click on any icon on the Desktop, like the trash can or your disk, *or* press Command UpArrow).

▾ From the File menu, choose **Print Desktop...** (it's the very last item; if the command you see is "Print Window...," then you are not at the Desktop level).

▾ In the Print dialog box, change any of the options to suit your fancy, then click OK (or hit the Return key).

## Print Other Windows or the Screen

**Picture 1**

*If this picture doesn't open in TeachText, it is because you don't have the current version of TeachText. TeachText is free, and most people have about fifteen copies floating around in their computer. Just find a friend with the newest one, or look on any of your software disks—it's almost always included on a disk so you can read the important "ReadMe" files.*

If you want to print a picture of a window in an application, see if there is a command called "Print Window" in one of the menus. If not, then you can create and print a screen shot, or screen dump, of the entire screen.

▼ While the image you want to print is on the screen, press Command Shift 3. You will hear a nerve-wracking little sound as if a tiny fuse is breaking inside your computer and your screen will freeze for a moment. Don't worry—it's okay. The computer is taking a picture of the screen. *(Jimmy, one of my sons, tells me that the disturbing sound is the sound of a picture being taken. That one went right over my head.)*

▼ Now go to your Desktop and look in the window belonging to the hard disk. You will see a new item called "Picture 1." (If you can't find it, use "Find File," Chapter 26).

▼ Double-click on "Picture 1" and it will open in the application called TeachText, a tiny word processor.

▼ From the File menu, choose "Print…" and then click OK.

▼ After you print it, choose "Quit" from the File menu, *or* press Command Q.

## Outline View

If you are wondering about those little triangles to the left of folders in a list view, please see Chapter 10 on Folders, pages 72-73 in particular. The triangles in this **outline view** collapse and expand the folders so you can see what is inside each one without having to open a new window. There are some great tricks to working with these, all of which are explained in that chapter.

# CHAPTER NINE

# ICONS

**Icons**—the little pictures you see on the screen—are an intrinsic part of the look and feel of the Macintosh. Instead of having to type a code to get into an application or document, you simply click on the icon representing it.

> A note about clicking on icons—if you're trying to select or open it, don't click on the *name,* or the icon thinks you want to change the name.

The icons offer rich visual clues. At first they may look like an odd collection of junk, and many people instantly change their view to a list so they're not overwhelmed by all the pictures. But once you really look at them, you will see how much information an icon instantly provides. This information is valuable to you, and that's the purpose of this chapter—to help you take advantage of these clues. I suggest you leave your windows in the icon view for a while in the beginning. After you start seeing the patterns and noticing the clues, after you are comfortable with copying and moving and organizing your icons, go ahead and view your windows in whatever sort of list is useful to you (pages 45-48).

If you have a color or grayscale monitor, your icons will look fancier than the ones you see here in the book. I used black-and-white icons because they are clearer. *(Personally, I prefer a black-and-white monitor in general because it is so much easier to read, as well as the fact that it puts out less radiation than color.)*

**Icons**

System System

*If your icons are in color, they will look fancier than the black-and-white ones shown here in the book.*

### Disk Icons

*Hard disk*

*Floppy disk*

When you initially turn on your machine and get to the Desktop (as on page 23), you'll always see an icon of any **disk** you're using, whether it's a hard disk or a floppy (your hard disk icon may look different than this one shown, depending on where it is and what kind it is).

▼ Single-clicking on a disk icon will select it.

▼ Double-clicking on a disk icon will open it to show you a window displaying all the files.

*Note:* If a disk icon is gray, it is either already open (page 61) or has been left in RAM after being ejected (page 119).

### Folder Icons

Whenever you have a window open, most likely you'll see **folder icons**. They act just like folders in your filing cabinet in that you store items in them for organization, and you can open them to see what's inside. Be sure to read the following chapter on Folders, as they are an important tool.

▼ Single-clicking on a folder will select it.

▼ Double-clicking will open it to show you a window with all the files that are stored in that folder.

For Shannon

*This folder icon means I will share its contents with another computer.*

If a folder icon has a little dark bar across its tab, or if it has wires coming out the bottom, or if it has happy little faces on it, these are all visual clues indicating that this folder is being or is capable of being shared.

For Shannon

*When the **other** computer turns on file sharing, **my** folder gets happy faces.*

The icon that looks like a platter of items being served (shown below), indicates a file server. When a folder on one computer is being shared through a network, that folder appears on the *other* person's computer as this file server icon. This icon is like a folder in that you can double-click on it and there are things stored inside.

For Shannon

*On the **other** computer, the folder I am sharing is seen on **their** computer as this file server icon.*

For details on simple networking and sharing folders with other people in your home or office, see Chapter 27 on Sharing.

The **application** (or **program**) **icons** are the fancy ones. These belong to the actual applications (the software programs that you work in). Each application has its own design, so they all look different, but what they have in common is that they all try to give some sort of visual clue as to what they do. For instance, in the icons to the right you can see that SuperPaint is an art program; MacWrite II is a word processing program.

▼ Single-clicking on an application icon will select it.

▼ Double-clicking will open to either a new, blank page within that program, or at least to a dialog box where you can choose to *create* a new, blank page.

**Document icons** represent documents, or files, that you have created in any particular application. Whenever you are working in an application and you save your document with a title, a document icon is created for you on your Desktop.

Document icons almost always look like a piece of paper with the top right corner folded down, or perhaps a sheaf of papers or a stack of cards. Typically they have some resemblance to the application they were created in, as you can see by the SuperPaint and the MacWrite icons on the right, which match their corresponding programs as shown above.

▼ Single-clicking on a document icon will select it.

▼ Double-clicking will usually open the application in which the document was created, with that particular document on the screen. (If you get an error message, check page 234, "Can't open a file.")

▼ Dragging a document icon and setting it on top of its application will open the document. Actually, if there is another application that is capable of opening a file of this type, you can drop it onto *that* application icon. If it opens, it works. If it doesn't open, that particular application cannot open a file of that sort.

## Application Icons

MacWrite II

SuperPaint

*Application icons are typically rather fancy.*

## Document Icons

Article

Zamoura

*Document icons almost always have the top right corner turned down.*

## Blank Document Icons

Zamoura

*This is the same file as on the previous page. The fact that it is blank gives me a clue that the program it was created in is not installed in this computer.*

Letters

*This blank document icon, however, with the **bottom right corner turned up**, is a stationery pad (page 68).*

Microsoft Word

*Drag the icon on top of various applications and see if any of the others will open the file.*

Occasionally you will see a **blank document icon**. This usually means that the application in which this document was created is not in the computer. For instance, the blank document shown to the left is the same as the SuperPaint file on the previous page. When this file is in a computer that has SuperPaint installed, it looks like it belongs to SuperPaint. But when I copy the same file to a computer that does not have the application SuperPaint installed, the icon is blank. (But if the blank document icon has a *bottom* corner turned up, that's a visual clue that the document is actually a *stationery pad;* see page 68.)

If you double-click a blank document icon, you will see this message:

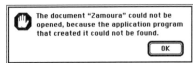

You can try dragging the document icon on top of various application icons. If an application can open a file of this type (Microsoft Word, for instance, can open almost any text file), the application icon will become highlighted (as shown at left). This is your clue that this application can open this file; let go of the document and it will open in that program.

It's difficult to find the source of a blank document icon without special utilities that tell you those sorts of things. If this is something you need to do often, ask for help at your local user group.

## System Icons

System   Finder   Finder Help

*Icons that are part of the operating system appear in all manner of sizes and shapes.*

Inside the folder named System Folder are **system icons** that help run the Macintosh, as well as a variety of icons that are for extra or fancy options. System icons represent programming that performs essential operations. You'll see a variety of types of system icons. You'll see one called System and one called Finder—if those two are not inside the System Folder, you won't even be able to use your machine.

▾ Single-clicking on a system icon will select it.

▾ Double-clicking will give you a message that "This file is used by the system software. It cannot be opened." That's because system icons are just visual representations of the data on your disk that makes them work—there's really nothing to look at besides the cute little icon. (Although you *can* open the System file itself; see page 127).

Your System Folder has quite a grand collection of icons, doesn't it? The System Folder is so important that it earns its own special chapter, page 127, and you should probably actually read it.

When an **icon is dark**, like the one on the right, that means it is *selected,* or *highlighted*—it got selected by someone clicking once on it. Once an icon is selected, you can press-and-drag it somewhere. Menu commands, such as Open or Put Away, will only affect highlighted icons.

## Highlighted (dark) Icons

Scarlett

▾ Single-clicking is what selected this icon in the first place.

▾ Double-clicking a selected icon will open it just like any other icon.

When an **icon is gray**, as the ones shown on the right, that means it's *already open.* Maybe you don't see the icon's window because it's hidden behind another open window, but you know it's open somewhere.

## Open (Gray) Icons

*An open folder icon*

Jargon

▾ Single-clicking on an open **folder icon** will select it.

▾ Double-clicking on an open *folder* icon will bring its window to the front as the active window.

Now, if the icon is not a folder, but a **disk icon**, one of two things is causing it to be gray: If the disk is still in the computer, its window is open somewhere, in which case you can just double-click on the gray icon to bring the window forward. But if the disk is not even in the computer, it means you have ejected the disk but the

*An open disk icon*

Fonts

computer is holding information about the disk in *memory*. See pages 119-120 for details on why this happened, what to do about it, and how to prevent it from happening.

Microsoft Word

*An open application icon*

If the icon is an **application icon**, it means the application is still open. If you double-click on its gray icon, the application will become active. So you double-click on it, and you say nothing happened? It did. Look at your menu bar. When you are at the Finder (Desktop), your menu bar will have the item "Special" in it, and the File menu does not have"Quit" at the bottom. Read Chapter 30 called Very Important Information. You need that information to have control over your Mac. And that control will make you happy and powerful.

## Moving Icons

To **move icons**, simply press-and-drag them. You can put any icon into or drag any icon out of any folder icon. For details, see Chapter 11 on Copying and Selecting.

## Renaming Icons

Rich Life Experiences

*When an icon is ready to be renamed, you'll see a border around the name.*

To **rename any icon**—a folder, a document, a program, a disk—just click once on the icon's name, not on the icon's graphic; then simply type the new name. A box appears around the name so you know you're changing it. Or instead of clicking on the name, you can select the icon and press Return to get that box around it. (The box and the insertion point do seem to be annoyingly slow to appear; be patient.)

Use standard word processing procedures to set an insertion point—double-click a *word* to select it, backspace to delete, etc., as detailed in Chapter 14 on Typing. As soon as you click somewhere else, or hit the Return or Enter keys, the name is set.

## Undo Icon Name Change

If you do **accidentally change the name** of an icon (which is very easy to do—files have been known to mysteriously change their names to \\\\\\\\\\\\ or `````` while you weren't doing anything but leaning on the keyboard), you do have one chance to restore the name to its original form: Undo. As soon as you see this mistake has been made, from the Edit menu choose "Undo." *If you haven't done anything* since this minor catastrophe (and things could be worse), Undo will restore the original name, even if you forgot it. If you are too late to catch Undo, you'll just have to rename it yourself (if you know what it was). Remember, the keyboard shortcut for Undo is Command Z.

You **cannot change the name** of a folder, disk, or application that is being **shared** (see the chapter on Sharing Files, page 181) or that is **locked**. A shared folder is indicated by a little black bar along the top of the tab, as shown to the right. A *disk* has no visual clue that it is being shared; the clue will be the fact that you don't get a border around the name when you click on it. If you really need to change the name of a shared item, you need to first turn sharing off (page 184). Even though a disk or folder may be shared, you can still change the name of any of their contents that are not being shared.

To unlock a *file* (folder, application, document, etc.), see page 67. To unlock a *disk,* see page 14.

If you have a color monitor, you can **color your icons** You can do this just for the heck of it, or to make your dull life more colorful, or you can use the color as an organizational tool. For instance, you may want to apply a passionate red color to all the love letters you have written and received. That way no matter what folder they are stored in or what sort of file they are (maybe you keep a database of all your lovers and letters, a stationery pad for multiple copies, a faxable version, and a graphic file of your photograph for sending over the modem), you can instantly recognize any file belonging to the passionate red classification.

To color an icon, use the Label menu. Just select the icon (click once on it), then from the Label menu, choose a

## If You Can't Change the Name

For Shannon

*The little black bar on the tab indicates that this folder is being shared.*

## Color Your Icons

Scrapbook of Lovers

*Color can be a very effective organizational tool.*

color. This will also apply the corresponding label to the file, which you can use for searching. For details on labeling and changing the color of the labels and thus the icons, see the chapter on Control Panels, page 163 in particular.

### Create Your Own Icons

Scarlett    Robin

*Click here to select the icon's image.*

Scarlett Info

Scarlett

**Kind**: DeskPaint® document
**Size**: 5K on disk (3,989 bytes used)

**Where**: Hard Disk: Robin:

**Created**: Wed, Sep 2, 1992, 9:21 PM
**Modified**: Wed, Sep 2, 1992, 9:42 PM
**Version**: n/a

**Comments**:

☐ **Locked**    ☐ **Stationery pad**

You can **create your own icons** and apply them to any existing icons. This is too cool.

▾ Open a graphic program like SuperPaint or MacPaint.

▾ In the graphic program, create the little picture that you want as your icon. You can also use any clip art or Scrapbook image. No matter what size you make the art, the Mac will reduce it to an appropriate size as it becomes the new icon. (If you create it too large, though, it will be unrecognizable when reduced.)

▾ Select the image you just created or found; copy it (from the Edit menu).

▾ Quit the graphics program. Go back to the Finder (press the Application menu in the far right corner of the menu bar; choose "Finder").

▾ Click once on the icon you want to replace. From the File menu, choose "Get Info" (or press Command I).

▾ Select the icon that appears in the upper left of the Get Info window (click once on it).

▾ From the Edit menu, choose "Paste" (or press Command V).

▾ Close the Get Info window (press Command W).

*Really, although this can be a wonderful trick, I don't like to encourage beginners to run around changing all their icons, because that original icon tells you so much information. If you start changing icons, how do you know what will happen when you double-click? Is this object a folder that will open to a window, or is it an application, or a document, or a system icon, or what? Just be sensible.*

To **change an icon back to the original**, select its tiny icon in the Get Info window and choose Clear or Cut (Command X).

Occasionally you will see or create an icon that is named Picture 1 or Picture 2, etc.; this is a **screen shot**, also known as a "screen dump" or "screen capture." A screen shot is a picture of the computer screen at the time you pressed the special key combination.

In the original edition of this book, I created all the pictures using screen shots. With the image on the screen in its natural habitat, I pressed Command Shift 3. Then I opened MacPaint and opened the Picture 1 file (it was called Screen 0 at that time) that had been created. Since the screen shot took a picture of the entire screen, I had to erase all the excess stuff around the image. Then I could change, resize, rotate, flop, etc., the graphic. I put the images in the Scrapbook (page 152) and later pasted them onto these pages. Now I use a screen capture program so I can selectively choose which portion of the screen I want to make a copy of, but screen shots still come in handy for many things, like when you want to capture the image of a dialog box or a warning message for later reference, or when you want to print an image or a window that you see on the screen.

**To take a screen shot**, press Command Shift 3. You will hear an unsettling noise, like a tiny fuse shattering, and your screen may freeze for a moment. Don't worry—the computer is just taking a picture of the screen. In the window for your hard disk you will see the Picture 1 icon as shown above. Every time you take a shot, the icon will have another number. You should rename the icons so you'll know what they are.

You can open the Picture 1 in most paint or draw programs and view/change the image just like you would any other graphic image. You can **print a screen shot** from the paint or draw program, or you can paste it into another document, like a letter or a newsletter. Or you can print a screen shot as is: simply double-click on the icon at your

## Screen Shot

Picture 1    Picture 2

*These icons represent screen shots. In case you wanna know, they are in the PICT format.*

*How to take a screen shot*

*How to print a screen shot*

**TeachText**

*You can open a screen shot in TeachText.*

Desktop. It will open in the utility called TeachText, which is a tiny, limited word processor that you probably have a dozen copies of. A screen shot in System 7 will only open in version 7.0 or later of TeachText (see the next entry for how to tell which version you have). To print it, just choose "Print..." or press Command P.

If you get a message when you double-click on Picture 1 that TeachText cannot open this kind of file or that you should try opening the document within the application, then first open TeachText (find it and double-click on it). An open window automatically shows up; close it by pressing Command W. From the File menu, choose "Open...," or press Command O. Find the name of the picture you want to open and double-click on its name. Now you should be able to print the image.

## Get Info

**Get Info** is not an icon, but a menu item that can give you important information about any file represented by an icon on your Desktop, be it application, document, system, folder, or any kind at all.

**Rich Life Experiences Info**

Rich Life Experiences

**Kind:** PageMaker 4.2 document
**Size:** 33K on disk (32,896 bytes used)

**Where:** Hard Disk : Robin :

**Created:** Wed, Jul 29, 1992, 1:12 PM
**Modified:** Wed, Jul 29, 1992, 1:12 PM
**Version:** n/a

**Comments:**

Socrates said the only thing we take with us when we die are our experiences. I say that it is therefore my moral obligation to collect as many rich life experiences as I can.

☐ **Locked**          ☐ **Stationery pad**

*This is the box in which you can type your own notes.*

Select an icon, any icon (or of course any file name in a list) by clicking once on it; then from the File menu choose "Get Info." You'll get a little information window that tells you interesting things about the file, such as how big it is, when it was made, which software program it was created in, which software version you have.

Another nice thing about this window is you can type your own information in the box at the bottom (the insertion point flashes, waiting for you to type). This comes in very handy: you can write notes to yourself about that particular file and what it contains, briefly detail this budget file from that budget file, make note of further changes you want to employ, leave notes for your lover, etc. The information is automatically saved.

You can also take advantage of the fact that Find File can search through these comments. Perhaps you have a great habit of making notes in this box about which files need to be updated. You can then search for all the files that need to be updated. See Chapter 25 on Find File.

*Use Find File to search comments*

You can also choose to view your Desktop window with these comments displayed (as shown below). Use the Views Control Panel to set this up (details on page 48).

*View comments in your Destop windows*

| Shakespeare | | | | |
|---|---|---|---|---|
| 1 item | | 76.3 MB in disk | | 2.5 MB available |
| Name | Size | Kind | Last Modified | Comments |
| MerryWives | 17K | Microsoft Word do... | Sat, Sep 12, 1992, 9:19 PM | Great story of strong women. |

*The comments will appear here.*

If at some point you choose to rebuild your Desktop (see page 228), the rebuilding process will unfortunately destroy any Get Info notes. Darn it.

There is a **Locked** checkbox in the lower left corner of the Get Info window. If you check this box (click once on it), this file cannot be renamed or inadvertently thrown away—as soon as it hits the trash a dialog box will come up telling you a locked file cannot be thrown away. It also becomes a *read-only* file: anyone can open and read the file, but no one can save any changes to it. This is handy for sending around copies of a document and ensuring no one accidentally changes anything. You can't even change the Get Info notes.

**Locking the File**

☒ **Locked**

*This file is now locked.*

> If you hold down the Option key, you *can* throw away a locked file. Uh oh.

!

To **unlock the file**, click in the checkbox again. If there is no X, it is unlocked. (To unlock a *disk,* see page 14.)

☐ **Locked**

*This file is now unlocked.*

## Stationery Pads

Fax Cover   Fax Cover

*On the left is the original PageMaker document. On the right is the stationery pad created from the PageMaker document. The visual clue is the turned up corner on the* **bottom** *right instead of the top right. Sometime a pad icon is* **plain white,** *as shown here.*

Letters

*This little button will eventually appear in most software.*

Also through the Get Info box you can make a template out of any document, called a **stationery pad**. The icon for it looks like a sheaf of papers, as shown on the left. Whenever you double-click a pad to open it, you'll open an *untitled* copy of the file (you may get a little dialog box telling you to name it before it opens). The original template, or stationery pad, remains unchanged so you always have a clean master copy.

To make a stationery pad, you need to be at the Desktop (Finder). Select a *document* icon by clicking once on it (this doesn't work on any other sort of file except a document). Press Command I to get the Get Info box, and click the checkbox at the bottom called "Stationery pad." If you don't see the checkbox, it's your clue that you can't make a template out of that file.

If your software application can make a template, then this stationery pad is no different than that template; it's just another way to do it. Eventually most applications will give you the option to create a stationery pad from within the Save As dialog box (as shown on the left). To create a stationery pad or template, click the icon that looks like a sheaf of papers.

## Putting Away Wayward Icons

Have you ever dragged a file out of its folder, left it on the Desktop, then forgot where it came from? Or perhaps someone else pulled it out and forgot to put it away and you don't know where it belongs. Or maybe you're just too lazy to do it yourself. Simply select the icon (click once on it), then from the File menu, choose **Put Away** (or press Command Y). A little invisible person grabs the file and puts it right back where it last came from.

You can also ask this little guy to put away a file that you stuck in the trash can and then changed your mind. Double-click the trash can to open it, select one or more files (hold down the Shift key to click on one or more), then press Command Y.

# CHAPTER TEN

# FOLDERS

## Folders

**Folders** are essential to the organization of your work on the Mac. They are, of course, visual representations of our office and home environment, and they function in much the same way.

You can consider your disk to be the main filing cabinet. When you store items in a filing cabinet, you don't just toss them in the drawer, do you? Can you imagine what a mess your filing cabinet would be without folders? Many Macintoshes become just as messy and just as difficult to find work in. It's very important to learn to take advantage of the folders.

**To create your own** new, empty folders, choose "New Folder" from the File menu, or use the keyboard short-cut, Command N. The new folder will appear in the *active* window (the window in front, the one with the stripes across the top), so make sure the window in which you want a new folder is active (click on it).

When the new folder appears in the active window it is already *highlighted,* or selected (it's dark), with the title "untitled folder." The Mac assumes you want to **change the name**, so while the folder is black with a white border around the title, you can just type the name you want it to have and the new name will appear. Yes, really, all you do is type. If you type an error, just backspace over the error (use the Delete key [Backspace] in the upper right of the keyboard) and continue typing. You can use up to 31 characters, but you can't use a colon. If you *try* to type a colon, the Mac will substitute a hyphen. After

## Creating a New Folder

## Naming the New Folder

*If you view your window "By Icon," this is what a new folder looks like.*

▷ ■ untitled folder

*If you view your window as a list, this is what a new folder looks like.*

you name the new folder, the border disappears as soon as you click anywhere else or hit the Return or Enter key. When the border disappears, you are no longer in the naming mode.

**Where did my new folder go?** If you are viewing your window in a list view, such as By Name or By Size, the new, *untitled* folder will appear in the list according to your view. For instance, if you are viewing your window By Name, the untitled folder will appear near the bottom of the list, alphabetized as "untitled." If you are viewing your window By Date, the untitled folder will appear first in the list because it is the most recent. After you name the untitled folder and click or hit the Enter key, *the new folder gets arranged in the list according to the view you have chosen.* That is, if you are viewing By Name, the folder will instantly get alphabetized into the existing list, which means it may disappear from your sight. You can use the scroll bars to go find it, or just type the first letter or two of its name and it will pop up again right in your face.

**Changing the Name of a Folder** If you accidently un-highlighted the new folder before you changed its name, or if you want to change the name of any other folder (or any icon of any sort, actually), it is still very easy to do: simply click on the *name* and the icon will turn dark with a border around the name. The border is a visual clue that whatever you type now will replace the title that is already there. So go ahead and type the new name while you see the border.

Once you click on the name, it seems to take a long time for the border to appear. For some reason, if you click on the name and then instantly move the mouse away, the border appears faster than if you click and don't move the mouse.

Use standard word processing procedures to type the new name: press-and-drag to select text; click to insert an insertion point; backspace to delete characters, etc. If you are careful, you can even double-click to select one word of the title, *after* the border has appeared.

**To put something inside** the folder, press-and-drag any icon over to it; when the folder turns black or changes color, let go and the icon will drop inside. You can have folders inside of folders inside of folders, which is technically called the *Hierarchical File System* (HFS). You can drag an item from one window and put it into a folder in another window.

The folder does not have to be open to place an item inside of it, and the folder can be gray. It does not even have to be an icon; you can use the same technique in any list of files in the window. The only trick is that you have to be able to see both the item you want to drop in *and* the folder you want to drop into. Sometimes this requires moving your windows around the screen so you can see both items at once.

**Putting Something Inside a Folder**

Double-click on any folder to **open** it to a window that displays all the valuable files you have stored inside. You can also, of course, select a folder (click once on it) and then choose "Open" from the File menu. Or select the folder and press Command O as a shortcut.

**Opening a Folder**

To **remove** something from a folder, you must *open* the folder first (see above) so you see its window and the icons inside. Then simply press-and-drag the icon(s) out, either to the Desktop or to another folder or window.

**Removing Something From a Folder**

If you are moving the file to someplace else on the *same* disk, the file will just pop out of that one folder and into the other. BUT if you are moving the file to a *different* disk, the original icon will stay put in the original folder and a *copy* of the file will be placed on the other disk. (See the tips on pages 75-76.)

**Note: Moving as opposed to Copying**

!

**Organizing Your Disk Using Folders**

Below is an example of a well-organized hard disk; there isn't a bunch of junk lying around making it difficult to find things. *(I wish it was this easy to keep a house organized.)* It's basically arranged the same way a filing cabinet would be.

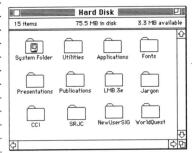

*Everything on the disk (the "filing cabinet") is tucked into a folder. The folders may each contain more folders to further organize their contents.*

**Outline Mode**

You may prefer to view your window as some sort of list, as described in the chapter on Desktop Windows (pages 45). When you choose any sort of list (by Name, Kind, Size, etc.) your folders are displayed in what is known as **outline mode**. There's a tiny triangle next to each folder's name, and if you click on that triangle you will see what's in that folder without opening another window. The items contained within a folder are indented just a little from the left, as you can see in the folder called "CCI" shown on the left.

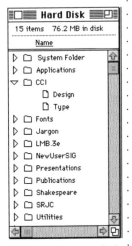

*When you see little triangles next to your folders, you are in outline mode.*

You can keep opening folders within folders until you are all the way to the bottom level of your filing system, *with everything displayed in the same window.* (If you accidentally double-click on the folder's *icon* instead of single-clicking on the *triangle,* you'll open a new window showing what's in the folder, as usual.)

Using the outline view, you can see at a glance exactly how your files are organized and what's in them. You can move items from one folder to another, even if the folders are several levels apart. You can Shift-click (page 79) to select items from any number of different folders. All of these techniques are explained in detail in Chapter 11 on Copying and Selecting.

To **expand**, or open a folder, single-click on the little sideways-pointing triangle (or select the icon and press Command RightArrow).

To **compress** or close a folder, single-click on the downward-pointing triangle (or select the icon and press Command LeftArrow).

To simultaneously **compress all the folders** that are expanded, press Command A to select everything in the window. Then press Command LeftArrow.

Or you can choose "By Icon" from the View menu. Then choose your preferred list view again. When you return to the list view, all the folders will be closed.

One of the best ways to keep windows tidy is to **create a specific new folder** for a new project *before* you create the documents for the project, and then *save the documents right into their own folder.* For instance, if you are about to create a budget report with seven variations, or a news-letter in which there will be ten to twelve separate stories, then follow these steps:

## Creating Project-Specific Folders

▼ **At your Desktop, before you open the application** to start creating the reports, make your new folder and name it (let's name this one *Budget News*). This new folder can be inside of another folder, of course.

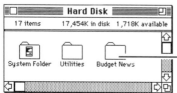

*This is the new folder in the hard disk window, waiting for you to save new stories inside.*

▼ Open your application and create the first report.

▼ When you choose "Save As…" and name the story, find the folder *Budget News* in the Save As dialog box (shown on the next page). *If you have trouble finding the folder, read the details in Chapter 15 on Saving, page 101.*

▼ In the list box you'll see the name of the folder you created earlier. Double-click the name ("Budget News" in this example) to open the folder.

*In this example, here in the list box is the folder Budget News; double-click the name to open it.*

*If you don't see the folder listed here, perhaps you have it tucked inside of another folder, in which case you will need to open that other folder first. Or click the Desktop button to see if the folder is on another disk.*

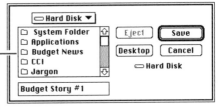

▼ After you double-click on the name of the folder, you will see its name and an open folder icon in the label above the list box, as shown below. If you choose to Save right now, it will be saved into *that* folder.

*Make sure this **label** shows the name of your folder.*

*If you see the name of your folder in this list box beneath the label, double-click on that name to open the folder and make its name appear in the label.*

**Whenever you save a file, it is always saved into whichever folder or onto whichever disk appears in this label.**

*This is the list box.*

▼ When you go back to your Desktop you'll find that everything is tucked away right where it belongs, right into its own folder, and nothing will have been misplaced.

If you refuse to read and follow these directions and have lost files because you don't know where you saved them, do read about Find File in Chapter 26. And when you really get frustrated with losing files all the time, read the special chapter on Navigating (finding your way around these dialog boxes), Chapter 29.

# CHAPTER ELEVEN

# COPYING AND SELECTING

**Copying files** is an everyday task. You may need to copy an application from its original disk onto your hard disk; copy a report to give to a co-worker; copy a document to take to a service bureau for printing; create the ever-necessary backup copy; etc., etc., etc.

Apple has made it as easy as possible to copy files on the Mac (which is why *pirating,* or copying software without paying for it, has always been such a problem for software developers). Copying files has no effect on the original file, nor is there any loss of quality in the new version—there is absolutely no difference between the original and the copy.

Actually, the copying process only works when you copy a file *from one disk to another disk.* When you drag an icon into another position on the same disk, you are simply *moving* the file, not *copying* it.

**To copy** a file from your hard disk to a floppy disk, simply click on the icon representing the file you want to copy; then press-and-drag that file to the icon of the disk you want to copy it onto. A little message comes up telling you it's being copied.

*This message will appear when you copy. Notice there are lines in the title bar; this is a visual clue that you can drag this message box around on the screen.***If you have a large file to copy, you can go back to work on something else during the process; from the Application menu, choose the program you were previously working in.**

### Why Copy?

### Copying from the Hard Disk to a Floppy Disk

!

*The trick to working while something is copying is that the work must be already open; you cannot open anything new while copying.*

You can copy from your hard disk onto a floppy disk, or from a floppy disk onto your hard disk, or into a folder on any other disk. In every case, make sure that the icon of the place you are copying *into* turns *black*. When the icon is black, that means it's ready to accept the file/s. If the icon is not black, you'll just be placing it *next* to the icon, not *inside* of it. The *tip of the pointer* is what turns any icon black. (When you copy straight into an open window, though, the window will not turn black. That's okay—it still works.)

**Copying from a Floppy Disk to a Hard Disk**

When you **copy from a floppy disk to your hard disk**, it is possible to press on the icon of the floppy disk and drag it onto the icon of your hard disk. The Mac will copy all the contents of the floppy disk. But unless you are absolutely sure that you want to copy every single item from the floppy disk, don't do it this way. Double-click on the disk icon to open its window. Take a look at the files on the disk, then selectively choose the ones you need to copy.

*Never copy another System Folder onto the hard disk! This isn't as common a problem as it used to be because now the System is so big it can hardly fit on a floppy disk. But just in case you have an older disk, perhaps with a game on it, that you want to copy onto your hard disk, keep in mind that you want to copy only the program and its related files, not another System file or System Folder.*

**Duplicate/Copy File on Same Disk**

The *copying* process, remember, only takes place if you drag the file to another *disk*. If you want to **make a copy of the file on the same disk**, first click *once* on the file icon to select it. Then from the File menu choose "Duplicate" (or press Command D). This creates a second version in the same folder named "Copy of _____." When you duplicate or copy *folders,* every item contained within that folder is also copied.

> If you want to put a *copy of a file into another folder* **on the same disk,** hold down the Option key while moving the file. This does *not* rename the file "Copy of _____."

Sometimes you need to copy information from one floppy disk onto another floppy disk. If you have two floppy disk drives, this is no problem, right? You stick a disk in each drive and do it. But most people do not have two floppy drives. There is a little trick to **copy from floppy to floppy with one floppy drive**

▼ Insert the floppy disk you want to copy *onto.* While the disk is selected (click once on the icon if it isn't), choose "Eject Disk" from the Special menu (*or you can press Command E*). This should eject the disk but leave a gray icon on the Desktop.

▼ Insert the disk to be copied *from.* Open this disk (double-click on the icon) and select the files to copy. Press-and-drag the files over to the gray icon of the ejected disk.

▼ As the Mac reads info from one disk and copies it onto the other, it will spit out each disk and tell you which one to insert next. Just follow the directions; this is called *disk swapping.* It will eventually end.

▼ If you end up with a gray disk icon on the screen, just drag it out through the trash can.

Instead of copying selected files, you can just drag the icon of the inserted disk itself onto the gray disk, which will **replace** everything that was ever on the gray disk with the entire contents of the inserted disk. When you replace the contents of one disk with the contents of another, it's called a **disk-to-disk copy** (*details on the next page*).

**Copy From Floppy to Floppy with Only One Floppy Drive**

Ejected Disk

*When you eject a disk using the menu, the icon turns gray. This is a visual clue that the computer still knows about this disk.*

*Disk-to-disk copying*

*If you drag the icon of one disk on top of the other disk (as shown by the shadow under the pointer), you will replace **the entire contents** of the other disk. Be careful!*

If you *want* to replace the contents of the disk, this is a tidy way to do it. Fortunately, the Mac knows that sometimes you do things you didn't really mean to, so when you drag the inserted disk icon and drop it onto the ejected disk icon, you will get a thoughtful message:

> ⚠ Are you sure you want to completely replace contents of
> "Ejected Disk" (not in any drive)
>
> with contents of
> "Inserted Disk" (internal drive)?
>
> [ Cancel ]  [  OK  ]

Notice that the dark border is around the Cancel button. Whenever you see a dark border you can press the Return or the Enter key to activate that button, and that button is usually the safest thing to do (Cancel, in this case).

### Copying More Than One File at a Time

To **copy more than one** file at a time, *select* more than one file (detailed in the next paragraph). When more than one file is selected, dragging one file will drag them all together, either to the trash can, into another folder, onto another disk, or simply to clean up the joint. Just make sure when you drag that you press on one of the black items; if you click anywhere else, all the items will be deselected.

### Selecting More Than One File at a Time

You may have noticed in a Desktop window that when you *press in an empty space and drag the pointer,* a dotted rectangle comes out of the tip—this is the **selection marquee**, common in many Mac programs. On the Desktop, any file that is even partially enclosed in this marquee will be selected.

*The selection marquee—
just press-and-drag with the pointer tool.*

Selecting all the icons this way will of course turn them all black.

▾ When you press-and-drag on the *black* area of one of the selected items, they will all drag together.

▾ Clicking in any *white* space or on any unselected icon or on the Desktop will *deselect* all the files.

You can also drag to select files that are next to each other while viewing a window in one of the list views (by Name, Date, Size, etc.). Press in a white space in the window next to a file name and start to drag. The selection marquee will appear when you drag, and any item that is even partially enclosed within the marquee will be added to the selection.

**Selecting more than one file in a list view**

*Press-and-drag to select adjacent items in a list view. Click anywhere else to deselect all the items in the group.*

Another method of selecting more than one item is to **Shift-click**. You may have noticed that once a file is selected, clicking on another file deselects the first one. *But*, if you hold down the Shift key while clicking, every one of the files you click will be selected. This way you can select several files in different corners of your window.

**Shift-Clicking to Select More Than One File**

In the same manner, you can **deselect** one file at a time. For instance, if you group a bunch of files within the selection marquee but you don't want the one in the middle, simply hold down the Shift key and click once on that one—it will be the only one deselected.

**Shift-Clicking to Deselect**

*Hold the Shift key down and click once on a selected file to deselect it.*

**Selection Shortcuts**

To select any single file (no matter how you are viewing the window), just **type the first letter** of the name of the file and you'll be taken right to it. If there are several files with the same first letter, quickly type the first couple of letters. This makes it a lot easier to find your folder named Waldo in an alphabetized list, for instance, or a file that starts with Z, or any icon in a crowded folder. *This technique also works in any dialog box with a list of files, such as in an "Open" dialog box.*

**Arrow keys**

You can also use the **arrow keys** to select files. Once you have a file selected, either by clicking on it or typing its first letter, the arrow keys will select the next icon or file name in the window. In a list, the UpArrow and the DownArrow select, of course, the next file in the list. In an icon view, all four of the arrows will select the icon to the left, right, up, or down, unless there is nothing else in that direction.

**Select the next file alphabetically**

To select the icon that would be alphabetically *after* the currently selected icon, whether you are in an icon view or a list view that is not alphabetized, press the **Tab** key.

To select the icon that would be alphabetically *before* the currently selected icon, press **Shift Tab**

**Edit keys**

You can also use the **edit keys** on an extended keyboard to scroll through a window, although this does not select anything. The edit keys (that little set between the alphabet keys and the numeric keypad) come in handy, though, if you want to get to the top or the bottom of a list instantly, where you might want to select something, or if you want to move the window past in a hurry.

**Home** rolls the window straight to the top.

**End** rolls the window straight to the bottom.

**PageUp** and **PageDown** roll the window one window-sized section up or down.

A common complaint about selecting a file name in a list by typing the first letter or two is that the name appears at the *bottom* of the window. It is much more convenient (really—you'll soon discover this) if the file name shows up at the *top* of the window. You can take advantage of the edit keys to solve this problem:

> If you have an extended keyboard you can force the selected file name to appear at the top of the window by pressing the **End** key before you type the letter of the file name.

**Selected file name at the top of the list**

!

If you are viewing your window By Icon, you can only select items from one window at a time. But if you view the window by any kind of list (Name, Date, Size, etc.), then you can **expand** the folders and **select** any number of files from any number of expanded folders.

## Selecting from Expanded Views

*The downward-pointing triangle indicates that this folder is expanded.*

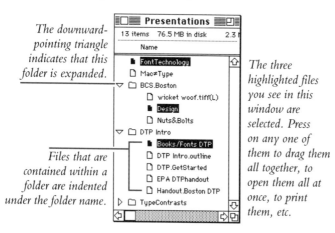

*Files that are contained within a folder are indented under the folder name.*

*The three highlighted files you see in this window are selected. Press on any one of them to drag them all together, to open them all at once, to print them, etc.*

Notice there are two files in the above window that are not in any folder. There are three folders, two of which have been *expanded* (I clicked on their triangles) to show the contents. By Shift-clicking I selected three separate items from three separate places. If I press-and-drag on any one of these three items, all three of them will move. I can copy them, trash them, print them, move them, etc., etc,. etc.

**Using Find File to Select Files**

You can also **use Find File to select files** from all over your hard disk (see Chapter 26 on Find File for all the intimate details). Even if there are so many files that Find File cannot display all of them at once on the screen, they are all selected. Dragging one of the selected icons to the Desktop will actually drag all of the found files to the Desktop, even if you can't see them.

I often use Find File to select a file even when I know where it is because it is so much faster than digging through layers of folders. If I need a document, I hit Command F, type in a few letters, hit the Return key, then lo and behold there is my file in front of my face. I hit Command O to open it (since Find File *selects* it for me) and off I go.

# CHAPTER TWELVE

# TRASH CAN

The **trash can icon** works just like the trash can in your yard—you put things in it you don't want anymore and the garbage collector comes and takes it away and you never see it again. You can move the trash can around on your Desktop and it will stay where you last left it.

**To put something in the trash:** Press-and-drag an icon over to the can. *When the can becomes black,* let go and the icon will drop inside. Don't let go of the icon before the can turns black! If you find a bunch of garbage hanging around outside the trash, it's because you didn't wait for the can to turn black—you just set it down next to it. Try again.

The trick here is that the *tip of the pointer* must touch the can! Whether you are putting one icon in here or whether you have selected fifteen icons and are dragging them all together to the trash, the tip of the pointer is the thing that opens the lid (figuratively, of course). The shadows of the objects *have nothing to do with it*—forget those shadows trailing along behind; just make sure the tip of the pointer touches the can and turns it black. *Then* let go.

**To remove something from the trash:** If you double-click on the trash can you'll find that it opens up to a window, just like any other window. So if you decide you want that item you just threw away, you can go get it. Either press-and-drag the icon back to the disk/folder it came from, **or** click once on the file to select it, then from the File menu choose **Put Away** and the file will go right back where it came from.

## The Trash Can

*The famous trash can icon*

*It's the tip of the pointer, not the shadow of the icon, that opens the trash.*

*The bulging trash can is an obvious visual clue that there is something in the garbage.*

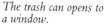

*The trash can opens to a window.*

**Emptying the Trash** Anything you put in the trash can will stay there, even if you turn off the computer, until you consciously **empty the trash**: from the Special menu, choose "Empty Trash." Once you do that, everything in the trash can is gone forever. No amount of crying or pleading or screaming or kicking will bring it back. Believe me.

*(Well, there is software and there are technicians who can often bring back your information, so if you lose something really important call your local guru or user group. But in general, consider it gone.)*

**The warning box** When you empty the trash, you'll get a **warning box** asking if you really want to throw the file away.

> ⚠ The Trash contains 1 item. It uses 123 K of disk space. Are you sure you want to permanently remove it?
>
> [ Cancel ] [ OK ]

▼ **If you don't want to see the warning box**, hold down the Option key while trashing the item.

▼ **If you want to throw away a locked item**, hold down the Option key when you trash the item.

▼ When trashing items to make more space on the disk, the trash must be emptied before the space will open up; watch the numbers in the information bar of the window when you empty the trash.

**Disable the Warning Box** If you find this warning box to be a nuisance (which I guarantee you will in about five minutes), you can **disable it** permanently (permanently until you choose to turn it back on again).

| Trash Info |
| --- |
| ((⦿)) Trash |
| **Where:** On the desktop |
| **Contents:** 0 files and 1 folder are in the Trash. |
| **Modified:** Sun, Oct 18, 1992, 11:13 PM |
| ☒ **Warn before emptying** |

*Uncheck this box to avoid the warning.*

▼ Select the trash can icon (click *once* on it).

▼ From the File menu, choose "Get Info."

▼ Click the checkbox "Warn before emptying" so there is no check in it.

▼ Close the Get Info window (click in its close box *or* press Command W.

# CHAPTER THIRTEEN

# OPENING APPLICATIONS

## OR DOCUMENTS

The term **application** is often used synonomously with **program** (although an *application* is only one form of programming). *Application* refers to the software package you use to create your documents, such as ClarisWorks, Aldus PageMaker, Adobe Illustrator, etc. They all do something different; they all have a particular function. Sometimes it takes a little research to find the software applications to meet your specific needs.

**What is an Application?**

To **open an application**, or software program, you will need to find its icon or file name, whether it's on your hard disk or on a floppy. Application icons, as noted in the chapter on icons, typically look fancier than anything else. If you view your window "By Kind," as shown below, the applications will be at the top of the list.

**Opening an Application**

PageMaker 4.2
*Application icon*

| PageMaker 4.2 | | |
|---|---|---|
| 8 items | 72.7 MB in disk | 6.1 MB available |
| Name | Size | Kind | Las |
| CheckList 1.0 | 204K | application program |
| PageMaker 4.2 | 1,797K | application program |
| Table Editor 1.01 | 215K | application program |
| Recipe.script | 6K | Microsoft Word do... |
| Coupon.PT4 | 47K | PageMaker 4.2 doc... |

*Notice there is an underline below the heading "Kind" in the information bar, which is a visual clue that this list is organized by Kind.*

▼ From the Desktop, double-click on an application icon or file name to open to a blank page, ready for you to create a new document.

▼ Some applications open to a commercial, or at least to an Open dialog box. In either case you can choose to create a new document at that point from the File menu.

**Opening a Document from the Desktop**

P▣ 4.2
Secrets
*Document icon*

To **open a document** that has already been created and saved in an application, find its icon or its file name on your Desktop. (A document icon, remember, typically looks like a page with the right corner turned down.)

Double-click on a document icon; most of the time this will open the application, placing your document on the screen as you last saved it.

**Important Note!**

Now, just because you have an icon representing a document you created in a certain software application doesn't mean you can open up that document just anywhere. Double-clicking on a document icon will only open it **IF** *the application itself is also in the computer,* either on the hard disk or on a floppy disk that is inserted into one of the drives. If the application isn't there, then the document doesn't have anywhere to put itself!

And then again, some programs won't *allow* you to open their documents from the Desktop. If you know the software program is really installed *in* the computer, either on the hard disk or on a floppy, and you get a message telling you an application can't be found, then you must *open the application first* and *then* open the document from the File menu by choosing "Open."

*(See the section on the following page for tips on using the Open dialog box.)*

> 🖐 The TouchBASE document "DataBase.NUSIG" could not be opened, because the application program that created it could not be found.
>
> [ OK ]

*Even though the application TouchBASE is installed in the computer, I get this message if I try to open a TouchBASE database document by double-clicking on the TouchBASE icon. I have to open TouchBASE itself first, then open the document. (Actually, in this case TouchBASE knows to open this document for me.)*

Also see the next page, the double exclamation tip.

You can also open a document by **dragging the icon** and **dropping it** on top of its application icon. You'll notice that the application icon will turn black, which is the visual clue that if you let go your document will open.

Now, a cool thing about this trick is that you can open a document in an application other than the one it was created in! For instance, MacWrite is able to open documents created in several other word processing applications. If you have a word processed document that someone gave you but you don't have the program they wrote it in, you can drag the foreign document on top of the MacWrite application icon. If MacWrite turns black, let go of the document and MacWrite will open it for you.

So if you ever get those blank document icons with no clue where they came from, or even whether they are paint files, or text, or spreadsheets, drag them over every application program you own. Whichever application turns black will open the document. Check Chapter 25 on Aliases, page 169, for a tip on creating an alias of each application you own. You can store these aliases in one folder on your Desktop and thus make them easily accessible for opening all files, strange or not.

Once an application is up and running, in the File menu you see two choices: **New** and **Open**. This confused me at first because I thought, "Well, I want to *open* a *new* one." The difference is this:

- ▾ **New** creates a clean, blank page on which you can begin a *new* document.

- ▾ **Open** takes you to a dialog box (shown on the next page) where you can choose to *open* a document that has been previously created and saved.

**Drag-and-Drop to Open a Document**

!

!!

**New vs. Open**

**An "Open" Dialog Box**

Finding your way around an Open dialog box is called "navigating." It's one of the most important skills you can learn, and you'll need this skill in other dialog boxes, like when you Save documents or when you import or export text. Take a good look at this illustration, and also check out the one in Chapter 29 on Navigating. Try to take the time to understand and absorb what each part of the dialog box is telling you. Your friends will be impressed.

*When the icon in the **title** or **label** here is a **folder**, this is a **menu**. Press on the label to see the hierarchy. As shown here, this menu indicates that the folder **Robin** is on the **Hard Disk**, which is on the **Desktop**.*

*The name shown here is the specific folder or disk that contains the files you see in the list below.*

🗀 Robin
🗀 Hard Disk
▣ Desktop

*This is the name of the disk you are looking at.*

🗀 **Robin** ▼          🗀 **Hard Disk**

🗋 **bar of pattern.tiff**          ⬆
🗀 **CCI**                         **Eject**
🗀 **For Drew**
🗀 **Guy**                         **Desktop**
🗀 **Mailing list**
🗀 **Warning**                     **Open**
🗀 **Zamoura**          ⬇          **Cancel**

*Single-click on any name to **select** that file.*

*Double-click the name to **open** the file.*

*When you **double-click on a folder**, it opens here to show you a list of the files inside that folder.*

*When you **double-click on a document**, it opens that document on your screen.*

*The only documents you will see in this list are documents that the current application can open.*

*Click **Eject** to eject a disk so you can insert another.*

*Click **Desktop** to see what's on the Desktop level, including disks in other drives.*

*Click **Open** to open the selected file; **or** you can double-click on the file name.*

*Click **Cancel** to take you back to wherever you were without opening anything.*

# CHAPTER FOURTEEN

# TYPING

In some applications **typing** is the main idea, as in a word processor. In some, it is the way to input the data whose purpose is to be manipulated, as in a database or a spreadsheet. In others, it is a sideline that is occasionally necessary, as in a paint program. And everywhere you find dialog boxes where you type some answer or other, and even on your Desktop you type the names of files and folders. Fortunately, in the consistent Mac environment, every program reacts to typing in the same way.

## Typing

You may already be familiar with the Macintosh word processing **I-beam** (pronounced eye-beam): ⌶

## The I-Beam

⌶

In the Macintosh, the I-beam is a visual clue that you are now in a typing mode, as opposed to having an arrow or a cross-hair or any number of other cursors that appear in various programs.

*The I-beam is simply another pointer.* And just like the pointer, it doesn't do anything until you *click* it.

When you move the I-beam pointer to a spot and click, it sets down a flashing **insertion point** that looks like this: | (but it flashes).

## The Insertion Point

After you click the mouse to set the insertion point, then you can move the I-beam out of the way (using the mouse)—**the insertion point is what you need to begin typing**. With the insertion point flashing, anything you type will start at that point and move out to the right. This is true whether the insertion point is at the beginning or the end of a paragraph, in the middle of a word, in a field of a dialog box, under an icon at your Desktop, or anywhere else. (The only time the words will not move to the right is if the alignment has been set to align right or centered, or if a tab other than left-aligned has been set.) At any time you can take the mouse, move the I-beam pointer somewhere else, click it, and start typing from the new insertion point.

**Delete (or Backspace)**
Also from that insertion point, press the **Delete** key (found in the upper right, called the **Backspace** key on older keyboards) to backspace over text and remove any letters along the way. So you can backspace/delete to correct typos as you go, or you can click to set the insertion point down anywhere else in your text and backspace/delete from there.

**Highlighting Text**
**Highlighting text** is a shortcut to backspacing over letters to remove them. If you double-click on a word anywhere in the Mac environment with the I-beam, the entire word is selected, indicated by the highlighting.

This **word** is highlighted.

If you want to select more than one word, press-and-drag over the entire area you wish to highlight.

**Part of this line** is highlighted.

What does highlighting do? Well, once a word is high-lighted (selected), anything you type will *entirely replace* the highlighted text. Or you can now change the font (typeface) or style or size of the text using your menu commands. Or you can copy or cut or delete that text. Or you can paste something in to replace it. In fact, you *cannot* do any of these things *unless* the text is first highlighted. (Each of these procedures is explained in this chapter.)

To **unhighlight,** click once anywhere, even in the black or colored space.

**Word wrap:** In a word processor, you *never* want to hit the Return key at the end of your line, *unless* it is the end of the paragraph or unless you *really do* want the line to end there, as in an address. This is because word processors *word wrap*—the words just wrap themselves around onto the next line when they get to the right margin. Why is that? Well . . .

**Hard return:** When you press the Return key you insert what is called a *hard return.* Then when you change your margins, your line will *always* break at that hard return, even if there are only two words on the line. So, just keep those nimble fingers moving along and only hit the Return key when you want a new paragraph.

**Double-space:** Hitting the Return key twice is like pushing the carriage return on a typewriter twice—you get a double space between the lines. This is for extra space between paragraphs (although in most word processors you can ask for an automatic increase of space between paragraphs). If you want the entire document, or even just a piece of it, double-spaced—that's different; there is always an instant way to change your spacing to double-spaced. Check your manual for the method for your particular application.

**Removing a Return:** The computer sees a Return as just another character, which means to remove a Return you simply *backspace over it,* just as you would to remove an unwanted character. The problem is, in most programs you can't *see* the Return character. So you must set the insertion point just to the left of the first character on the line and backspace/delete, like so:

|Set the insertion point at the beginning of the line (as shown here) and backspace to *remove the empty line* above this one. Backspace/delete *again* to *wrap the sentence back up* to the one above.

**When to Use the Return Key**

!

*A word wrap is sometimes called a soft Return.*

*Most word processing programs have a command for showing these invisible characters, which makes it easier to get rid of them. It might be something like "Show invisibles" or "Show ¶" or "Display ¶."*

**Blank Spaces**     The computer deals with **blank spaces** just as it deals with the characters you can see. Every tab, return, spacebar space, etc., is a character on the Mac. This means you can select blank spaces, blank lines, blank tabbed spaces, or Returns in order to delete them. Select and delete them just like you would any other character.

> The space between
> these███████words is highlighted.
>
> In many applications
> you can also select the blank space
> ██████████████████████████
> between the lines to delete it.

Also, since these blank spaces are characters, you can actually change the size of them (font size, that is), as well as the *leading* (space between the lines), the style, the paragraph spacing, etc. This comes in handy for manipulating space.

**Centering Text**     And a most important thing: when you **center** a word or line, Mac takes all those blank spaces into consideration, so any spacebar spaces or any first-line indents or any tabs you've inserted will be used to calculate the center of the line, making the line not *appear* centered.

> This line is centered.
> ───── **This line is also centered**
> but it includes a tab.

*I hit the Tab key before I typed the first word in this centered line. The line appears not to be centered.*

> The invisible tab character
> that is disrupting the alignment
> must be highlighted
> and removed, like so:

*I selected the tab space to delete it.* ───── ██████**This line is also centered.**

> Then it will be centered just fine:

*After I deleted the invisible space, the line was centered just fine.* ───── **This line is also centered.**

Throughout the entire Mac environment, to make any changes to anything you must follow Rule #2:

### Select First, Then Do It To It.

For instance, **to change to a different font**, or typeface: first *select* the characters you want to change (press-and-drag over the word/s), then *choose* the font name you want to change it into. The font list is found in your menu under various labels, depending on your program.

> Notice that the insertion point picks up whatever font and style and size and alignment *is directly to its left*. No matter where you set the insertion point, you will type in the font, etc., of that character, even if that character is an empty space (unless you proceed as in the following paragraph).

Now, let's say you know that the next thing you're going to type is going to be in a different font. Do you need to type the text first and then select those characters and change the font? No. Set your insertion point down (that is, click with the I-beam positioned) where you want to type with the new font. *With no text selected*, go up to the menu and choose the font (and style and size, if you like); *when there is no text selected, all the formatting gets poured into the insertion point*—whatever you type next will be in the font you just chose. As soon as you place the insertion point elsewhere, though, it will again pick up all the formatting of the character to its left.

**Style** refers to whether the type is plain, bold, outline, italic, etc. To change the style of the type, you need to follow Rule #2: *select first, then do it to it*. Select the type you want to change (highlight it), then choose the style you want from the menu. You can choose more than one of these; for instance, you can have a face that is bold–italic–outlined–shadowed type. Yuk.

**Changing Style**

> To remove all of the style choices at once, simply select the text and choose Plain or Normal.

As mentioned in that last section about changing *fonts*, you can choose the style you want from the menu *before* you type it (as long as you don't move the insertion point after choosing). But even that's a pain if you just want to italicize the next word and then return to normal text. This is an easier method:

**Changing Styles Mid-Sentence— Without Using the Menu**

Notice the keyboard shortcuts in the style menu? They are almost always Command **B** for Bold, Command **I** for Italic, etc. (Some programs may use Command Shift B and Command Shift I, etc.).

As you're typing along, simply press Command **B** and the next word you type will be **bold**; when you want the next word to be *not* bold, press Command **B** again and it will take *off* the bold (that's called a *toggle switch*—when choosing the same command turns that command *off* ). Logically, you can press Command **B I** to create a word that is (guess!) ***bold italic.***

**Changing Type Size**

**Size** in type is measured in *points*. There are 72 points in one inch. In your menu you see different numbers referring to the size of type; logically, the bigger the number, the bigger the type. Again, to change the size of characters: *select first, then do it to it.* Or set your insertion point down and choose the size from the menu *before* you type (see the last two sections on changing fonts and styles). For more information on type sizes, see Chapter 21 on Fonts.

**Alignment**

**Alignment** refers to where the margins are lined up: *align left* has the text lined up on the left margin; *align right* is on the right, obviously; *align center* has everything centered on a vertical axis *between your margins; justified* has both the left *and* right margins lined up. To change your alignment, you know what to do! That's right: *select first, then do it to it*—highlight the text, then choose the alignment.

A note when centering: If you have a first-line indent or tabs in the text that is to be centered, or if you have inserted blank spaces either before or after the text, then those spaces are taken into consideration when centering (see page 92). Also, *alignment affects the entire paragraph;* it is not possible to make one line align left and another align right in the same paragraph. If you want to do that, you must insert a hard Return between the two lines.

Almost anywhere you can type, you can cut or copy text. When you **cut** text (or graphics), it is *removed* from your document and placed on the Clipboard. When you **copy** text (or graphics), the original text *is left on your document* and a *copy* of it is placed on the Clipboard. Well, what the heck is a Clipboard?

**The Clipboard**: The Clipboard is an invisible "container" somewhere in the depths of the Mac. In some programs, including the Finder, you'll find a menu command called *Show the Clipboard,* in which case it appears as a window with its contents displayed. In most programs, though, you never see the actual Clipboard; you simply trust that it's there. (If you have the Clipboard file in your System Folder, which you do unless you consciously threw it away, then the Clipboard is available in every application.)

The Clipboard holds whatever you have cut or copied, be it text, spreadsheet data, graphics, etc. Once something is on the Clipboard, it waits there until you paste it in somewhere (you'll get to that in the next paragraph). **The most important thing to remember about the Clipboard** is that it holds *only one thing at a time;* that is, as soon as you cut or copy something else, whatever was in the Clipboard to begin with is *replaced* with the new selection.

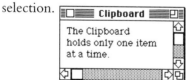

*The Clipboard appears as a window (if it's available for looking at in your program).*

**Cut, Copy, and the Clipboard**

***The Clipboard***

Clipboard

*This is the Clipboard icon that lives in the System Folder. If you double-click on it, you'll see what is currently being stored.*

Items will stay on the Clipboard even when you change applications; you can put something on the Clipboard in a paint program, then open up a word processing program and paste it into a new document. Items will leave the Clipboard all by themselves if the computer is turned off or if there is a power failure; the contents are stored in RAM, so anytime RAM gets wiped out, so do the contents of the Clipboard. (RAM info on pages 101– 102; plus read Chapter 30, Very Important Information.)

**Cut**

**How to Cut**: Simply select, then do it to it. For instance, select the text you wish to remove from the document (press-and-drag over it). Then from the Edit menu choose "Cut." The text will be *eliminated* from your document and placed on the Clipboard. (Be sure to read about "Delete" further on in this section.)

**Copy**

**How to Copy**: Simply select, then do it to it. For instance, select the text you wish to copy (press-and-drag over it), then from the Edit menu choose "Copy." The text will *remain* in your document and a *copy* will be placed on the Clipboard.

OK, it's on the Clipboard. Now what? Well, the Clipboard holds objects for **pasting**. You can take text or a graphic out of one place and paste it into your document somewhere else, just as if you had a little glue pot.

**Paste**

**How to Paste**: From the Edit menu choose "Paste." If you are working with text, whatever was on the Clipboard will be inserted in your document *beginning at the flashing insertion point*. If you have a range of text selected, the pasted item will *replace* what was selected. Spreadsheet data, graphics, etc., all can be pasted in also. In some programs, especially graphic programs, the pasted object will just land in the middle of the page.

As long as something is on the Clipboard, you can paste it in a million times.

Now, the **Delete** key (found on the upper right, called **Backspace** on older keyboards) works a little differently: if you hit this key while something is selected, whatever is selected is *deleted* and is *not* placed on the Clipboard. This means if you are holding something in the Clipboard to paste in again, whatever you *delete* will not replace what is currently being held. But it also means that you don't have that deleted item anymore—whatever you delete is really gone. **Clear**, found in the Edit menu, does the same thing.

**Undo** can sometimes save your boompah (no, that's not computer jargon—it's Grandma's euphemism). When you do something that makes you scream, "Aack! Oh no!" then try Undo. It's always the first command in the Edit menu (or press Command Z).

> What Undo can undo is *only the last action that occurred*. For instance, if you selected two paragraphs of brilliantly witty text that you spent three hours composing and just then the cat walked across your keyboard and obliterated the entire work, Undo could give it back to you **IF** you ask to Undo before you touch *anything*. If you start fiddling around with the keys and the mouse, then what you will undo is that fiddling around. So if something goes wrong, don't scream—**UNDO**. Then scream if necessary.

Thoughtfully, the Mac designers have made the keyboard shortcuts for the cut/copy/paste/undo commands very handy. Notice on your keyboard the letters **Z**, **X**, **C**, and **V**, all in a row right near the Command key.

- ▾ Command **Z** will Undo (the closest to the ⌘ key).
- ▾ Command **X** will Cut (X like eXiting or Xing it out).
- ▾ Command **C** will Copy (C for Copy, easy mnemonic).
- ▾ Command **V** will Paste (V because it is next to C).

It's nice to get familiar with these. Remember, select first (*except to Undo*); then hold down the Command key and lightly tap the other letter.

## Accessing Special Characters

**Special characters** are the symbols you have access to on the Macintosh that aren't available on a typewriter, such as upside-down question marks for Spanish (¿), the pound symbol for English money (£), the cents sign (¢), the registration or trademark symbols (® ™), etc. You can view all these with your **Key Caps** desk accessory. (If you aren't sure what Key Caps is, please read page 150.)

## Using Key Caps

To get special characters into your document, follow these steps:

*Some special characters and the keys to access them in any font:*

| | |
|---|---|
| Option 8 | • |
| Option g | © |
| Option 2 | ™ |
| Option r | ® |
| Option $ | ¢ |
| Option Shift 8 | ° |
| Option ; | ... |
| Option hyphen | – |
| Option Shift hyphen | — |

▼While working in your document, pull down the desk accessory Key Caps from the Apple menu (far left; press on the apple).

▼From the Key Caps menu (a new item that appears in your menu bar!) choose the font you wish to view.

▼Find the character you want by pressing Shift **or** Option **or** Shift-Option together; press the character key. Notice which combination of keystrokes produces the character you want. For instance, Shift Option k in the font Times will produce an apple: 🍎

▼So *remember* that keystroke combination. Close Key Caps and go back to your document (remember, you can access desk accessories in any program).

▼In your document, click to set your insertion point. Choose the font Times and press Shift Option k. The apple will appear!

If the character you need is in a different font than you are using, such as a ♥ in Zapf Dingbats, you can also do this: Through Key Caps, find the keystroke combination for the character (Option 6 in this case). Press Option 6 in whatever font you are currently using; some strange character will appear. Select the strange character and change it into Zapf Dingbats; it will turn into a ♥.

You can also select and copy the character showing in the Key Caps entry bar—select as you would any text, and copy from the Edit menu. Back at your document, set the insertion point and paste it in. Unfortunately, if your document text is another font, the Key Caps characters will pick up the font already on your page. If the character you need is in a different font, you will still have to select the new characters and change them into the font that holds those characters you wanted. It seems easier just to do it the other way.

> Remember, the insertion point picks up the *formatting of any character immediately to its left, even if it's a blank space*, so anything else you type will be in that character's font, style, etc. To continue in your *original* font, leave your insertion point right where it is; from the menu just choose the font specifications you were originally using.

Included in your special characters are **accent marks**, such as those in résumé and piñata. You can find them in Key Caps, but it's easy to remember that they're accessed using the Option key and are hiding beneath the characters on the keyboard that would usually be under them. For example, the acute accent over the **e** is **Option e**; the tilde over the **n** is **Option n**.

To type accent marks in your document, follow these steps (using the word résumé):

▼ Type the word until you come to the letter that will be *under* the accent mark; e.g., **r**

▼ *Before* you type that letter (the letter **e** in this case), type the Option combination (**Option e** in this case) —*it will look like nothing happened.*

▼ Now type the character that is to be *under* the accent mark, and both the mark and the letter will appear together; e.g., **r é s u m é**

▼ That's easy, huh!

## Using Accent Marks

*A list of common accent marks:*

   ´   Option e
   `   Option ~
   "   Option u
   ~   Option n
   ^   Option i

**One Space After Periods**

What?! One space after a period? If you grew up on a typewriter, this is not an easy habit to change, I know. But characters on a Macintosh are not *monospaced* as they are on a typewriter (except for Monaco and Courier), so there is no need to use two spaces to separate two sentences. Check any book or magazine on your shelf; you will never find two spaces after periods (except publications produced on a computer typed by someone still using typewriter rules). If you find this hard to accept, read the following commercial.

**A Commercial**

*If you are typing on a Macintosh, you must face the fact that it is not a typewriter and that some of the standard conventions developed particularly for that wonderful little mechanical appliance do not apply to the kind of type you are now creating. A very important book to read is* The Mac is not a typewriter. *It's small, it's cheap, it's easy to read, and it's true. Well, yes, I did write it myself, but that's beside the point. I didn't make up anything in the book—I just report the typographic facts.*

# CHAPTER FIFTEEN

While you are in the process of creating a document of any sort within any program, the information you put into that document is floating around in the depths of the computer. If you were to turn off the computer, that document would disappear. Usually, though, you want to keep a permanent copy of it, right? So you need to **save the document** onto a disk.

**Save the Document**

Until you actually go through the process of naming a document and saving it, the document hangs around in **RAM**, which stands for **Random Access Memory**. RAM is sort of like the top of the desk in your office, and you can consider your *disk* as a filing cabinet where you keep all your folders of information.

**RAM: Random Access Memory**

When you are working on a project, you don't keep running to the filing cabinet every time you need a little piece of information, do you? No, you take out all the applicable info and put it on your desk, then when you're finished you put it all away again and take out something else. RAM is sort of like that: when you open an application the computer puts a copy of that application into RAM, also called *memory*. When you quit that application and open another one, Mac puts the first one back where it came from and puts the new application into RAM. That way the computer doesn't have to keep going into the filing cabinet to do its work and it can operate much more efficiently.

When you create a document, it sits in RAM, too, until you put it in the filing cabinet—your disk. You put the document on your disk by **saving** it. Once it's on your disk, either hard or floppy, it will stay there until you trash it yourself.

**Danger!** All that time your document is in RAM, it is in **danger** At any moment, if there is a power failure, even for a split second, or you accidentally hit the wrong button, or you have a system crash, or the screen freezes, or a virus attacks, or your child pulls out the power cord, or any other catastrophe of considerable dimension happens to befall, then everything in RAM *(memory)* is gone. Just plain gone. No way on earth for a mortal person to get it back.

**Rule #1: Save Often!** The prevention? **SOS**: Save Often, Stupid. Well, that's a little harsh—how about Save Often, Sweetie. Save Save Save. Every few minutes, when you're just sitting there thinking about your next marvelous move, Save. In most programs it's as easy as pressing Command S. Then if there *is* a catastrophe, you will have lost only the last few minutes of your work. Of course you won't listen to me until you have experienced your own catastrophe.

**Save As... vs. Save** To save a document for the first time, it must be given a name. Under the File menu are the commands **Save As...** and **Save**. At first the subtle difference can be confusing.

**Save As...** **Save As...** is the command you must use *first* in order to give the document a name, as a document cannot be saved without a name. "Save As..." gives you a dialog box such as the one shown on the next page (they're slightly different from program to program).

**Save** **Save** is the command to use *after* you have named the document and you want to save the new changes onto that same document. *Save* just goes ahead and does it— you won't see or hear anything. Get in the habit of typing Command S (the keyboard shortcut) regularly.

There is no keyboard shortcut listed in the menu for "Save as…." But if you have not yet given the document a name, then choosing *Save* (Command S) will give you the *Save As…* dialog box because the file must have a name. Most programs will not allow you to name a document "Untitled."

Sometimes you might want to create changes in a document, but you still want to keep a **copy of the original without the changes**. For instance, you write a witty letter to Uncle Jeff, then decide you also want to write to Uncle Cliff. You have a few things to tell Cliff that Jeff isn't interested in, but you don't want to have to retype the entire letter. That's when you'll use *Save As…* a *second* time to give the document a *new* name.

▼ Save the letter to Uncle Jeff. You've probably named it "Witty letter to Uncle Jeff."

▼ Now from the File menu, choose "Save As…."

▼ Change the name from "Witty letter to Uncle Jeff" to "Witty letter to Uncle Cliff."

This puts the original document (to Uncle Jeff) safely away on your disk and opens a new one (the copy to Uncle Cliff) right on the screen. You'll notice the name in the window title bar of your document will change to what you renamed it. Any changes you make to *this* document (Uncle Cliff's) will not affect the original (Uncle Jeff's).

If you made a bunch of changes you don't want, simply close the document and *don't save the changes*. Reopen it and everything will be exactly the way it was last time you saved.

Some programs have an option to **Revert** in the File menu. Choosing Revert will remove all changes you made since the last time you saved, without having to close the document.

**The "Save As..."
Dialog Box**

Below and opposite are illustrations of a typical **"Save As..." dialog box**. This is a very important box for you to understand because you will be using it every time you start a new document. I know all this information looks intimidating, but it's really not that bad. If you spend a few minutes here, *you* will be in control instead of being at the mercy of the computer system.

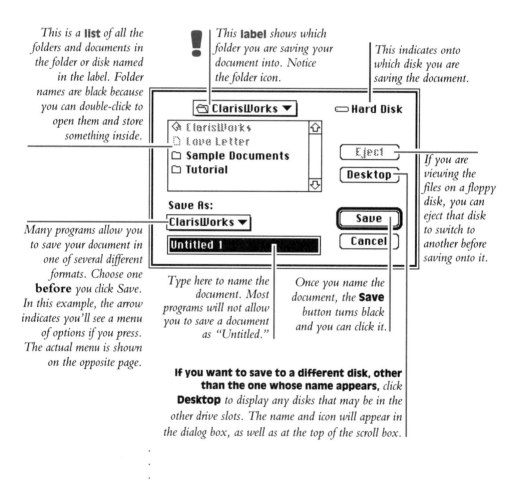

*This is a **list** of all the folders and documents in the folder or disk named in the label. Folder names are black because you can double-click to open them and store something inside.*

*This **label** shows which folder you are saving your document into. Notice the folder icon.*

*This indicates onto which disk you are saving the document.*

*If you are viewing the files on a floppy disk, you can eject that disk to switch to another before saving onto it.*

*Many programs allow you to save your document in one of several different formats. Choose one **before** you click Save. In this example, the arrow indicates you'll see a menu of options if you press. The actual menu is shown on the opposite page.*

*Type here to name the document. Most programs will not allow you to save a document as "Untitled."*

*Once you name the document, the **Save** button turns black and you can click it.*

**If you want to save to a different disk, other than the one whose name appears,** *click* **Desktop** *to display any disks that may be in the other drive slots. The name and icon will appear in the dialog box, as well as at the top of the scroll box.*

As is typical on the Mac, the dialog box has many **visual clues** that tell you what to do or what to expect.

*As soon as you click in this list box to select a folder, this list box becomes selected. Do you see the* **double border★** *around it? Compare this list box with the example on the previous page, where the* **name** *is highlighted.*

*If the list box is selected, you can* **type the first letter or two of a file to select the file.**

*If the list box is not selected, press the* **Tab key**.

*Press on this label to get the menu (as shown) showing the hierarchy, or the levels in which the files are stored. Any level you choose (other folders, the hard disk, or the Desktop) will display a list that tells you what else is on that level (in that folder, on the hard disk, or at the Desktop which includes any inserted floppy disks). Learning to navigate through these folders and disks is a required skill, although it does seem to take some time to get the concept. See Chapter 29 for more details.*

    ☐ ClarisWorks
    ☐ Applications
    ☐ Hard Disk
    ▓ Desktop

*If you press on this label, you will see this menu.*

***Instead of clicking the buttons, you can:***

*Click the name here to go up one level (in this example, you would next see all the items in the Applications folder).*

    ☐ ClarisWorks ▼          ☐ Hard Disk

    ◇ ClarisWorks                    ⬆
    ☐ Love Letter
    ☐ Sample Documents          [ Eject ]
    ☐ Tutorial                  [ Desktop ]
                                ⬇

★*double border*

*Press Command E (if there is a floppy disk inserted).*

*Press Command D or Command UpArrow*

    Save As:                    [ Open ]
    ☐ClarisWorks ▼              [ Cancel ]

    Untitled 1

*Press the Return or the Enter key. These keys always activate the button with the dark border.*

*Most programs offer you a choice of file formats in which to save your document. For instance, if you created this document here in ClarisWorks and you need to give it to someone who uses WriteNow, you could actually save it here directly as a WriteNow file. The list shown here is what you see if you press on the label "ClarisWorks."*

    Save As:
    ✓ClarisWorks
    ClarisWorks Stationery

    AppleWorks 2.0
    MacWrite 5.0
    MacWrite II
    Microsoft Word
    Microsoft Word 4.0
    Microsoft Word PC
    Microsoft Works 1.1
    Microsoft Works 2.0
    Microsoft Write 1.0
    RTF
    Text
    WordPerfect 1.0.2
    WordPerfect PC 4.2
    WriteNow 1.0
    WriteNow 2.0-2.2
    WriteNow NeXT

*Press Command Period.*

*If this box is white and there is no insertion point flashing, no matter what you type it will not appear in this edit box. Instead, you will select files in the list box that begin with the first letter.*

*To select this edit box so you can type in it, press the* **Tab key**

*When the text in this box is highlighted,* **anything you type will replace the highlighted text—** *you do not have to click or delete first. You can impress your friends with this information.*

**Navigating**
The key to using a "Save As..." dialog box effectively is in knowing how to navigate, how to get from one place to another in the computer. This is such a basic and important skill, and one that seems hard to grasp for many people, that I have devoted an entire chapter to the topic. If you don't quite get it yet, check out Chapter 29 on Navigating. Trust me, it will be worth your while to spend some time learning to navigate.

# CHAPTER SIXTEEN

# PRINTING

**Printing** is the process of reproducing the data that is inside the Macintosh onto a piece of paper. This piece of paper, then, in computer jargon, is called "hard copy."

**Printing**

There are basically two types of printers: **QuickDraw printers** and **PostScript printers**.

**Printers**

**QuickDraw** is a computer programming language that your *Macintosh* reads. It creates what you see on the screen. A printer that can only reproduce what is on the screen is usually called a QuickDraw printer (although there is really nothing "QuickDraw" in the printer itself). The ImageWriter, the HP DeskWriter, and the Apple Style-Writer are all examples of QuickDraw printers, with *resolutions* ranging from 75 to 400 dots per inch (the higher the resolution, the smoother the printed image).

*QuickDraw printers*

**PostScript** is a page description programming language that a *PostScript printer* can interpret. A PostScript printer doesn't care what the heck you have on your screen. If the font or the graphic image is created with PostScript, it can look dreadful on the screen but will print beautifully on the page. Personal PostScript printers are the expensive ones, typically around $3,000. They're expensive because they have a computer built inside, complete with memory and a CPU (central processing unit, the tiny chip that runs the entire process).

*PostScript printers*

There are also very expensive (like $80,000), very high-end PostScript printers with resolutions of around

*Imagesetters*

1270 or 2540 dots per inch, such as the **Linotronic**. These machines, called *imagesetters,* output onto film, not paper, and the hard copy looks virtually like traditional typesetting, limited only by the professional expertise of the person who input the type. This book was output on a Linotronic.

**Service Bureaus**

Since the high resolution machines are so expensive, you only find them in **service bureaus**—shops where they offer the output as a service. You take the disk containing your document to them, leave it there, and they print it up for you. It can cost from $5 to $10 a page, but it's beautiful.

**Chooser**

The very first time you print on your machine, or if you are hooked up to more than one printer, or sometimes if you go somewhere else and print, or if you find you are having difficulty printing, you need to go to **Chooser** to direct the computer to the printer. If none of these situations apply to you, then you can skip this information, go right to "OK OK Let's Print" (page 111) and remember these details are here if you ever need them.

You'll find the Chooser under the Apple at the top left of the menu bar.

*This is the Chooser. If you are connected to a non-PostScript printer or to a network, your Chooser may look a little different.*

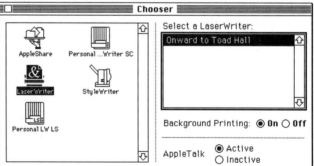

**Printer drivers**

On the left side of the Chooser window you will see printer icons. These printer icons represent the *printer drivers* that are installed in your System (a printer driver is the program that tells the printer what to do; it *drives* the printer). For every printer driver in your System Folder (specifically, in the Extensions folder within the System Folder), there will be a matching icon in your Chooser. *Even if you have a printer hooked-up right next to you, you won't be able to print to it unless its driver is in your System Folder.*

StyleWriter

*This is the printer driver for the Apple StyleWriter.*

▾ Click on the icon representing the machine you want to print to.

If you don't see an icon for your printer, you must close the Chooser (click in its close box) and **install the driver**:

If you have an Apple printer, find the disk that came with your printer and drag the driver icon onto the top of the closed System Folder; the Mac will put the driver into the Extensions folder. (You could, of course, put the icon directly into the Extensions folder yourself.)

If your printer is not an Apple printer, read the manual that came with your printer for directions on installing the driver. It should be very similar.

**If you selected a QuickDraw printer,** then on the right side of the Chooser you should see a *port* icon, asking which port, or plug, the cable connected to the printer is plugged into. **If you selected a PostScript printer** or **if you are on a network,** then on the right side of the Chooser you should see the names of all printers that are connected to your Mac and turned on.

*Printer port icons. The cable to your QuickDraw printer is plugged into one of these (check the little pictures on the plugs on the back of your Mac).*

▾ Click on the port that your printer is connected to.

▾ **If you are on a network** (which you would be if more than one computer is going to the same printer) or **if you are connected to a PostScript printer,** then make sure the AppleTalk button is clicked **Active.**

If you are the only one connected to a QuickDraw printer, AppleTalk should be **Inactive.**

If AppleTalk was previously Inactive, then the Active button says "Active On Restart." This means that if you click this button, AppleTalk will not really be active until you restart the computer. (Either wait until next time you turn on the Mac, or go to the Special menu and choose "Restart.")

▾ Notice in the illustration that two things are *highlighted:* the icon representing your printer, *and* the name (or the port) of your printer. **These two items must both be selected!** Select each one by clicking once on each.

▾ It feels like the Chooser should have an OK button, but it doesn't. I have always wondered why not. So now that you've told the Mac which printer to print to, just close the Chooser window (click its close box or press Command W) and proceed with printing your work.

*Background printing*
*Also see "PrintMonitor"*

**Background Printing** allows the Mac to print to a laser printer while you go on with your work. If you do *not* check this button, then you have to wait until the computer has sent all the information to the printer before you have control of your screen again. If you *do* check this button, then the computer sends the information into a "buffer," then lets you use your screen. The buffer sends the information to the printer at the slower rate the printer requires, while you continue with your work. You will notice, during background printing, that occasionally your cursor may freeze or your typing may stop. This is normal behavior as the computer tries to do two things at once.

PrintMonitor    LaserWriter

You will only see the Background Printing option if you have the PrintMonitor icon and the LaserWriter driver icon in the Extension folder within your System Folder.

Printing to your personal printer is very simple. You may see different print dialog boxes depending on which printer you are connected to, and the dialog boxes within different applications may look slightly different, but basically all you need to do is answer the questions they ask.

**OK OK Let's Print!**

The first thing you want to do is to **Save** again—as a preventive measure always save just before you print. Also, make sure the printer is turned on (an ImageWriter must have its "Select" button on as well).

*1. Save again*

In many programs you should next check the "Page Setup" command under the File menu. This sets certain parameters for printing pages. Here is an example of a LaserWriter Page Setup dialog box. Because this box and any Options box that comes with it may vary from printer to printer, I can only suggest that you check your printer's manual for specific details on all the buttons, although some options are explained below.

*2. Check the Page Setup*

```
┌─────────────────────────────────────────────────┐
│ LaserWriter Page Setup              ┌──────────┐ │
│                                     │    OK    │ │
│ Paper: ◉ US Letter  ○ A4 Letter     └──────────┘ │
│        ○ US Legal  ○ B5 Letter ○ ┌Tabloid    ▼┐┌──────────┐│
│                                  └───────────┘│  Cancel  ││
│ Reduce or ┌───┐%   Printer Effects:   └──────────┘│
│ Enlarge:  │100│    ☒ Font Substitution?  ┌──────────┐│
│           └───┘    ☒ Text Smoothing?     │ Options  ││
│ Orientation        ☒ Graphics Smoothing? └──────────┘│
│  ┌──┐┌──┐          ☒ Faster Bitmap Printing?│
│  └──┘└──┘                                     │
└─────────────────────────────────────────────────┘
```

Now just go up to the File menu and choose "Print...". Depending on which application and which printer you are using, you'll get some sort of dialog box (an example below) asking you questions. (If you get a message telling you it's not possible to print, check the previous section on Chooser.)

*3. Choose "Print"*

```
┌─────────────────────────────────────────────────┐
│ StyleWriter                        ┌──────────┐  │
│                                    │    OK    │  │
│ Paper: ◉ US Letter   ○ A4 Letter   └──────────┘  │
│        ○ US Legal    ○ Envelope (#10) ┌────────┐ │
│                                       │ Cancel │ │
│ Orientation: ┌──┐ ┌──┐   Scale: 100%⬍ └────────┘ │
│              └──┘ └──┘                            │
└─────────────────────────────────────────────────┘
```

***A few details*** Most of the options in these dialog boxes are self-explanatory; the following items are some terms that may not be so obvious:

**Quality**: Draft quality on the ImageWriter prints very quickly, but eliminates any graphics you may have had and produces really awful stuff; you can generally ignore this option unless you're in an extreme hurry and don't care at all what it looks like.

You can adjust the draft quality with the button on the ImageWriter itself. If you turn off the Select light, you can push the Print Quality button to one of the three levels shown. You'll get three levels of terrible type, from awful to worse.

**Orientation**: Your application may use another term for it, but what the Mac wants to know is if it should print upside right or sideways (8.5 x 11 or 11 x 8.5); also known as **Tall** or **Wide, Portrait** or **Landscape.**

**Pages: All** or **From __ to __**: You can choose to print *all* the pages contained in your document, or just pages 3 through 12 (or whatever your choice is, of course). Choosing **All** will override any numbers in the **From/To** boxes.

**Reduce or Enlarge; Scale**: Regardless of the precise term your printer driver uses, you can enter a number or press the arrows here to enlarge or reduce the printed page. For instance, enter 50% to print your work at half size. Remember, half of an 8.5 x 11 is 4.25 x 5.5 —you must halve *both* directions. On paper, this looks like the image is ¼ the original size; it isn't—it's half of *both* the horizontal *and* the vertical.

*The shaded portion is 50% of the larger size— half of both the width and the length.*

**Tall Adjusted:** The Macintosh screen generally has a resolution of 72 dots per inch (72 across x 72 down); the ImageWriter prints at 72 x 80 dots per inch. Thus the ImageWriter tends to print large circles, such as pie charts, in oval shapes, unless you choose Tall Adjusted. Tall Adjusted will also make the letter-spacing more closely resemble laser printer spacing; if you're using the ImageWriter as draft copies for eventual reproduction on a laser printer, this will help you judge the work a little better. And it looks nicer.

**Computer Paper:** *This does not refer to pin-fed paper!* Computer paper is 11 x 13 inches. The pin-fed paper that fits through a printer such as the ImageWriter is 8.5 x 11 (letter-size, just all strung together).

When you click the last "OK" or "Print" button in the last dialog box (sometimes there are up to three dialog boxes), the messages will be sent to the printer and your brilliant document shall come rolling forth.

**4. Click those buttons**

You can select one or more **documents** from windows at the **Desktop** (Finder) and choose to **print** them. The Mac opens the applications in which the documents were created, prints the files, then quits the applications and returns to the Desktop.

**Printing from the Desktop (Finder)**

▼ All you need to do is select the file you want to print by clicking once on it. If you want to select and print more than one file, see Chapter 11 on Selecting, page 75. Just make sure that you don't select too many files from so many *different* programs that the Mac cannot open all these applications all at once. You can usually, however, open several publications that all belong to *one* application without experiencing difficulty.

▼ Once the file/s is selected, you may want to choose "Page Setup…" from the File menu to set some parameters.

▼ To print the file/s, press Command P (*or* choose "Print" from the File menu, the third command down the list).

**Print the Window**

When you are at the Finder (Desktop), you can also **print the contents of the active window** (the active window is the one with the horizontal lines in its title bar). Just click once on the window whose contents you want to print. Then from the File menu, choose "Print Window" (it's the very last item in the list). If your window is showing icons, then the Mac will print the icons. Even if not all the icons are visible on the screen, all of them will print. If your window is in a list, the entire list and all the details will print, even if all the details are not visible on the screen.

**Print the Desktop**

You can also **print the contents of the Desktop**. Click once on any icon on the Desktop level, such as the trash can, *or* press Command Shift UpArrow. From the File menu, choose "Print Desktop" (it's the very last item in the list). (If this item still says "Print Window," then you have not selected the Desktop level. Try again.) The Mac will print up as many pages as necessary to display everything that is on your Desktop.

**Save Laser Printer Toner & Paper**

Most laser printers spew forth a sample page every time you turn them on, useful for checking the toner level and quality, as well as letting you know how many pages have been printed since you bought the printer. If you don't want to waste paper or toner on this page every-day, simply pull the paper tray partially out before you turn it on. After a minute or two push it back in.

This is, obviously, a temporary measure. If you would like to turn it off permanently (well, permanently until you decide to change it back), you can use the Laser-Writer Font Utility that should be on your hard disk somewhere. If it isn't on your hard disk, it's on one of your original disks for System 7 (if you have "More Tidbits," it's on that disk). If you don't have the original disk, ask to borrow someone's. It's free.

LaserWriter Font Utility

*This file is probably in your computer somewhere.*

**To turn off the start-up page**, follow these steps:

▼ Double-click on the LaserWriter Font Utility.

▼ Click OK on the commercial.

▼ From the Utilities menu, choose "Start Page Options...."

▼ In this little dialog box, click the button "Off." Then click OK.

▼ From the File menu, choose "Quit," *or* press Command Q.

*Notice you can also use this utility to restart the printer without having to turn it off.*

*Just click the "Off" button.*

The **PrintMonitor** is a utility that lets you control background printing, the printing that goes on in the background while you work on something else (see page 110). Through the PrintMonitor you can check on the status of the printing jobs you've requested, cancel documents that are in the process of printing, cancel any that are waiting to print, set a time (the hour and the date) that you want a job to print, or postpone the time indefinitely. You can tell the PrintMonitor to alert you when the printer is out of paper or when to feed in a new sheet of paper during a manual feed.

*After you have started printing a document*, you will be able to choose "PrintMonitor" from the Application menu (far right of the menu bar). This means if it's a very short print job you won't have much control over it. If you send several files off to print, their names will be listed in the dialog box in order of scheduled printing. You can select a document name, then cancel it or set the print time. From the File menu you can also choose to "Stop Printing," which just *stops* the process (rather than cancels it) until you tell it to resume, also from the File menu. The PrintMonitor will automatically go away when all printing is complete. You can't make it go away before that.

## PrintMonitor

*While the PrintMonitor is open (if you are not printing, you can double-click on the PrintMonitor icon in the Extensions folder), you can get this Preferences dialog box from the File menu.*

*Choose "PrintMonitor" from the Application menu to get this dialog box:*

**Align
ImageWriter
Pin-Fed Paper**

Most applications let you determine how far down from the top of the page you want the document to begin. Unfortunately, the ImageWriter doesn't know where the perforation of the pin-fed paper is; it just assumes the paper is aligned at the top of the printer and adjusts itself according to your specifications. In order to keep the printing consistent, so your documents always begin where you expect and line breaks will occur at perforations rather than in the middle of documents, do this:

1. Turn the printer on.
2. Make sure the Select light is **off**.
3. Press the line feed button until the perforation is just at the top of the printer head (if you hold the button down, after four lines it will form-feed until you let go).
4. Print your work (take notice if you need to arrange that first adjustment higher or lower; that is, above or below the printer head).
5. **When your work is finished printing, don't ever roll the paper forward manually in order to get to the perf to tear it off! That's exactly what causes the problem because then the paper isn't lined up any more.**
6. Instead, turn the Select button **off**.
7. Press the **form-feed button**; this will roll one entire sheet out of the printer, leaving the perforation lined up exactly how you just set it in step #3.
8. Turn the Select light back **on** now so you don't forget, since you cannot print with the Select light off.
9. Now you can tear off your page, leaving one full sheet hanging out of the printer.

Obviously, this is going to waste one page of paper per document, but it actually wastes *less* than if your document printed right over the perforation marks and you had to reprint the whole thing! Another advantage is that with that whole sheet hanging out of the printer, the paper doesn't get curled around the roller and roll back inside itself when you try to print.

# CHAPTER SEVENTEEN

# CLOSING AND QUITTING

When you are finished working on a document, you can **close that document** window by clicking in its close box or by choosing "Close" from the File menu. Either way, you are just *closing the document* and remaining *within the application (the software program)*. You still see the menu belonging to the application, even though the rest of your screen may look gray or colored, just like your Desktop, and even if you see windows that belong to other programs or to the Desktop.

**Closing a Document**

> If you just *closed* a document window and now you see "Special" in your menu, it does not necessarily mean you *quit* the program—you have just *closed,* but not *quit.* A simple click on the screen will pop you into the Desktop, deluding you into thinking you have quit the application!

!

To really **quit an application**, you must choose the Quit command. This is always done from the File menu, the very last item. In most programs you can use the keyboard shortcut: **Command Q**.

If you haven't saved all your changes, the Mac will politely ask if you want to save them at this point, whether you are closing or quitting. Thank goodness.

**Quitting an Application**

> Save changes to "Article" before quitting?
>
> [ Yes ]
> [ No ]     [ Cancel ]

*The item "Quit" is always the last command in the File menu. If you don't see Quit in the File menu, you are probably at the Desktop/Finder.*

If you click Yes and you haven't yet even saved the document with a name, you'll get the "Save As..." dialog box (page 104) to name the document before quitting, because nothing can be saved without a name. Click the No button if you decide at this point you don't want the changes (or the document, if you've never named it). Click Cancel to return to your document without saving any changes.

**!** If you hold down the Option key while choosing "Quit," *and keep holding it down,* when you arrive at your Desktop all the windows will be closed!

**Shutting Down** See Chapter 19 about Shutting Down, if you are all done for the day. That chapter also explains how to check for any programs whose documents you may have closed when you really meant to quit.

# CHAPTER EIGHTEEN

# EJECTING DISKS

There are actually many ways to **eject a floppy disk** (remove it from the floppy disk drive), some of which are preferable to others. Let's start at the Desktop.

**Ejecting**

If you are done for the day and are planning to **shut down** the whole system, then close up all your windows (press Command Option W). From the Special menu choose "Shut Down." This will close any open applications, eject any floppy disks, and reassuringly notify you that it is now safe to turn off the computer.

**Shutting Down**
*Also see page 123.*

Even if you're not ready to shut down, you may sometimes need to eject a floppy disk in order to trade it with another, or simply to take your disk and go away. Beginners usually go through the routine of selecting the disk (by clicking once on it) and choosing "Eject" from the File menu (or using the keyboard shortcut **Command E**). This will certainly work, but it is actually not the best method.

**From the Menu or the Keyboard Shortcut**

*Gray disk icon left on the screen after being ejected.*

You may have noticed when you eject a disk by using the menu that a gray version of the icon stays on the screen. That's because the memory of this disk is still in RAM (see page 101). If someone else comes along to use this machine while the icon is still showing, when they insert their disk the Mac will very often spit theirs out and ask for the one that just left. That's not a problem if the disk is sitting on the desk, but if Mary took that disk and left for a meeting in Chicago, then you may have a problem.

**Try this!** If the computer asks you to insert a disk and you don't have it, try pressing **Command Period**. This will often force that rude question to disappear. You may need to do it a few times, along with clicking OK to a dialog box or two. If the message won't go away with Command Period and you don't have the disk (the disk must be named exactly the same and have exactly the same data on it—you can't fool the System), then the only thing you can do is to turn off the computer. If you see a gray disk icon on your screen, you can try sticking it in the trash, but oftentimes even then you'll get that dialog box asking for it to be inserted.

**Through the Trash**

To avoid the problem of gray disk icons being left on the screen, it is actually preferable to **eject your disk through the trash.**

Aack, you say! Yes, that's a frightening thought, but calm down; it's quite all right. *The trash can doesn't erase anything off your disk.* First make sure you have closed any documents and quit any applications that you used on that disk. Then simply press on the disk icon, drag it down to the trash and put it in. Your disk will safely pop out and leave no gray icon on the screen. The computer now has no recollection of the existence of that disk and you can merrily be on your way and no one will be mad at you for leaving yourself behind. This is especially important if more than one person uses the computer, as in an office or in a classroom.

Or the best shortcut of all is **Command Y**, which is actually the command for "Put Away."

Some **dialog boxes** give you an option to eject a disk while in an application, such as "Save As…" and "Open." When you want to eject a disk while working, just choose something like "Save As…" even though you don't really want to rename your current document. Choose the disk you want to eject and click the Eject button (if you don't see the name of the disk, click the Desktop button to find it in the other drive slot). Then click the Cancel button to get back to your document.

After ejecting a disk through this dialog box, you can of course insert a new disk if you like. If something from the ejected disk is still open on the screen, though, the Mac will ask for the ejected disk again so she can put it away.

**Through Dialog Boxes**

▼ To eject a disk from the internal drive at any time, in any application, press Command Shift 1 (one).

▼ To eject a disk from the external drive at any time, press Command Shift 2.

▼ For a Mac with two internal drives and an external: Command Shift 1 ejects the bottom internal drive; Command Shift 2 ejects the top internal drive; Command Shift 0 (zero) ejects the external drive.

**More Keyboard Shortcuts**

If for some reason, perhaps because of a power outage or a system error, when you turn off the computer your disk is still inside, do this:

Hold down the mouse button. *Keep holding it down* and turn the computer back on; your disk/s should pop out like toast.

**The Mouse Trick**

If all else fails, notice that tiny hole next to the drive slot? That's paper clip size. Unbend a paper clip and push it in. It's pretty safe, as all you're doing is releasing the mechanism that holds the disk in place—push firmly.

**The Paper Clip Trick**

**Mounting and Dismounting**

You may hear talk of **mounting** and **dismounting** disks, rather than inserting and ejecting them. The terms *mount* and *dismount* typically refer to hard disks. It is possible and very common to have more than one hard disk attached to your computer. It is possible to have removable cartridge hard disks that you insert into a cartridge drive sort of like inserting a video tape into a VCR. But even though the hard disk is attached to the computer or you have inserted a cartridge hard disk, that does not guarantee that its icon will show up on the screen. If the icon does not appear (which means the computer cannot "read" the disk), we say that the disk did not *mount*. (You can sometimes hear power users muttering under their bated breath as they wait that suspenseful moment for the computer to find and read the disk, "Mount, baby, mount." Why is it suspenseful? Because sometimes they don't. But that is another book.)

You cannot eject these hard disks as you do floppy disks. The cartridge hard disk must be *dismounted* before it can be removed from the drive. Drag the icon to the trash to dismount it, then follow the directions for your drive on how to actually eject the disk.

# CHAPTER NINETEEN

# SHUTTING DOWN

**Shutting down** is the process of the computer tying up all the loose ends inside itself and parking the hard disk before it's turned off. It is certainly possible to turn the computer off without shutting down, but you run the risk of losing data and possibly damaging mysterious but important elements.

When you're done with the Macintosh, it's **good house-keeping** to close up all your windows on the Desktop. Press Command Option W and all the windows will fly away home. This is an especially nice thing to do if more than one person uses the machine, because any windows left open will reopen the next time the computer is turned on. However, you can take advantage of these windows staying where you left them and perhaps leave your nice, neatly organized hard disk window open so when you return to the Mac you can skip the step of double-clicking the hard disk to see your files.

Check to make sure all your applications are also closed: Press on the **Application menu**, which is the icon in the far upper right of the menu bar (the *menu bar,* not the Desktop; look *above* the icon of your hard disk). If there is any application or utility listed in the bottom portion of that menu other than "Finder," it means that program is still open. The checkmark indicates which program you are currently in. All other programs listed will have a tiny gray icon; the gray icon means it is open somewhere but you are not there.

## Shutting Down

## Good Housekeeping

*This is the Application menu. Watch it change.*

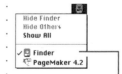

*Any programs listed here are still open. The check-mark shows which one you are currently in, whether you believe it or not.*

## Quit All Programs

*The tiny icon on the upper far right of the menu bar changes, giving you a visual clue as to what program you are currently using. Compare this icon with the one on the previous page, or the one on your own computer.*

**To quit a still-open program** (application or utility) select it from this Application menu. It may seem that nothing whatsoever happened and you are thinking, "So what?" *But something did happen!* Look at your menu bar. I bet it is different than it was twenty seconds ago. And in the far right of the menu bar, the tiny icon has changed. Even though you may see no other indication of your program —no window, no document, in fact, you may see windows from *other* programs—*the program you chose from the application menu is open and ready for you to work.* Really. (If this confuses you, be sure to read Chapter 30, called Very Important Information.)

So now that you're in the open program, from the File menu choose "Quit," which should be the very last item. (If the File menu does not have "Quit," then you probably clicked on the Desktop and popped yourself back to the Finder. Check the Application menu again.)

Repeat this process for every program listed in the Application menu (except Finder).

## Shut Down

Now from the Special menu choose **Shut Down** (Actually, if you had left any applications or documents open, the Mac would take care of putting them away, but it is safest to do it yourself.)

When you shut down, all your floppy disks will pop out and any extra hard disks will dismount. If you are using a smaller or older Mac, you'll get a reassuring dialog box that says you can now turn off your computer safely. In that case, turn it off with the same button you turned it on. On the larger Macs, "Shut Down" will also automatically turn off the computer.

*Well, that was fun, wasn't it?*

# PART THE SECOND

This section explains features of the Macintosh beyond the basic things you need to know just to get your work done. Many of the items in this section are for customizing your Mac, making your work much easier, and helping you to be more efficient. Everything in this section is important for you to understand, but you may want to take it in small chunks. For instance, read through the Desk Accessories chapter and play with each of the desk accessories. Then in a couple of days read about the Apple Menu and Aliases, and make some aliases to put into your Apple Menu. Next week spend some time with the Find File. Oh, you have many treasures to discover!

*You will do foolish things, but do them with enthusiasm.*
*—Colette*

# CHAPTER TWENTY

The **System Folder** is a magical thing. It's in charge of running your Mac, and a great number of items work simply because they are inside the System Folder. If you take a look inside the System Folder, you'll see other important folders; each folder takes care of some detail of working on the computer.

You need to know just what these folders are and what they do because you install many items (such as fonts, desk accessories, sounds, printer resources, extensions, and cdevs) simply by dragging them to your System Folder. Each item goes in a particular folder within the System Folder, but the Mac will usually take care of that for you (see "Installing Items" on page 131).

**These are some of the icons and folders you will see in your System Folder:**

The **System file** (the file that actually runs your Mac, as opposed to the System *Folder*) may be a little different from computer to computer, depending on which version of System 7 you use. You can actually double-click on

## What is the System Folder?

*Notice the information bar tells us there are 33 items in this folder, plus the scroll bars are gray. Both of these visual clues indicate that there is a lot more stuff in here than I'm showing you at the moment, items from applications I use or other utilities I have installed.*

## System File

System

the System file icon to see the list of fonts (typefaces) and sounds you have installed in your System. Each font is represented by a document icon. You can double-click on the name of a font to see a sample of what it looks like, or double-click on the name of a sound to hear it.

*This is what you will see when you open the System file (double-click on it). Double-click on a sound icon to hear it. When you double-click on a font icon (any file with one or three 'A's on it), you will see the little window shown in the left column.*

*Double-click a font icon to see what it looks like.*

In **version 7.1** and above, most fonts are not stored in the System file; they are stored in a **Fonts folder** in the System Folder. You can still view the fonts from the Fonts folder by double-clicking on their icons. Both the screen fonts and the printer fonts are stored in this folder. When you are ready for greater details about fonts, see Chapter 21.

Fonts

*System 7.1 and above uses a Fonts folder inside the System Folder.*

Don't let these simple icons fool you into thinking this is all the System file does—those fonts and sounds may take up about 150 kilobytes of space, but if you check the Get Info window for the System file, you'll find it consumes at least a megabyte and often more. All the rest of the space is for the inner magic that makes the machine work. *The System file must remain inside the System Folder or you will not be able to start up the computer!*

**Finder**

Finder

The **Finder** is the program that runs the Desktop and keeps track of all your files. This icon is just as important as the System file, and *it must stay in the System Folder or you won't be able to start the Mac!* If you try to open the Finder icon, you'll just get a message telling you it's none of your business. (Well, not in exactly those words, but that's the effect.)

**This file is used by the system software. It cannot be opened.**

OK

*If you double-click on the Finder icon, you'll get this message.*

The **Clipboard** and the **Scrapbook file** are stored in your System Folder. See page 152 for information about the Scrapbook, and pages 95–97 for information about the Clipboard. You can double-click on either icon to see what is stored within each file.

**The Clipboard and the Scrapbook File**

Scrapbook File          Clipboard

The **Note Pad File** keeps track of the notes you write into the Note Pad desk accessory, as detailed in the chapter on Desk Accessories, page 151.

**Note Pad File**

Note Pad File

The **Control Panels folder** holds all your control panels. A control panel lets you customize your Mac and the features of many utilities; you can alter your Desktop pattern, set the mouse speed, or change the number of colors displayed on your monitor. Because control panels are so important to you and your work, you really should read Chapter 24.

**Control Panels**

Control Panels

The **Apple Menu Items folder** contains the icons of every item on your Apple menu (the menu on the far left of the menu bar). You can put documents, programs, folders, desk accessories—anything you like—in your Apple menu by dragging their icons to this folder. Of course you should put *aliases* of most files into the folder—not the original files! (See Chapter 25 on Aliases for details.)

**Apple Menu Items Folder**

Apple Menu Items

If you are accustomed to using a previous operating system, you may recall that *desk accessories* lived in suitcases (if you don't recall this detail, then ignore this paragraph).When you double-click on a suitcase that contains desk accessories in System 7, the suitcase opens to a window, and each accessory has its own icon. Desk accessories don't even need to live in suitcases anymore; they can just hang around on a disk as a file.

You can double-click the icon of any desk accessory to open and use it, whether it is stored in the Apple Menu Items folder or not. See Chapter 22 for details on desk accessories.

(Because the Apple Menu is a key to organizing your work and making your life simpler and happier, it would behoove you to read Chapter 23.)

## Startup Items Folder

Startup Items

The **Startup Items folder** can be very handy. Any documents or programs that you store in the Startup Items folder will automatically open each time you start your Mac. (Use aliases, though! See Chapter 25 on Aliases.) This is great, for instance, if you are busy for weeks on the same project—every time you turn on your computer, you can have that particular project open automatically for you, or at least the folder that contains all the files. Or you can put an alias of your hard disk icon in here and then every time you turn on your Mac your hard disk window will open.

You can also put sound files in the Startup Items folder, and when the Mac arrives at the Desktop, this sound will play. If your Mac arrived with a microphone, it is extraordinarily easy to make your own sounds (see page 167). You could leave sweet messages for your lover or reminders to your kids, but of course you would never leave a nasty sound to surprise and terrify that boss you don't like. (You can't make an alias of a sound, though.)

## Extensions Folder

Extensions

The **Extensions folder** holds certain System-related files that help run your Mac or your peripheral equipment. These "system extensions," previously called INITs, should be stored in the Extensions folder. This folder also contains utilities that let you share files on a network. If you have a PostScript printer, you should store your printer font icons (page 134) here, *unless* you have a system version that also has a Fonts folder here in the System Folder (7.1 and above). See "Installing Items," below, for details on how to tell if something belongs in the Extensions folder.

The **Preferences folder** contains files that have settings about how your programs think you want them to work. You can't open the icons in this folder because they're created by your programs. Don't worry about putting anything in here—your application program and System 7 will take care of that.

When you're ready to add, or **install**, something to your Mac's system, like a font or a desk accessory or a new control panel device (cdev; see page 129) or an extension (see page 130), don't worry about which folder it is supposed to be stored in. Here's what to do:

Select the file or files you want to install. Press-and-drag the icon to your *closed* System Folder. The Mac will ask if it's OK to put the item in the appropriate folder. Yes, it's OK. Let the Mac figure out which folder it belongs in. If you have several different sorts of files, the Mac will put each one where it belongs, then tell you where they were placed. How thoughtful.

**Important Note:** When installing items, drag the new item to the *closed* folder icon (even if it's gray) of your System Folder, not to the *open window* of the System Folder. If you drag files to the open window, they will be placed inside the System Folder, yes, *but not in the places they belong.*

**Another Important Note:** This method of installing files does not work for anything that you want to be placed in the **Apple Menu Items folder** or in the **Startup Items folder**. If you want anything to go into either of these folders, you must drag it there directly.

**Preferences Folder**

Preferences

**Installing Files into the System Folder**

System Folder

*Drag the files and drop them on top of this* ***closed*** *folder, not to the open window of the System Folder.*

**Just a Note** If you find that you are using your Apple Menu Items folder regularly, or the Startup Items folder, or that you often use certain desk accessories, you can create aliases of these and put them somewhere where they are easier to access, instead of digging into the System Folder. You could put aliases of the folders on the Desktop, for instance, and just drop things into them as you need. *The files you put into the alias folder will actually drop into the real folder.* See Chapter 25 on Aliases for details.

# CHAPTER TWENTY-ONE

In the Macintosh user environment, the term **fonts** refers to the typefaces available. Technically and traditionally, that's not exactly what "font" means, but we'll let it pass for now rather than confuse the issue.

It used to be so easy. Now font technology and font management has become so complex that I have written a separate book on the subject. In this chapter I'm going to tell you only the very basic things you need to know. And maybe you don't even need to know these. **If your fonts are working fine and this information bores you or makes you quiver, just skip this chapter.** My sister calls font technology "the F word."

At the moment there are two basic font technologies on the Mac: PostScript and TrueType. First I must explain a little about PostScript printers and non–PostScript printers so the font information makes more sense.

**PostScript** is a "page description language" from Adobe Systems, Inc. that allows a printer to interpret certain fonts and graphics. See, certain fonts and graphics are created in the computer using mathematical formulas and outlines. Printers print *dots,* though, not outlines or math formula descriptions. They print tiny dots in "resolutions" of, for instance, 300 dots per inch. The more dots per inch, the smoother the edge of the object because the dots are smaller and closer together. Some PostScript printers, called **imagesetters**, print 1270 or 2540 dots per inch (the type you are reading right now was set by an

## Fonts

*I'm serious—ignore this chapter unless you really want to know the technology of fonts. Just read pages 142–143.*

## Printers: PostScript and QuickDraw

### PostScript

*This is a visual example of a PostScript outline character. You can read the code for this in a word processor.*

### Imagesetters

imagesetter). Anyway, when a font or graphic comes down the pike from the computer to the printer, the printer freaks out at these outlines. The PostScript interpreter takes over and translates, or *rasterizes,* the outlines into dots so they can be printed. PostScript printers are the expensive ones because they have a computer inside of them (sometimes the computer inside your printer is more powerful than the one on your desk). The Apple LaserWriter IINT and IINTX, the TI OmniLaser, or the QMS-PS are examples of PostScript laser printers.

**QuickDraw printers**

Printers that are not PostScript are often called **QuickDraw printers**. This is not because there is anything called QuickDraw inside the printer, but because the images you see on the Macintosh screen are displayed using the QuickDraw language. A printer that can only reproduce what it sees on the Macintosh screen is therefore called a QuickDraw printer. The HP DeskJet, HP DeskWriter, and the Apple StyleWriter are all QuickDraw printers.

OK. Got that? Now for the F information.

**PostScript Fonts**

A **PostScript font** has two parts to each font. There is a *screen, bitmapped* part which is what appears on your screen: little electronic *bits* of information are *mapped* to the pixels (dots) on the screen, turning the dots on or off so you can see the shape of the letters. The screen font is also what shows up in your menu. Screen fonts (bitmapped fonts, same thing) are usually stored in little suitcase icons, although they can actually be kept almost anywhere now.

Centennial

*Screen fonts are usually contained in suitcases. Screen fonts appear on your screen and their names appear in the font menus.*

The second part of a PostScript font is the *outline* part, which is what a PostScript printer reads. This outline portion is actually a mathematically derived outline of the shape of the letter. See, on your screen you're viewing the bitmapped font. When this page goes to the printer, the printer says, "Oh, I don't understand QuickDraw. I'll go find the outline of that font." It finds the outline, which

CenteLig

*The outline portion of a PostScript font is what the PostScript printer reads.*

is sometimes called the *printer font* because that's what the printer needs. The PostScript interpreter rasterizes that outline into dots.

*Printer font icons may look different, depending on which vendor they are from.*

If you have a PostScript printer and you use PostScript fonts, then it doesn't matter what your type looks like on the screen.

The type can look like this on the screen:

but it will print like this: Q

That's because the *bitmapped* font displays on the screen, but the printer creates the type from the *outline* font.

(If you have a non-PostScript printer, though [a Quick-Draw printer], then if it looks crummy on your screen it will look crummy when it prints. Don't worry—there are a couple of wonderful and easy ways around this. Read on.)

- ▼ All PostScript fonts are also known as *outline* fonts.
- ▼ All PostScript fonts are *scalable,* meaning they can be scaled, or resized, to any size you like and they will still print nicely.
- ▼ Almost all PostScript fonts are *Type 1* (and *all* Type 1 fonts are PostScript).

**PostScript fonts**
**Outline fonts**
**Scalable fonts**
**Type 1 fonts**

When you buy PostScript fonts, you will get both parts. You will get a suitcase that contains the screen fonts, plus you will get a printer font for each style of screen font. For instance, if you have Centennial Light, Centennial Light Italic, Centennial Black, and Centennial Black Italic screen fonts in the suitcase, you will have four printer fonts, one for each of those styles. To install them, see page 138.

## What Do You Get on a Font Disk?

*This disk contains both the screen fonts and the printer fonts.*

**TrueType Fonts**

**TrueType fonts**, created by Apple, are also *outline* fonts, although their outline uses a different mathematical system from PostScript's. TrueType fonts are also *scalable*, in that they can be resized to any size you like. TrueType is *not* PostScript, and TrueType is *not* Type 1.

Geneva

*This is a TrueType font icon.*

The TrueType screen information and the printer information are built into one unit so you don't have two separate icons for each font. This means that the screen can use the same information that the printer uses and can simulate the look of the printed type on the screen. TrueType fonts, at any size, will look smoother that you thought your monitor would allow. TrueType fonts, when printed to a PostScript printer *or to a non-PostScript printer,* will print at the resolution of the printer. That is, if you use an Apple StyleWriter with a resolution of 360 dots per inch, your type will print at 360 dots per inch. It's beautiful on the screen and on the page.

# Geneva

*This is what TrueType Geneva looks like right on the screen. This is 19.3-point type.*

This makes it sound like TrueType is better than PostScript, yes? Well, in some cases it is and in some it isn't. Let me explain Adobe Type Manager first and then suggest some optimal combinations of font technology and printers.

**Adobe Type Manager (ATM)**

**Adobe Type Manager** is a small program, a "utility," that costs about $7.50 at the moment and may even be free by now. You drop it into your System Folder and it works. Adobe Type Manager, affectionately called **ATM**, finds the printer font portion (the outline) of the PostScript fonts. It *rasterizes* this outline (turns the outline into dots) and outputs it to the screen. Basically, ATM does the same thing the PostScript *printer* does, but instead of outputting it to paper like the printer would, ATM outputs it to the monitor. So your PostScript fonts look as beautiful on the screen as they do on paper.

~ATM 68020/030     ~ATM™

*Drop both these icons on the System Folder, restart, and you've got ATM.*

In fact, ATM will also rasterize the outlines and output them *to a non-PostScript printer* at the resolution of the printer. With ATM, your HP DeskWriter will create smooth type at 300 dots per inch, which looks as good as any type from a PostScript Apple LaserWriter.

On the screen without ATM

On the screen with ATM

Well, ATM combined with PostScript fonts sounds just like using TrueType, yes? It's true. It is. And it is possible to use both TrueType fonts and PostScript fonts on the same machine and in the same document.

*PostScript and TrueType together*

> *Just don't keep two fonts with the same name from the two different technologies in your computer!* That is, don't keep both TrueType Times and PostScript Times in your Mac. I'll come back to this later.

Here are suggestions for optimal combinations of font technology and printers.

**Which Font Technology For You?**

**If you have a non-PostScript printer** (DeskWriter, DeskJet, StyleWriter, etc.), you will be able to create beautifully typeset pages and see beautiful type on your screen using **TrueType**. If you already have TrueType fonts that came with your machine, then when you begin to invest in more fonts you may want to continue to invest in TrueType fonts.

*Non-PostScript printer: one option*

**If you have a non-PostScript printer**, you will be able to create beautifully typeset pages and see beautiful type on your screen using **ATM and PostScript fonts**. If you already have PostScript fonts, you may want to continue investing in PostScript. There are currently many more typefaces available in PostScript than in TrueType.

*Non-PostScript printer: another option*

> Keep in mind that both TrueType and ATM technologies are centered around type, not graphics. Many graphics use PostScript, and if you have a QuickDraw printer, neither TrueType nor ATM

can help create those graphics on the printed page. You will not be able to get high-end, smooth graphics on a QuickDraw printer, but then if you are in the market for high-end graphics you would not have bought a non-PostScript printer.

**_PostScript printer_**   **If you have a PostScript printer**, the general consensus is to ignore TrueType and use **ATM and PostScript fonts**. One of the reasons for this is that the PostScript interpreter understands perfectly the PostScript fonts; they speak the same language, but the PostScript interpreter has to figure out what to do with TrueType. Life is just smoother and easier and pages print with fewer hassles when you keep the similar technologies together.

**_Imagesetters_**   And if you plan to eventually have your **pages printed on an imagesetter**, keep in mind that service bureaus (see page 108) and imagesetters _really_ don't like to deal with TrueType fonts. Those $100,000 PostScript imagesetters are even fussier than our $3000 laser printers. Check with your service bureau before you show up with a document containing TrueType.

**How to Install Fonts**   Fonts, PostScript or TrueType, must be installed into your System before you can use them. I'm going to tell you **how to install fonts**, but then you really must read the Important Note after the directions.

_If the Application menu shows any other applications open besides "Finder," you must close each one first._

▼ First make sure all applications are closed. Check the Application menu (far right of the menu bar) and make sure there is no other application listed except the "Finder." If there is, select the application, then press Command Q. Do this even if you don't know what I'm talking about and even if, when you choose the application, you don't see any change on your screen. Trust me.

▼ Make sure your System Folder is closed. Make sure you can see both the closed System Folder *and* the fonts you want to install at the same time.

*This is a closed System Folder.*

▼ Whether you have a suitcase or a series of bitmapped fonts, select them and drag them over to the System Folder. When the System Folder is highlighted, let go of the fonts. You'll get a message asking if you want the Mac to put them where they belong. Of course you do.

▼ If you are installing PostScript fonts, find the printer font icons and drag them, all of them, over to the System Folder and drop them inside also. The Mac will put them where they belong.

You can drop a combination of screen, printer, and TrueType fonts onto the System Folder simultaneously and the Mac will place each one where it belongs.

▼ If you have an AFM file (Adobe Font Metrics), ignore it. Do not install it anywhere on your Mac. Leave the AFM file on the floppy disk on the *very* off chance you may ever need it. If you do need it, the application you are using will tell you so.

*Ignore the AFM files.*

▼ You might have some sort of font downloader utility also on a disk of fonts. If you don't already have a downloader in a folder somewhere, copy this one onto your hard disk, *but not into the System Folder!* If you have a downloader already, you don't need this one unless this one is a more recent version (check the Get Info notes on each file; see page 66).

*Even if you don't know what to do with it yet, keep a recent version of a font downloader on your hard disk.*

In System 7.0, bitmapped screen fonts and TrueType fonts are stored in the System file; printer fonts for PostScript are stored in the Extensions folder. In System 7.1 and above, all fonts and all parts of fonts are stored in the Fonts folder within the System Folder. You will need ATM version 3.0 (at least) to use ATM with the Fonts folder.

**Note on installing fonts**

**Important Note:** What I just described is the standard, typical way of installing fonts, the way you read about in all the magazines and literature about the Mac. "Oh, just drag those fonts and drop them into the System Folder." The truth is, though, once you start adding fonts to your collection you need to become responsible and knowledgeable about how to manage those critters. Once you start adding fonts, you must buy and use a font management utility because *your fonts really should not be kept in the System Folder!* If you buy maybe two or three or four font families, you'll be safe enough with all of them in the System. But any more than that and you need help. You need to manage them. You need to buy either Suitcase or MasterJuggler and you need to learn how to use it. All of this is the topic of another book.

**Resident Fonts**

Now, this following bit of information will only pertain to you if you use PostScript fonts and ATM, and it will pertain whether you use a PostScript printer *or* a Quick-Draw printer.

PostScript printers have RAM (random-access memory) and ROM (read-only memory) inside, just like your computer. Permanently built into the ROMs is the printer font information for the standard laser printer fonts: Avant Garde, Bookman, Courier, Helvetica, Palatino, New Century Schoolbook, Times, Zapf Chancery, Symbol, and Zapf Dingbats. These fonts are considered **resident** in the printer. When you buy a PostScript printer you are given a disk with the corresponding screen fonts to install in the Mac. Whenever you print using one of these fonts, the printer looks in its own ROM first, finds the printer font information, and prints.

If you use PostScript fonts and ATM, you may notice that ATM does not affect these standard, resident laser fonts—they still appear rough and jaggy on the screen (although they will print smooth on a PostScript printer, they will print jagged on a QuickDraw printer). Well, remember, ATM uses the printer (outline) font to produce the smooth shapes on the screen. *But ATM cannot find the printer fonts for these standard laser faces because the printer fonts live in the ROM of the PostScript printer!* If you want to see these fonts rendered beautifully on your screen, or if you want to print them to a non-PostScript printer, then you need to buy the printer fonts from Adobe. At the moment you can buy those outlines for $199. Personally, I would rather take that money and buy some new fonts.

Now, *this* following bit of information will only pertain to you if you use a PostScript printer.

System 7 automatically installs TrueType Times, Courier, Helvetica, and Symbol. *It is not possible, though, to print TrueType Times, Helvetica, Courier, or Symbol to a PostScript printer.* Most applications call on a font by name. If a document goes down to the PostScript printer and asks for Times, the printer looks in its own ROM first for an outline called Times. It finds one there, of course (see the paragraphs above).

So you may see TrueType Times on your screen, but you will print PostScript Times. *They are not exactly the same face.* You may end up with different spacing, different line endings, different page breaks. If you have a PostScript printer, then you also have the PostScript versions of these four fonts. *Remove the TrueType versions.*

This is what Palatino looks like on the screen.

But this is how Palatino prints to a PostScript printer.

## Fonts of the Same Name

**City-Named Fonts**

Then there is the situation with **fonts that have a city name**, such as New York, Geneva, Monaco, Cairo, San Francisco, Chicago, Los Angeles, London, Venice, etc. If you use TrueType versions of city-named fonts, you won't have the following problems, with three font exceptions—see "Font substitution," below. But if you are not using TrueType versions, then city-named fonts, almost 100 percent of them, are neither PostScript nor TrueType. They are simply bitmapped screen fonts with no corresponding printer font. They were the original font standard on the Mac, before PostScript was invented.

City-named fonts were designed to take advantage of the original resolution of the screen (72 pixels per inch) and the reigning resolution of the only printer, the Image-Writer (75 dots per inch). Because the letterforms were designed for these lower resolutions, city-named fonts are actually easier to read on the screen, *especially* (sometimes only) if you use a size that has been installed in your Mac. See the following page for discovering which sizes are installed. I always use a city-named font when word processing or databasing (databasing?).

If you are printing to an ImageWriter or other Quick-Draw printer, go ahead and use a city-named font. Your page will look just like it does on the screen.

But if you are printing to a PostScript printer, *change the font to a PostScript (or TrueType) font before you print!* Seriously. PostScript printers don't know what to do with city-named fonts. They get confused when they look for the matching printer font and there isn't one. Depending on the application you're using and which boxes in the Page Setup dialog box you have checked (see next page), the printer will either substitute fonts (see next page) or try to create a bitmapped version that usually looks pretty dorky.

If you are printing to a PostScript printer and you use the city-named fonts New York, Geneva, or Monaco, your application may automatically **substitute fonts**. This is true even if you are using TrueType city fonts. While in your favorite application, choose "Page Setup" from the File menu. Most applications will display this dialog box:

```
┌─────────────────────────────────────────────────┐
│ LaserWriter Page Setup            7.1.1  ┌──────┐│
│                                          │  OK  ││
│ Paper: ⦿ US Letter  ○ A4 Letter          └──────┘│
│        ○ US Legal   ○ B5 Letter  ○ ┌────────┐ ▼ │
│                                    │ Tabloid│    │
│ Reduce or ┌───┐%    Printer Effects:  ┌────────┐│
│ Enlarge:  │100│     ⊠ Font Substitution?│Options││
│           └───┘     ⊠ Text Smoothing?  └────────┘│
│ Orientation         ⊠ Graphics Smoothing?        │
│  ┌──┐┌──┐           ⊠ Faster Bitmap Printing?    │
│  └──┘└──┘                                         │
└─────────────────────────────────────────────────┘
```

Notice the first checkbox button, "Font Substitution?" This box is checked as a default (an automatic selection). Unless you consciously uncheck it, this box makes the printer substitute certain fonts. It will substitute Times when it finds New York, Helvetica when it finds Geneva, and Courier when it finds Monaco. Because the city-named fonts are designed for a much lower resolution (sort of like trying to build letterforms out of bricks), the words take up more space. The PostScript substitution tries to keep the line as long as it was in the city-named font, but to do that it must add more space to fill out the line. Have you ever noticed printed pages with too much space between the words? Or numbers that looked like there were supposed to align but didn't? Or an underline that was dashed? That's the result of trying to print a font with a city name to a PostScript printer.

Try this yourself. Type a page with Geneva, New York, and Monaco. Print it once with font substitution checked, then print it again without font substitution checked. Put the two pages together and look at them against a light.

TrueType Chicago prints very nicely on a PostScript printer, because there is no corresponding substitute or similarly named printer font living in the printer.

## Substitute Fonts

This is a sample of 10-point New York printed with no font substitution.

This is a sample of 10-point New York printed with automatic font substitution.

This is a sample of 10-point Times printed. It needs no font substitution.

This is a sample of 10-point TrueType New York.

## Is It TrueType or PostScript?

**Type Size**

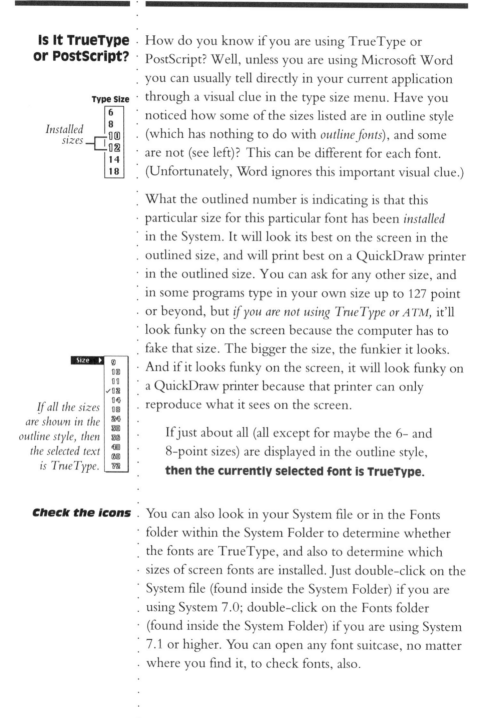

*Installed sizes*

| 6 |
| 8 |
| **10** |
| **12** |
| 14 |
| 18 |

*If all the sizes are shown in the outline style, then the selected text is TrueType.*

**Size ▶**

| 9 |
| 10 |
| 11 |
| ✓**12** |
| **14** |
| **18** |
| **24** |
| **30** |
| **36** |
| **48** |
| **60** |
| **72** |

How do you know if you are using TrueType or PostScript? Well, unless you are using Microsoft Word you can usually tell directly in your current application through a visual clue in the type size menu. Have you noticed how some of the sizes listed are in outline style (which has nothing to do with *outline fonts*), and some are not (see left)? This can be different for each font. (Unfortunately, Word ignores this important visual clue.)

What the outlined number is indicating is that this particular size for this particular font has been *installed* in the System. It will look its best on the screen in the outlined size, and will print best on a QuickDraw printer in the outlined size. You can ask for any other size, and in some programs type in your own size up to 127 point or beyond, but *if you are not using TrueType or ATM,* it'll look funky on the screen because the computer has to fake that size. The bigger the size, the funkier it looks. And if it looks funky on the screen, it will look funky on a QuickDraw printer because that printer can only reproduce what it sees on the screen.

If just about all (all except for maybe the 6- and 8-point sizes) are displayed in the outline style, **then the currently selected font is TrueType.**

**Check the icons**

You can also look in your System file or in the Fonts folder within the System Folder to determine whether the fonts are TrueType, and also to determine which sizes of screen fonts are installed. Just double-click on the System file (found inside the System Folder) if you are using System 7.0; double-click on the Fonts folder (found inside the System Folder) if you are using System 7.1 or higher. You can open any font suitcase, no matter where you find it, to check fonts, also.

**If the icon has three "A"s on it, it is TrueType.**

**If the icon has only one "A", it is a bitmapped font.** The icons with a single A will have a number after the name, such as Zapf Dingbats 12. This means it is the 12-point screen size.

*TrueType font icons have three "A"s; screen fonts have only one A.*

Well, now, I bet you might be wondering why, if you have TrueType New York, you also see screen fonts for New York 10 and New York 12 in your System. Yes, I did say earlier that TrueType combines screen and printer font information into the one icon. These screen fonts for TrueType New York (and any others you find that match your other TrueType fonts) are simply there because it is faster for the Mac to create the font on the screen if it can use the already-created screen font in that size, rather than having to use the TrueType technology to *create* that size. Since most people use sizes 10- and 12-point type most of the time, the screen fonts are merely to speed the process. You could remove these screen versions from your System, which gives you a little more space if RAM is crowded, and you might not notice the slight loss of speed.

Anywhere you find a TrueType icon or a screen font icon, you can double-click on it to see what that font looks like. If it is TrueType, you'll see it in three sizes. If it is a screen font, you see it just in that size screen font.

## Why Do You See Both Icons?

## You Can See What Any Font Looks Like

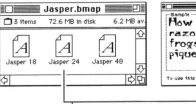 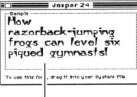

*Double-clicking on the 24-point size screen font icon displays the font in 24-point.*

**Font Sizes**   Below are two PostScript fonts shown in several sizes to give you an indication of what to expect in a particular size. They have been printed on a Linotronic. Times is a *serif;* Helvetica is a *sans serif.* (This book is set in 11 point Bembo, with heads in 10 point Antique Olive Black.)

This line is set in 6 point Times.

This line is set in 8 point Times.

This line is set in 9 point Times.

This line is set in 10 point Times.

This line is set in 12 point Times.

This line is set in 14 point Times.

This line is set in 18 point Times.

This line is set in 24 point Times.

This line is 30 point Times.

This line is set in 36 pt.

This line is set in 6 point Helvetica.

This line is set in 8 point Helvetica.

This line is set in 9 point Helvetica.

This line is set in 10 point Helvetica.

This line is set in 12 point Helvetica.

This line is set in 14 point Helvetica.

This line is set in 18 point Helvetica.

This line is 24 point Helvetica.

This line is 30 pt. Helvetica.

This line is set in 36 pt.

# CHAPTER TWENTY-TWO

# DESK ACCESSORIES

**Desk accessories**, affectionately known as **DA**s, are handy little tools found in your menu under the Apple. Their purpose is to make life easier. Access them like any other menu item—slide down the list until the name of the DA is highlighted, then let go. Desk accessories all appear in windows, so they can be moved around the screen from their title bars and closed with their little close boxes. They all work from within the System, so you can open any DA while you are in any application.

The Apple menu used to hold nothing *except* desk accessories, but now it can hold anything you want to put in it so not everything you see in the menu is a DA (read Chapter 23 on the Apple Menu for details). You can buy an amazing number of desk accessories, many for very low prices. They do all manner of useful and useless things. The following information, however, explains just the DAs that come standard with any Mac.

The **Alarm Clock** won't wake you up in the morning, but it will beep at you while you're sitting at your computer. After it beeps once, the apple in the corner flashes from an apple to an alarm clock. The problem with this alarm is that it doesn't turn itself off—even if you turn off the computer and come back next week, the alarm clock is still flashing; you have to go get it and turn it off yourself.

## Desk Accessories

## Alarm Clock

*Press on the numbers, (which is essentially the title bar) to drag this clock anywhere on your screen.*

When the clock is the *active window* on your screen, you can press Command C and **create a copy of the date and time**; set your insertion point down anywhere, even under an icon at your Desktop, and press Command V; the date and time will paste into your document, like so: 1:38:07 AM   11/30/93.

*flag*

*time clock*
*calendar*
*alarm clock*

❏ **To change the settings:** begin by clicking on the tiny flag on the right; it will open up to a little control panel. After changing a setting, click anywhere in the clock window to put it into effect.

❏ **To change the time:**
  ▼ Click on the time clock icon on the bottom left.
  ▼ Click on the number in the middle panel that you wish to change (this will cause little up and down arrows to appear on the right).
  ▼ Click on the arrows to move the time forward or backward **or** you can *type* in the numbers once you select them, either from the keyboard or the keypad.
  ▼ Change the AM or PM notation the same way.
  ▼ *Note:* you can press the Tab key to move the selection from hours to minutes to seconds, etc.

❏ **To change the date:**
  ▼ Do the same as for the time, details above, *after* clicking on the little calendar icon.

*Arrows with which to change the numbers*

*The switch to turn the alarm on or off*

❏ **To set the alarm:**
  ▼ Click on the alarm clock icon.
  ▼ Change the time to when you want it to go off, as detailed above (check the AM or PM notation).
  ▼ Click the little switch on the *left* to the up position (you'll notice the zingers around the icon now).
  ▼ When the alarm goes off, you'll get a beep and/or your menu will flash, and the little apple in the menu will flash on and off.

❏ **To close up the clock:**
  ▼ To just get rid of the control panel, click on the flag in the upper right again.
  ▼ To put it away altogether, click in its close box.

❏ **To turn off the alarm:**

▼ To turn it off *temporarily,* but leave the alarm set for the next day at the same time, simply get the alarm clock and then click in its close box.

▼ To turn it off *permanently,* you must go in and reverse the process of turning it on; that is, click on the alarm clock icon and turn off the switch.

The **Calculator** is a very handy item to have. It operates just like your hand-held calculator, although it has only the four basic functions. Remember, this calculator is a window so it can be dragged around like any other window and put away with its close box. Access it within any application.

## Calculator

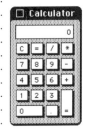

▼ Operate the calculator with the mouse, keyboard, or numeric keypad.

▼ If using the keyboard, make sure you use the real numeral 1 (one) and not a lowercase l (el).

▼ The division sign is the slash: /.
The multiplication sign is the asterisk: ★.

▼ The answer can be copied and pasted into your document using Copy and Paste from the Edit menu. You don't need to select the numbers first—if the Calculator is the active window, the Copy command knows what to copy. You can also copy numbers from your document and paste them into the Calculator.

The **Chooser** is where you choose which printer you wish to use. If you are working at home or at work and are hooked up to only one printer, you need to use the Chooser only the very first time you print. If you have the option of printing to more than one printer, then you need to go to the Chooser each time you want to switch to another printer. For all the gory details on using the Chooser, please see the Chapter 16 on Printing.

## Chooser

**Key Caps**

Key Caps

**Key Caps** can show you the keyboard layout for every font in your System. On a Macintosh keyboard you actually have four separate sets of keys, two of which you know already and two of which only a few people know about. You are about to become In The Know.

▼ After you open up Key Caps, you have a new menu bar that includes "Key Caps."

▼ Pull down the Key Caps menu—this is a list of the fonts that are installed on your System.

▼ Select the font you want; the characters of that font will appear on the keyboard (these are the characters everybody knows about).

▼ To see the Shift characters, press the Shift key (everybody knows these, too).

▼ To see the Option characters, press the Option key (Ha! You are now In The Know).

▼ To see the Shift Option characters, press the Shift and Option keys simultaneously.

Different fonts have different characters in the Option and Shift Option keyboards—some have more, some have less. Most of the Option key characters are consistent in every font, so you can always find, for instance, the accent marks or copyright, trademark, and monetary symbols, etc., in the same place.

**How to use Key Caps**

Key Caps is only for finding the *placement* of all the available characters on the keyboard. Hold down the Option key, for instance, and note where the ¢ sign is located. Once you discover that it is found under the 4 (the $ sign, logically), then you can go back to your document and press Option and 4; the ¢ will appear. It's exactly the same idea as pressing Shift 8 to get an asterisk!

It's possible to type the characters on the Key Caps keyboard, copy them (select the characters first, then choose Copy from the Edit menu), and then Paste the

characters into your document (they will paste in wherever the insertion point is flashing). This works fine as
long as the font you are using in your document is the
same font you chose from Key Caps, or at least that they
share the same character. Otherwise when you paste the
character it will take on the *format* (font, size, style) of the
character to the left of the insertion point, which may
not be what you want at all.

> ▼ At the Key Caps keyboard, find the character
> you want to use.
>
> ▼ Remember what font and what keys to press to
> get that character.
>
> ▼ Go back to your document, select the font you
> want, and press the appropriate keys.
>
> ▼ Can you find the apple?

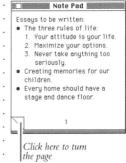

*Very interesting—
this apple won't print
on an imagesetter.*

Also see pages 98–99 for more info, including how to
type accent marks over letters. There is a very tricky
method for discovering the keyboard combination for
many of the accent marks that take two steps to create,
such as Ê, which takes Option i, and then Shift e. But
that detail and some others will be in *The Font and File
Book*. For now, you can use the chart of special characters
at the end of the book as a quick reference for typing.

The **Note Pad** is a nice little accessory that allows you
to write up to eight pages of notes. This is a great place
to leave prearranged messages, notes about particular
formatting used in a document, reminders, or more love
notes. Any messages in the Note Pad are automatically
saved (they will *not* be destroyed on rebuilding the
Desktop, as Get Info notes will, page 66).

The insertion point is flashing; type into it just as you
type anywhere else in the Macintosh. You can backspace/
delete, cut, copy, paste, etc. Turn the pages by clicking
on the little turned corner on the bottom left; click on
the *very* bottom corner to turn the pages backwards.

## Note Pad

```
┌─□═══════ Note Pad ═══════┐
│ Essays to be written:     │
│ ● The three rules of life: │
│   1. Your attitude is your life. │
│   2. Maximize your options. │
│   3. Never take anything too │
│      seriously.           │
│ ● Creating memories for our │
│   children.               │
│ ● Every home should have a │
│   stage and dance floor.  │
│                           │
│               1           │
└┐                          │
 └──────────────────────────┘
```

*Click here to turn
the page*

**Scrapbook**

The **Scrapbook** is a place where you can store text or graphics permanently from virtually any program; then in any other program you can take a copy of it back out from the Scrapbook and paste it into your document. Once you put something in the Scrapbook it is saved to your disk automatically. The Scrapbook holds the entire object or text, even though you can't always see all of it in the window.

*See pages 95–97 if you want more information on the Clipboard.*

*You must go through the Clipboard to put items into the Scrapbook and to take them out.*

❑ **To paste something into the Scrapbook:**
- ▼ From your document, *select* and *copy* the item you want to place (this puts a copy on the Clipboard).
- ▼ Open the Scrapbook.
- ▼ Paste the item into the Scrapbook (from the Edit menu choose "Paste")—it will be pasted onto the page that is visible, and everything else *will move over one; nothing is being replaced.*
- ▼ Close the Scrapbook to get back to your document.

❑ **To copy an item out of the Scrapbook:**
- ▼ Open the Scrapbook.
- ▼ Scroll through until the item you want *is visible.*
- ▼ Copy it (from the Edit menu choose "Copy").
- ▼ Close the Scrapbook.
- ▼ Go to your document and paste it in (usually any text that is pasted, and sometimes graphics, will insert itself wherever the insertion point is flashing; in some programs it will just be pasted into the middle of the page).

❑ **To delete an item from the Scrapbook:**
- ▼ Scroll through until the item you want is *visible.*
- ▼ From the Edit menu choose "Clear" (Clear *removes* it *without* putting it on the Clipboard).

*See the illustration at the top of the next page.*

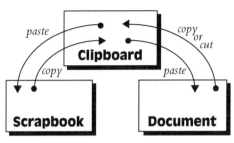

To get things into the Scrapbook, cut or copy them from a document and paste them in.

To get things into the document, copy them from the Scrapbook and paste them in.

The **Puzzle** is a great relaxer. Be sure to have your sound turned on so you get the prize at the end.

**Puzzle**

The completed Apple puzzle. No, I didn't cheat; I really did it!

- ▼ **To switch the Puzzle** from the Apple logo to the numbers, choose "Clear" from the Edit menu while the puzzle is active (click once on it to make it active). Choose "Clear" again to get the Apple logo.
- ▼ **To view the finished puzzle,** choose "Puzzle" from the Apple menu.
- ▼ From the Edit menu, choose "Copy."
- ▼ Put the Puzzle away by clicking in its close box (or press Command W).
- ▼ From the Edit menu, choose "Show Clipboard" to see the completed puzzle. Press Command W to close the Clipboard.
- ▼ **To paste different new pictures** in the Puzzle to entertain your kids or yourself:
- ▼ Create a graphic in your painting or drawing program, or open some clip art or the Scrapbook.
- ▼ Select the graphic and copy it.
- ▼ Quit the graphics program or close the Scrapbook.
- ▼ Open the Puzzle.
- ▼ From the Edit menu, choose Paste. Zap. A whole new Puzzle.
- ▼ **To get the original Puzzle back,** choose "Clear" from the Edit menu.

The numbers puzzle is much easier.

When you solve the puzzle, you get a prize!

This is a custom-made puzzle. Too cute.

## Installing Desk Accessories

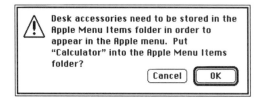

*The Get Info box will tell you if the file is actually a desk accessory.*

Remember, not all of the items in your Apple menu are desk accessories. You won't often need to know which ones are or aren't except when you are **installing** them and want to know where to put them. If you need to know, click once on the icon, then choose "Get Info" from the File menu. If the file is really a desk accessory, meaning the Mac knows it is a desk accessory and not just something you want to put in your Apple Menu Items folder, then you can just drag the icon and drop it onto the top of the *closed* System Folder (see details on page 156 of the Apple Menu chapter). You'll see this polite message:

> ⚠ Desk accessories need to be stored in the Apple Menu Items folder in order to appear in the Apple menu. Put "Calculator" into the Apple Menu Items folder?
>
> [ Cancel ]  [ **OK** ]

You can also place the desk accessory icon directly into the Apple Menu Items folder, found inside the System Folder. As soon as you drop it in, it appears in the Apple Menu and you can use it.

Keep in mind that desk accessories can also be stored right on the Desktop, if you use one so much that you would like to have it available for instant clicking. You might want to keep an alias (Chapter 25) on the Desktop and the original file in the Apple Menu.

## Closing Desk Accessories

You can **close any desk accessory** by clicking in its little close box in the upper left, *or* by pressing Command W.

# CHAPTER TWENTY-THREE

# THE APPLE MENU

The **Apple menu** is under the tiny apple icon (picture) in the upper left corner of your menu bar. This menu is completely customizable, meaning you can add or delete any item at any time. You have access to anything in the Apple menu from within any other program on the Macintosh.

You can customize your Apple menu by adding files to it that you use frequently. Documents, folders, programs, desk accessories—stick 'em in the Apple menu. You'll see tiny icons next to the file name that attempt to give you some kind of visual clue as to the nature of the item.

If you install a *folder* in the Apple menu, selecting it from the menu will open the folder for you. If you install a *program* in the Apple menu, selecting it will open the program for you.

> Except for desk accessories (see Chapter 22 for details on desk accessories), you should put *aliases* of any item into the Apple menu—don't install the original file!

**Aliases** are the coolest little things—an alias is a "gofer." You know, kind of like your kids: "Jimmy, go fer this and go fer that." When you choose or double-click an *alias,* the alias goes and gets the real thing. Even though I will explain how to create aliases here, you should read Chapter 25 for details. Aliases are too cool. And a very important part of managing your work.

## The Apple Menu

*This Apple menu has been customized.*

## Aliases

## Installing Apple Menu Items

*The Get Info window (above) will tell you what kind of file it is, and the window viewed in a list (below) will also tell you.*

Follow these steps to **install any file**, *including desk accessories,* in the Apple menu. If you don't know whether it is an actual "desk accessory" or not, click once on the file, then press Command I to check the Get Info window, (shown on the left). Or you can check the window: when you view the window as some sort of list, the column "Kind" is usually showing.

▾ Unless the file is a desk accessory, first make an alias of it:

   ▪ Click once on the folder, application, document, etc., that you want in the Apple menu.

   ▪ From the File menu, choose "Make Alias."

   ▪ Press-and-drag this alias out of the folder and onto the Desktop. (While it's on the Desktop, I like to remove the word "alias" from the file's name.)

▾ Now to customize your Apple menu, open your System Folder.

▾ There is a folder in the System Folder called **Apple Menu Items.**

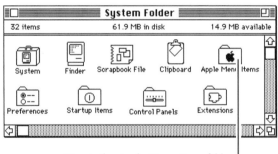

*Here is the Apple Menu Items folder, inside the System Folder.*

▾ The trick is that you need to be able to see both the alias of your file *and* the Apple Menu Items folder at the same time; you may need to rearrange windows and the alias file so you can do that.

▼ Drag the alias and drop it into the "Apple Menu Items" folder.

▼ The item will appear in the menu instantly; you don't need to restart the computer for it to take effect.

The Apple menu displays items alphabetically, as I'm sure you've noticed. When the Mac alphabetizes, blank spaces and punctuation are sorted in front of any other character. So if you add a blank space or a period as the first character in a name, that file will be first in the Apple menu list. The more blank spaces, the higher on the list the file will be located.(And then some utilities that put themselves into the Apple menu have an option to be alphabetized or to be placed at the top of the list, such as Suitcase, which you see in my example.)

## Alphabetized Apple Menu

Here are some **suggestions for customizing your own Apple menu**

## Suggestions for Customizing Your Menu

▼ The "Battery" tells you how much juice is left in the battery that is running your portable computer. If you are not using a portable Macintosh of some sort, you do not need the Battery file. Take it out of the Apple Menu Items folder and throw it away. If you do get a portable Mac, it will be in that Apple menu already.

▼ System 7 automatically places an alias of the Control Panels folder in the Apple menu. But if there are control panels that you use regularly, you can make it even easier on yourself by installing aliases of the individual control panels. For instance, if you switch grayscale and/or color levels on your Mac all the time, then install an alias of the Monitors control panel.

▼ Rather than dig into all those folders to get an application that you use regularly, put aliases of your favorite applications into the Apple menu.

▼ If you have a folder of important items that is filed within other folders, install an alias of the important folder into the Apple menu. When you choose it, the folder will open and you'll have easy access to all those related files.

**Hey—Let's Get Really Fancy**

If you really want to get fancy with customizing your menu, you can group the items into clusters and even create separators between the clusters, taking advantage of the fact that blank spaces are alphabetized first, then non-letters, such as hyphens or bullets ( • Option 8).

| | |
|---|---|
| **About This Macintosh...** | *(The font management utility "Suitcase" puts itself first and I let it.)* |
| **Suitcase** ⌘K | |
| **After Dark** | *I typed three blank spaces in front of the name of each of these aliases so my applications are grouped together.* |
| **DeskPaint** | |
| **PageMaker** | |
| **Word** | |
| ---------------- | |
| **PageMaker fax** | *I typed two blank spaces in front of the names of these template aliases.* |
| **PageMaker Letter** | |
| ---------------- | |
| **At Ease Setup** | *I typed one blank space in front of the names of these control panels.* |
| **Control Panels** | |
| **Monitors** | |
| **SCSIProbe** | |
| ---------------- | |
| **Alarm Clock** | *I didn't change the name at all of these files (there are no blank spaces). This last section contains all the actual desk accessories— these are not aliases.* |
| **Calculator** | |
| **Chooser** | |
| **Key Caps** | |
| **Microtek B&W** | |
| **Note Pad II** | |
| **Puzzle** | |
| **SmartScrap™** | |
| **TouchBASE** | |

*I created the separators by making three aliases of a blank page. I typed one, two, or no blank spaces in front of the row of hyphens. They each "alphabetized" at the top of the different groups of files because a hyphen precedes an alphabetic character.*

# CHAPTER TWENTY-FOUR

# CONTROL PANELS

The **Control Panels** concept is a very important feature of the Macintosh that lets you customize the look and feel of your computer. A certain number of control panels are provided by Apple, and you will run into others provided by other vendors. Each one controls a certain aspect of the Mac, such as what you see in your windows and how the items are displayed, what sound you hear and how loud it is, whether or not you want to share folders and files with other people on other computers, and many other features.

Control panels are all stored in the Control Panels folder found within the System Folder. *A control panel will not work unless it is stored in this folder!* You can open the Control Panels folder and double-click on any file to open the panel itself. Most of the features are self–explanatory, but in this chapter I'll go through each one separately so you can quickly get an idea of what they do and how you can control your Mac.

Control panels are also accessible through your Apple menu (the System installed an alias of the Control Panels folder in the Apple Menu Items folder for you). When you choose Control Panels from the Apple menu, the Control Panels folder opens and you can double-click on any file. If you find you are using certain control panels regularly, you may want to put an alias of the panel itself directly into the Apple menu (see the previous chapter).

## Control Panels

Control Panels

*Control Panels are stored in this folder, found in the System Folder.*

*These are some of the Control Panels that are standard with the Mac.*

## General Controls

General Controls

The control panel called **General Controls** lets you control several details. You can change the pattern and the colors of your monitor.

*This is an enlargement of the selected pattern.* — *You can edit the existing pattern, or change it altogether, by drawing in this box with the mouse. The tiny bar above the colored box below indicates which color you will edit with. If you have a color monitor, double-click on one of these colored boxes to get the Apple Color Wheel, where you can choose another color.*

*Cick the tiny right or left arrows to view the existing patterns. Click on the pattern itself to change your screen. Double-click the pattern to save it; otherwise it will disappear when you view another.*

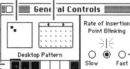

*Choose how fast the insertion point blinks whenever you are in a typing mode.*

*Choose whether, when you let go of a menu selection, the highlighted selection flashes or not. I like at least one flash to let me know I really did choose the menu item.* —

*Click on any of these numbers or dates, then type in the numbers you want to change them to, or use the tiny arrows that appear. Click the calendar or clock icons to set the changes. The time you set here will change the Alarm Clock, and vice versa.*

On the **Performa** models, your General Controls panel will not give you the option to edit the Desktop pattern. You will have a number of beautiful patterns, though, much more complex than these, to choose from.

## Brightness

Brightness

The **Brightness** control panel only works on computers that do not have brightness or contrast knobs on the monitor itself. If you have dials of some sort, use those to control the brightness of the screen. The dials may be on the side of the monitor, under the Apple logo on the front of the computer, or perhaps inside a panel similar to your television. If this Brightness control panel works on your Mac, just press–and–drag the slider bars to adjust the levels.

## Color

Color

The **Color** control panel only works if you have a color monitor or a grayscale monitor (a grayscale monitor is one that can show varying shades of gray instead of just black and white). Press on the arrow to get a menu of color choices. The color you choose for "Highlight color" will appear whenever you select text, whether you are in an application or in a dialog box. The color you choose for "Window color" will be the color of the border and sometimes a few details of the windows. Keep in mind that a colored border around your windows takes more time to create than a black-and-white window. If you choose "Other…," you will get the Apple Color Wheel where you can create and select any color possible. Just play with this wheel— move the scroll bars up and down, press on the arrows, drag around in the wheel itself. (To change the color of *icons*, use the Labels control panel.)

*· If you click on "Sample
· Text," you'll see the names
· of the programmers.*

Use the **Date & Time** control panel to change the date and time, if necessary (this will change the date and time in the Alarm Clock and in the General Control panels, and vice versa). Just click on the day or time and press the arrows or type the numbers. To accept the new information, click anywhere, close the control panel, *or* press the Return key.

**Date & Time**

Date & Time

This control panel also lets you change the *formats* for the date and time. Click the button "Date Formats…" or "Time Formats…" to get a list of options. As you change options here, a sample of the new format will appear in the bottom portion of the box. If you have any other language versions installed in your System, you can choose to display date and time in that language's standard format: choose the languge from the "Date Formats" menu by pressing on the arrowhead (it probably says "U.S." at the moment). As soon as you make any changes to these boxes, the Format menu will display "Custom."

When you use a program in which you can automatically insert the date or time, the numbers will appear in the format you have determined here.

### Keyboard

Keyboard

*If you notice you seem to type double spaces between words often, or perhaps double letters as in "tthe" or "yyou," you might want to lengthen the delay.*

The **Keyboard** control panel gives you control over several features on your keyboard.

▼ Every key on the Macintosh keyboard will repeat, meaning if you hold the key down it will continue typing that character across the page. "Key Repeat Rate" lets you control just how fast that key repeats across the page.

▼ If you click the "Off" button under "Delay Until Repeat," then the keys will not repeat at all, no matter how long you hold them down.

▼ From "Long" to "Short" gives you control over how long you can hold your finger on a key before it starts to repeat. This is wonderful for people who are heavy on the keys—set it for a long delay so even if your fingers plod along on the keys you won't end up with extra characters all over the place.

▼ If you have a file in your System Folder that provides you with another keyboard layout, perhaps for another language or for a Dvorak keyboard, the names of the different layouts will show up here and you will be able to switch between them.

### Labels

Labels

*The labels you create in the control panel, above, will appear in the Label menu on the Desktop, shown at the top of the next page.*

The **Labels** control panel allows you to set up a labeling system for the files on your Mac, which you can access and apply from the Labels menu at the Desktop. You can set up groups of icons that are related to each other, but that may be stored in different places. For instance, you may have a series of lectures you present in different fields. You can store the lectures each in the folders for the respective fields, but apply a "Lecture" label to them so you can search for and group them together.

The label is *in addition* to the icon's name. It's just attached to the file; it does not appear in the name. In your Desktop windows, you can choose to display the "Label" as another column in the list (use the Views control panel; see page 47). If you choose to display it in the windows, then your View menu will have the option to view "By Label." Perhaps you have a folder with lots of files in it from a variety of topics. You can label some or all of them, then when you view "By Label" all the files from each topic will be grouped together.

You can change the name of any of the existing labels:

▼ First open the Labels control panel (double-click on the panel "Labels" in the Control Panels folder).

▼ Select an existing label (you can press the Tab key to select each one).

▼ Type the name of the new label.

▼ Close the control panel window (click in its close box *or* press Command W). The revised label will instantly appear in the Labels menu.

▼ **To apply a label to an icon**, simply select the icon or group of icons. Then choose the label from the menu.

**Note:** If you apply a label one day and then later change the name of that particular label in the control panel, all icons with the previous label attached will change to the new label! For instance, say I labeled 12 documents with the label "Love Letters." If I go to the control panel and change "Love Letters" to "Dog Food," every document that had the label "Love Letters" will now have the label Dog Food."

You can also use the Labels control panel to **color your icons**. On a color monitor, the Label menu at the Desktop has colored boxes. Simply select any icon, then choose the color from this menu. Yes, this does also apply the label to it; it's simply another way of labeling— rather than by name, by color. You can search by color just as easily as by label.

*Color your icons*

**Launcher**

Launcher

The **Launcher** control panel is on the Performa models of the Macintosh and changes several features of the regular System. It brings up the Launcher window, where applications and documents are displayed as buttons that open with a single click; it prevents a user from accidentally slipping out of the application and landing at the Desktop through a misplaced click; it defaults all saved documents to a folder called "Documents." Details on the Launcher are in Chapter 34, The Performa.

**Memory**

Memory

Use the **Memory** control panel to set a *disk cache* (pronounced "cash") for your Mac, turn *virtual memory* on or off, and turn *32-bit addressing* on or off. The **disk cache** is a part of the memory your Mac uses to hold information about the most recent things it's done on your disk, like getting files and saving them. Getting this data from the disk cache is much quicker than going back to the disk to retrieve it. The Mac will set a default (an automatic choice) for the cache size, depending on how much memory is available. You can override this default by changing the Cache Size yourself. It might seem like setting a larger cache size would be better, but generally it actually isn't because then that much memory is unavailable to any applications you open.

*This control panel assumes you know what* **memory** *is in the first place. Read the chapter called "Very Important Information" for a better understanding of the difference between hard disk space, memory, and virtual memory.*

You should really read Chapter 30, called "Very Important Information," so you understand memory and **virtual memory**. The basic idea behind virtual memory is that you can use some of your hard disk space as memory. If after reading that chapter you want to turn on virtual memory, this control panel is where you do it.

If your Mac can hold more than 8 megabytes of memory, then you will see the section for **32-bit addressing**. If you don't know whether or not you have more than 8 megs of memory (RAM, random access memory) installed, choose "About This Macintosh..." from under

the Apple menu while you are at the Finder.
Next to the item "Total Memory," the Mac
will tell you how much RAM is installed. If this
number is more than 8,192K, then you should
turn **on** 32-bit addressing. If the Total Memory
is something like 12, and your System Software is taking
up something like 6 or 9 megs, the System is reporting
that high amount for itself because 32-bit addressing is
not on. (Look up 32-bit addressing in the Jargon section
if you're not quite sure what it is or does for you.)

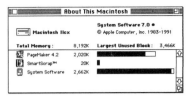

*You can only get this
dialog box if you are at
the Finder (Desktop).*

If you ever run old software that is not "32-bit clean"
(it's a long story, just trust me), you may run into problems
if 32-bit addressing is turned on. "Problems" like crashing your computer. Software that is not 32-bit clean will
often run okay if you turn off 32-bit addressing, although
if the software is really old it just may not work with the
System itself.

**Trivia:** *Hold the Option
key as you press on the
Apple menu. Choose
"About the Finder" to see
an interesting graphic (it's
actually the graphic for the
very first Macintosh Finder).
Wait a minute or two for the
secret message. If you hold
down the Option and the
Command keys before you
choose it, you'll get a very
interesting cursor in addition
to the secret message.*

Some machines (the SE30, Mac II, IIx, IIcx) cannot use
more than 8 megs of memory anyway, even if you install
it and turn on 32-bit addressing. You can get the software
called Mode32 from Connectix, now available from
Apple, user groups, and bulletin boards, to help one of
these Macs access more memory.

The **Monitors** control panel lets you choose how many
of the available shades of gray or colors your screen will
display, assuming you even have a choice. The number
of grays and colors to choose from depends on your
monitor, how much memory you have, and what kind
of video card is in your computer.

## Monitors

Monitors

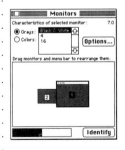

If you have **more than one monitor** attached to your
computer, this control panel also lets you determine
which one should function as your main monitor. You
can press on the tiny menu bar in the control panel and
drag it to another monitor. Whichever one has the menu

bar is the one that will function as your main monitor. This change won't take effect until you restart the Mac.

You can also drag the picture of the second monitor around and put it on the same side of your main screen as your second monitor is positioned on your desk. The mouse will move off the main screen in that direction. For instance, in the example on the previous page, the second monitor is positioned to the left of the main screen. When I move my mouse to the left, it goes off the screen over to the second monitor.

**Mouse**

Mouse

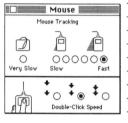

Use the **Mouse** control panel to switch to a tablet speed, if you use a tablet (a tablet is a pad on which you use a pen-shaped stylus; you would know if you had one). The terms "Slow" and "Fast" are a little misleading. The "slower" the "Mouse Tracking," the farther you have to move the mouse across the desk to get the cursor to move across the screen. Slower speeds are good for drawing. It may drive you nuts, though, to work on someone's computer who has the mouse tracking set to one of the slower speeds. Now you know what to do about it.

The "Double-Click Speed" lets you set the speed at which the mouse will interpret two clicks as a double-click (as opposed to two single clicks). If you're kind of slow with your finger, set it to the slow speed. If you set it to the fastest speed (the far right button), you may find that the mouse sometimes thinks a single click is a double-click.

**Numbers**

Numbers

Use the **Numbers** control panel to determine how numbers and currency will display. This can be important in international work, where numbers in the thousands may be separated with a period instead of a comma. The format you choose here will affect cells and fields and headers that use a currency or number format automatically.

Use the **Sound** control panel to determine the volume of
all the sounds that come out of your Mac. Just move the
slider bar on the Speaker Volume up or down. If you set
the bar at zero, the menu bar will flash instead of beep.
You can also choose what noise you want to hear instead
of the beep. Click on the name of a sound to hear it. The
last one you choose before you close the control panel is
the sound the Mac will use when you need to be beeped.

If you *don't* have one of the Macs that came with a
microphone, then your control panel won't have the
bottom portion you see in the example. If you *do* have
a microphone, then you can have lots of fun. Plug the
mike into the little port on the back of the machine
(there's only one spot the plug will fit into). (If you have
a phono jack adapter, you can directly record sounds
from other sources, such as music CDs and tapes.) Click
the "Add…" button, then record sounds using the
buttons as you would on a tape recorder. When you save
the sound, it will appear in the list and you can select it.

These sound files are actually kept in the System file
(the Mac puts them there for you). My uncle recorded
himself hollering, "Woman—get back in the kitchen!"
and moved the sound from the System file to the Startup
Items folder so when my aunt turned on the machine
she got yelled at. (Don't worry—she didn't get mad,
she got even.)

If you have more than one hard disk attached to your
Mac that has a System Folder on it, or perhaps more than
one *partition* to your hard disk, you can use the **Startup
Disk** control panel to determine which hard disk to use
to start your computer. Each attached hard disk that
contains a System will appear as an icon in the control
panel; click on one to choose it. You need to restart the
computer for the new disk to become the startup disk.

## Sound

Sound

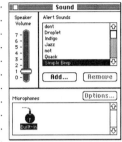

*If your Mac came with a
microphone, you'll have
the "Add" button and the
bottom portion shown here.*

*When you click the
"Add" button, you get
these controls for
recording the sounds.*

## Startup Disk

Startup Disk

## Networking Control Panels

Sharing Setup

Users & Groups

File Sharing Monitor

System 7 has several built-in **networking** features, and there are three control panels that let you change those settings. These are explained in Chapter 27 on Sharing Files, page 181.

**Sharing Setup** lets you set your user name, choose a password for yourself, and turn on your Mac's ability to share files over the network.

**Users & Groups** lets you restrict access to your computer to specific people or lets everybody see what you've been working on.

**File Sharing Monitor** shows you what's being shared and lets you know just who's looking in your folders.

## Views

Views

The **Views** control panel lets you customize the look of your Desktop (Finder) windows. This control panel is explained in detail in Chapter 8 on Desktop Windows.

# CHAPTER TWENTY-FIVE

**Aliases** are one of the greatest features of the Mac. An alias is a duplicate *icon* (not a duplicate *file*) that *represents* the real thing. Once you create an alias (which only takes up about 2 or 3K of disk space), use that alias as if it were the original file, but you can store an alias wherever it's easiest for you to use.

When you double-click on an alias that may be sitting on your Desktop, the Mac actually goes to the *original* file and opens the original. This is ideal for those applications that have to be in the same folder as their supplemental files, like their dictionaries or preferences, to open or to function properly. Having an alias hanging out on your Desktop just gives you a quick path to the original file.

Say you have a program you use frequently—your word processing program, for instance. You can make an alias of MacWrite or WriteNow or What-Have-You and put it just about anywhere. How about in your Apple menu? No problem. Out on your Desktop? Sure.

Store an alias of your hard disk icon inside the Startup Items folder within the System Folder. Then whenever you turn on your Mac, the window to your hard disk will automatically open. Leave an alias of the Chooser on your Desktop if you have to change printers often. Leave an alias of the Apple Menu Items folder open on the Desktop also, so you can double-click to access any desk accessory without having to go into the menu. And since you can make any number of aliases of any one thing,

## Aliases

*This alias sits on my Desktop so I can quickly pop in to check my mail.*

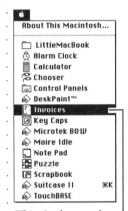

*This Apple menu has an alias of the PageMaker document I use for invoices; the original is nested deep within folders. There is also an alias of the folder for this book. I put a blank space before its name so it would appear first in the list.*

you can store aliases of your word processing program in folders all over your hard disk so you can locate it quickly, no matter where you are or what you're doing.

You can make aliases of programs, documents, desk accessories, disks, folders, control panels, etc. Aliases provide a wonderful tool for organizing your work; anything you want to use can be only one click away from wherever you are.

## Making Aliases

MerryWives  *Merry Wives alias*

*When you make an alias, the alias looks just like the original, but the name is italic.*

*Merry Wives*

*I like to remove the word "alias" so the name is shorter.*

*Merry Wives*

*Even when you view your windows by name, an alias looks like an alias.*

**Making an alias** is so easy.

▼ Select the item you want to make an alias of (click once on it).

▼ From the File menu, choose "Make Alias."

▼ The new alias icon will look the same and will be named the same, with the word *alias* added. An alias name is in italic so you can always recognize the file as an alias.

I like to remove the word "alias" from my files because otherwise the name too long. You have to move the alias out of the folder the original is in before you change the name because you can't have two files with the same name in one folder.

▼ Just drag the icon to wherever you want to keep it. Rename it if you like. The new file does not have to have the word "alias" in its name. *And it doesn't matter if you move the original file*—the alias can always find it.

▼ To put the alias in your Apple menu, drag the alias icon to the "Apple Menu Items" folder in your System Folder and drop it in.

Making aliases is easy, but there are a couple of **fine points** you should understand.

▼ An alias isn't really a *duplicate* of anything but the icon; it's just a *representation* of the real thing. If you double-click on an *alias* of Word, you'll start your *original* Word program running, even if the original Word is stored in a completely different folder.

▼ If you delete an alias of something, you don't delete the original—it's still stored on your hard disk. So you can keep on revising your filing system as your needs change. Don't want that alias of MacWrite cluttering up your MacDraw folder any more? Fine; throw it away. The original MacWrite is still where you left it.

▼ If you put an item into an *alias* of a folder, the item actually gets put into the *original* folder.

▼ You can move an alias and even rename an alias. The Mac will still be able to find the original and open it whenever you double-click on the alias.

▼ Even if you move or rename the *original* file, the Mac can still find it.

▼ If you eliminate the *original* file, the Mac does not automatically eliminate any of the representational aliases you created.

Here are other ideas for **using aliases**

▼ If you have a document you use frequently, put an alias of it in the Apple menu: just open your System Folder and drag the alias into the "Apple Menu Items" folder.

▼ In fact, if you find you use your Apple Menu Items folder regularly, make an alias of the folder and leave it on your Desktop. Dropping a file in the alias folder automatically puts it in the real folder.

▼ If you have a program or a document that you want to open immediately whenever you turn on your Mac, put an alias of it in your "Startup Items" folder, found in the System Folder.

▼ Leave aliases of applications neatly organized directly on your Desktop or in your hard disk window. This way you don't have to dig into folders to open the applications. It also makes all your apps available to you for the **drag-and-drop trick of opening files**, including files from other programs. Remember: you can drag any document onto the icon of the application to open the document. Many applications can open files created in other programs this way, so if you come across a file from a program you don't have, or perhaps you don't know where it came from, you can drag it over the top of all these aliases that are sitting on your hard disk. Any icon that changes color when you drag the document on top of it will open that document.

▼ Use the drag-and-drop trick mentioned above to open those ubiquitous "ReadMe" files that are on every disk of software. These files open automatically in TeachText, but I like to *print* the ReadMe files. I hate to print them in the font they show up in within TeachText because the type is too big and it takes too many pieces of paper, but TeachText doesn't let me change the font. So I drop ReadMe files onto an alias of my word processor and I am happy.

▼ Put an alias of a Control Panel that you use over and over again out on your Desktop or in your Apple menu.

▼ Use aliases to store documents in two or three places at once. For instance, you may want to keep budget reports in folders organized by months, as well as in folders organized by projects.

▼ Some of the more advanced uses for aliases aren't apparent unless you're on a network. For example, you can make an alias of your file server so you can connect to it quickly. And you can make an alias of your hard disk, copy it onto a floppy (since the alias is only about 2K), and take it to somebody elses's computer on the network. Then you can quickly connect back to your own computer just by clicking on the alias on the other computer (provided you have set up the sharing privileges first; see Chapter 27 on simple networking and sharing). This concept is sometimes called the "office-on-a-disk."

▼ **Use aliases to find files that you keep stored on floppy disks or cartridge hard disks.**

- Make an alias of an original file; *the original file must be on the floppy or the cartridge already*. Be sure this floppy disk or cartridge disk has an identifiable name, and be sure you put a label on the disk with this name.

- Drag the alias from the floppy to your hard disk. Now you can eject the disk and store it safely.

- When you double-click on the alias you have on your hard disk, you will get a dialog box asking for the floppy disk that contains the original file (that's why you named the disk memorably and actually labeled it, right?).

- Since aliases only take up about 2K, you can keep a folder of many of the files you use only occasionally but that you do want to keep track of. This folder of aliases is your secretary who knows just where everything is filed. (Also see "Finding the Original File," next page.)

**Finding the Original File**

If you need to **find the original file** belonging to an alias, follow these steps:

▼ Click once on the alias.

▼ From the File menu, choose "Get Info," *or* press Command I.

▼ The Get Info dialog box tells you where the original is located.

▼ If you want to have the Mac go get it and bring it to you, click the button "Find Original." The window the original is stored in will be displayed and the icon will be highlighted.

▼ If you click "Find Original" *or* if you double-click on an alias that has its original stored on a floppy disk or a cartridge hard disk (see previous page), you will get a message telling you which disk to insert.

```
┌─────────────────────────────────────┐
│ ▤ ▭▭ MerryWives  Info ▭▭▭         │
├─────────────────────────────────────┤
│    ╱W╲   Merry Wives                │
│                                     │
│   Kind : alias                      │
│   Size : 2K on disk (539 bytes used)│
│                                     │
│  Where : Hard Disk :                │
│                                     │
│  Created : Sun, Nov 29, 1992, 4:32 PM │
│ Modified : Sun, Nov 29, 1992, 4:36 PM │
│ Original : Shakespeare Stories : Merry Wives │
│                                     │
│ Comments :                          │
│  ┌───────────────────────────────┐  │
│  │                               │  │
│  │                               │  │
│  └───────────────────────────────┘  │
│                                     │
│ ☐ Locked      ( Find Original )     │
└─────────────────────────────────────┘
```

*Click here and the Mac will find and display the original file.*

*If the original file is on another disk and the disk is not in the computer, you will get a message telling you which disk to insert.*

```
┌──────────────────────────────┐
│ ▱▱  Please insert the disk:   │
│ ▱▱  Shakespeare Stories       │
│         ( Cancel )            │
└──────────────────────────────┘
```

**Find File** is a wonderful time-saving and frustration-reducing feature that allows you to search for any file on your disk. Have you ever saved a document and then wondered where it went? Or have you needed to find all the letters you wrote last Tuesday? Or do you want a file that is buried five folders deep and you're just too lazy to dig down? You can also do a search-within-a-search, like find all the letters you wrote last Tuesday whose titles start with "Memo to."

**You can find any file** if you know any of this information about it:

- ▼ A few characters in the file's name, or what characters start or end its name.
- ▼ Any of the words that may be in the file's Get Info comment box (see page 66).
- ▼ The date you last changed the file, or when you created it.
- ▼ What label you assigned to it.
- ▼ What kind of file it is (an application, a folder, an alias, etc.).
- ▼ The version number.
- ▼ Whether it's locked or not.
- ▼ Whether its size is greater than or less than so many kilobytes.

**Find File**

**You Can Find:**

**Simple Finding**

When you want to find a file and you know its name, or at least several characters (a "string" of characters) in its name, you can just do a **quick-and-easy simple find**

▾ From the File menu, choose "Find..." (*or* press Command F). You'll see this dialog box:

```
╔══════════════════ Find ══════════════════╗
║                                           ║
║   Find: [                            ]     ║
║                                           ║
║  ( More Choices )     ( Cancel )  (( Find ))║
║                                           ║
╚═══════════════════════════════════════════╝
```

▾ If you know the name or even part of the name of the file you're looking for, just type the characters in the Find box (it doesn't matter whether you use capital letters or lowercase letters).

▾ Click the Find button, *or* hit the Return key. When Find File finds a matching file, it will display it for you. If the file was deep in folders, Find File will put it right in front of your face. If a matching file can't be found, you'll hear a beep.

▾ If the file isn't exactly the one you want, just leave it there and press Command G (which is the shortcut for "Find Again"). This will put the wrong file away, back where it came from, and another file with the name you want will be displayed. Keep pressing Command G to put the wrong one away and find another one. When the Mac has found every file with that string of characters, you'll hear a beep.

Instead of searching for something one file at a time, you can click the button **More Choices** to bring up a fairly sophisticated Find utility.

*Click "More Choices" to really have some fun.*

Now there are a great many more options. Notice the downward-pointing arrowheads next to "name" and "contains," plus the tiny shadow behind the words. These are visual clues that if you press on these words you will see menus. These pop-up menus hold more choices. As you select different options in the first pop-up menu (currently displaying "name"), the options available in the other menus change. Try it and see.

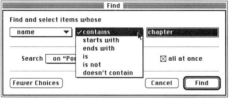

*When "name" is my search criteria, the second menu has options for text, and I can type into the third box.*

*Notice how the options change in all three spaces, depending on what you select in the first menu. Spend a few minutes checking this out so you have a better idea of what your options are for searching.*

*When "date created" is my search criteria, the second menu has options for dates, and I can click to change the date.*

*When "label" is my search criteria, the last box becomes a menu.*

*All At Once*

⊠ **all at once**

*Click this box
to display all the found
files simultaneously.*

*Even if your window was
in an icon view, Find
File creates a list, then
expands the folders that
have a file you want.*

If you check the **all at once** checkbox, Find File will find and display, simultaneously, every occurrence of whatever you've specified so that you can see all the matching files at the same time, without searching individually for each one. It does this by making a list of the items in your hard disk window (if that's where you searched), and then expanding the appropriate folders. When you scroll down the list, you will see that every matching file is highlighted.

Maybe you want to apply a label or a color to all of these files at once; since they are all selected, just choose the label or color from the Label menu. Maybe you want to throw them all away; drag *one* of the icons to the trash and they will all follow, whether you can see them or not (remember, *the tip of the pointer* must reach the trash can; it doesn't matter whether the icon reaches it or not). Maybe you want to store them all into a new folder; just drag one of the files into the new folder and they will all go. *As soon as you click anywhere except a highlighted icon, all the selected files will be deselected!*

If all the files cannot be displayed at the same time, the Mac will tell you this. When you press Command G to see the rest of the selected items, the first group of files is deselected.

**!** If Find File has expanded a lot of your folders (see page 73 for info on expanded and compressed folders) and you want them all compressed again, simply press Command A to select all the files in the window, then press Command LeftArrow.

You can also choose **where you want Find File to search**. Narrowing your search can save a lot of time. See the downward-pointing arrow in the label next to "Search"? You can press on the arrow to get the menu of places to search—just the Desktop, just your hard disk, just a floppy disk, just the active window, or perhaps just the files you've selected (select the files and folders *before you choose Find File)*. What you see in this menu is affected by what is selected on your disk and whether the "all at once" button is checked or not.

You can **get back to the simple Find box** by clicking the button "Fewer Choices."

In a **search within a search** you can look for items that meet one set of criteria. Then search just those selected files for the next set of criteria. For example, suppose you have a lot of files that have "Chapter" in their names, but you only want to locate the chapters you wrote after March 20, 1993. Here's how to do that.

▼ First, search "all at once" for all files whose "name" "contains" the word "chapter." Find File will find and highlight all the matching files.
*Don't deselect the files!* (Don't click anywhere.)

▼ From the "Search" pop-up menu, choose "the selected items."

▼ Change the search criteria to "date created" and "is after."

▼ When you choose "date created," today's date will be shown. To change the date to March 20, click once on the part of the date you wish to change, then click on the little arrows.

▼ Click the "Find" button, or hit the Return key. Find File will display only those files that have the word "Chapter" in their names that were created after March 20, 1993. It's too cool.

## Restricting Searches

*Widen or narrow your search as you choose.*

## Back to Simple Finding

## Search Within a Search

**Other
Search Ideas**

Don't limit yourself to using "Find…" only when you are looking for a particular file. This feature can also be a lot of help if you're reorganizing your filing system. For instance, you can search by "date created" to see which of your files are outdated. Or if you're making backups, you can first search by "date modified" to see which files you haven't backed up since the last time. Or you can search for a file you want to use simply because you don't want to go digging through folders to get to it: Hit Command F, type a few letters of the name, hit Return, when the file appears, hit Command O to open it. Oh, there are all kinds of ways to be lazy—I mean efficient.

# CHAPTER TWENTY-SEVEN

# SHARING FILES

This chapter is only for you if you have more than one Mac in the same house or office. If you do have more than one Mac, it is incredibly easy—in fact, it's so easy it's spooky—to **share files** between Macs. You can just drop a file into a shared folder and it instantly appears on the other computer. This works even if the other Macs are not using System 7.

You must be networked together (your Macs must have some sort of cable connecting them to each other or both to the same printer), but networking a couple of Macs is a simple procedure. There are entire books written on networking, and the procedure *can* get very complex, so complex that people make a living being network specialists and in a large office there is usually a *network administrator*. I am only going to explain the simplest method to get a couple of Macs talking to each other. I do this in my office with one other person and it is the coolest, most efficient way for us to get work done.

You need to have installed the **file sharing software** that came with System 7. If you didn't install it, you can run the Installer again from your original disk (have that power user friend of yours help you), click Customize, and install it. It's probably already there—if you see the control panels Network, Users & Groups, File Sharing Monitor, and Sharing Setup in your Control Panels folder, and if you see Network Extension, File Sharing Extension, and AppleShare in your Extensions folder, then you probably have everything you need.

**Sharing Files, Networking**

**File Sharing Software**

## AppleTalk and LocalTalk

System 7 has the **AppleTalk** networking software built into it that allows you to connect with other kinds of networks. The **LocalTalk**® network is a type of Apple-Talk network, and for our purposes here LocalTalk is all you're gonna need—the software and hardware is built into the System and into the computer. If you use EtherTalk® or TokenTalk®, you need other help.

## Network Control Panel

Network

*This control panel lets you choose between installed networks.*

The **Network control panel** is similar to the Chooser (where you choose which printer you are going to print to). In the Network control panel you choose which network you are going to use, *if* you are using EtherTalk or TokenTalk. *If all you're going to use is LocalTalk, which is what this chapter is about, you can ignore this control panel.* In fact, you don't even need it, so if you don't have it in your Control Panels folder, don't worry about it. If you have no idea whether or not you are connected to another type of network, you can open the Network control panel; it will have an icon for each network you are connected to. If all you see is the LocalTalk Built-in icon, then you're on LocalTalk.

## Step 1: Connect the Computers

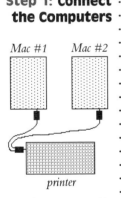

*This is one possible arrangement. Even if the printer is off, the two computers can talk to each other.*

So if you're still reading, you have checked that you have file sharing control panels and that you're only using LocalTalk. The first thing you must do before you can actually share files is connect the two computers together with a cable. All you need are LocalTalk-compatible cables that you can get at your computer store or through mail order. I use the PhoneNET kit from Farallon because it's much cheaper and then I can use plain ol' telephone cables from the hardware store when I need to rearrange things (you can get extra long telephone cables and connect computers in different rooms to each other and to the same printer). Just follow the directions in the kit you buy. Both the computers in my office have PhoneNET connectors plugged into the printer ports on the backs of the machines. Then telephone cables are plugged into the connectors. Both of these cables (one from each machine) plug into another connector that plugs into the printer (see the illustration on the previous page). It's really not much different from connecting your VCR and your CD player and your television together.

Now you must **name the Macintosh** and the owner. Generally the biggest computer will be your *file server,* or the one to which the other computers will connect. In large offices or school labs, there are one or more computers that do nothing except act as file servers. In your home or office, one of the Macs will be considered the file server, but to you it will still be your working Mac.

**Step 2: Name the Mac**

You name the Macintosh through the Sharing Setup control panel, found in the Control Panels folder in the System Folder. Double-click the Sharing Setup icon to open it.

*Sharing Setup control panel*

Sharing Setup

*If you can't open the Sharing Setup control panel, check that you have the File Sharing Extension and the Network Extension in your Extensions folder inside the System Folder. If not, install them and restart.*

▼ Type your name in the edit box "Owner Name."

▼ Make up a password, up to eight characters, so you can control whether other people have access to your files. I use my name because I can never remember a password.

▼ After you type the password, the letters turn into bullets (••••). You better remember this password, including which letters you typed capital or lowercase.

▼ Type a name for your Mac. This is the name that the person on the other computer needs to know to connect to you. This name will appear in their Chooser when they try to share your files.

**Turn on file sharing** | ▼Click the "Start" button to turn File Sharing on.

```
┌─────────────────────────────────────┐
│ □▭      Sharing Setup        ▤▤▤     │
│ ┌──┐                                 │
│ │▦ │  Network Identity               │
│ └──┘                                 │
│    Owner Name:   [Robin_____]  │
│    Owner Password: [•••••]           │
│    Macintosh Name: [Big One_____] │
│ ┌──┐                                 │
│ │▦ │  File Sharing                   │
│ └──┘     ┌Status──────────────────┐  │
│  ┌──────┐ File sharing is on. Click Stop to prevent other │
│  │ Stop │ users from accessing shared folders.  │
│  └──────┘                            │
│ ┌──┐                                 │
│ │▲ │  Program Linking                │
│ └──┘     ┌Status──────────────────┐  │
│  ┌──────┐ Program linking is on.  Click Stop to prevent other │
│  │ Stop │ users from linking to your shared programs. │
│  └──────┘                            │
└─────────────────────────────────────┘
```

*When you click the "Start" button, the button turns into "Stop." Notice in the message box to the right of the button it now says "File sharing is on." Notice also that the folder has a dark tab and has wires coming out the bottom, indicating that information is flowing in and out.*

**Program linking** | You probably don't need to worry about "Program Linking" right now. Program linking doesn't mean that *you* link to the program (that's just called "sharing"); this button allows *programs* to link to each other, to talk to each other, to instruct each other, to share information. Different applications implement this in different ways; most can't do it at all. Check your manual for details.

**Step 3: Make a Folder to Share** | **Make a folder** (or several folders) *or* select existing folders and give it sharing privileges (instructions below). Anything you put in this folder will appear to the person on the other Mac. The person on the other Mac can put items into this folder while they sit at their own computer, and the files will show up on yours.

> ▼Click on a folder to select it. You can select more than one folder at a time.

> ▼From the File menu, choose "Sharing…."

> ▼Click to put an x in the box "Save this item and its contents." Click the close box *or* press Command W to put this dialog box away.

```
┌─────────────────────────────────────┐
│ □▭      WorldQuest           ▤       │
│ ┌──┐                                 │
│ │  │  Where:    Hard Disk:           │
│ └──┘                                 │
│                                      │
│ ☒ Share this item and its contents   │
│                    See    See   Make │
│                   Folders Files Changes │
│  Owner:  [Robin___▼]  ☒    ☒    ☒    │
│  User/Group: [<None>▼] ☒   ☒    ☒    │
│       Everyone         ☒    ☒    ☒    │
│                                      │
│ □ Make all currently enclosed folders like this one │
│ □ Can't be moved, renamed or deleted │
└─────────────────────────────────────┘
```

*If you want the other person to be able to read these files and/or perhaps to make changes to the file, you can grant permission right here. Just check the boxes of your choice.*

▾ Now the folder will look like this:
The dark bar in the tab and the 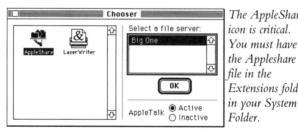 `For Shannon`
wires coming out the bottom are good visual clues
that this folder is willing to share. Anything you drop
into this folder will also share, even without specifically telling it to.

Now the *other* Macintosh needs to **connect** to *your*
Macintosh. Once you do this, you won't need to do it
again unless the file-serving Mac turned off the sharing.
If the sharing does get turned off, then you just need to
repeat this process (or use the alias trick, page 189). **The
file-serving Mac must be turned on.**

**Step 4: Connect
the Other Mac
to Yours**

▾ On the *other* Mac that wants to share from that folder
you just created on the file-serving Mac, get the
Chooser from the Apple menu. You should see this:

*The AppleShare
icon is critical.
You must have
the Appleshare
file in the
Extensions folder
in your System
Folder.*

▾ Click on the AppleShare icon. (If you were on a big
network with "zones," you would see all the zones
listed here also. But right now we're just talking two
computers.)

▾ You should see the name of the file-serving Mac you
just named a few minutes ago in the box on the right.
Click on that name.

▾ If the AppleTalk button is not on, click to turn it on.
You will have to restart, though, before AppleTalk
will be in effect, and you cannot share files without it.

▾ Click the OK button. This will give you the dialog
box shown on the next page:

▼ Since I am gearing this file-sharing information to the idea of two or three people who want to share files and be able to send things back and forth to each other, then I am going to suggest here that you just "log on" (connect) as "Guest" (that means click the Guest button). If you want, you can use the control panel Users & Groups to set up registered users and passwords so you can limit the access to your shared folders. If you are concerned about security, then you may want to do that. But today, you are a Guest.

**Users & Groups**

*Use this control panel if you want to set up users and groups of users to have password-protected access to the shared files.*

▼ After you click "Guest," you will see this dialog box:

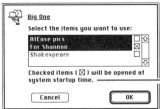

▼ Click OK and you will have the option of selecting which of the shared folders on the other computer you want access to.

*After the first time you connect to the other Mac, this shared item will only open at startup **if** the file-serving Macintosh has already been turned on.*

▼ After you choose the files you want, click OK. On your Desktop you should see an icon like this for each folder you have chosen to share:

For Shannon

You can now double-click on this file serving icon, which is a representation of the folder on the file-sharing Mac. It opens to a window just like any other folder.

All you need to do now to **share files** between computers is to put the file either in the shared folder on the file-serving Mac, or in the file-serving "folder" on the other Mac. Either way, as long as a file is in this place, both Macs can use it.

When you are using the file-serving Mac (the one with the happy faces), anything you move from your hard disk into this folder is just being moved—*that is, it is the original file that is being placed into the folder.* Keep that in mind and make copies (Chapter 11) or aliases (Chapter 25) of files as necessary for your purpose.

When you are using the *other* Mac, anything you move from your hard disk into the file server "folder" is a copy—*the original will stay on your hard disk.*

While working on the *other* Mac, you can use any file straight out of the shared, file-serving folder, but I usually like to first copy the file I want out of this folder and onto the hard disk of the other Mac. When the computers are file-sharing, you'll notice they go through little spasms and your typing will stop for a second or two, menu commands take longer to happen, and other little annoying tricks will irritate you because the computers are trying to do two things at once—the work you want, plus share a file.

▼ On the file-sharing Mac, the shared folder icon changes when the other Mac has chosen to share it:

For Shannon

*Can you believe how cute this is—little happy people sharing files?*

## Step 5: Share Files

For Shannon          For Shannon

*Whether you put the file in the share folder or in the file server folder, both computers can use it.*

**Disconnecting**

You can **disconnect** yourself from the "network" in several ways.

▼ When either computer shuts down, file sharing is automatically disconnected.

▼ You can drag the icon of the *file server* to the trash (*file server* meaning the icon on the *other* computer, not the shared folder on the file-serving Mac). This is similar to ejecting a disk through the trash. You will not see any icon of the file server in the trash can window, so you cannot go get it to reconnect.

▼ Click once on the file server icon to select it, then press Command Y (the keyboard shortcut for "Put Away" from the File menu).

▼ On the file-serving Mac, you can go back to the Sharing Setup control panel and click the "Stop" button to disconnect.

▼ You can selectively disconnect users through the File Sharing Monitor: From the Apple menu, choose "Control Panels." Double-click on the File Sharing Monitor control panel. Click once on the name of the connected user you want to disconnect, then click the "Disconnect" button. You will get an option to determine how many minutes before the person is actually disconnected.

For Shannon

*This is the file server icon on the other Macintosh.*

"Big One"
The file server has closed down [2:45 AM on 12/3/92].
OK

*If the file-serving Mac disconnects while the other Mac is still turned on, the other Mac will get this message.*

File Sharing Monitor

*This control panel keeps track of who is sharing what.*

File Sharing Monitor
Big One
Shared Items          Connected Users
For Shannon           Guest
Shakespeare

File Sharing Activity:
Idle    Busy          Disconnect

How many minutes until selected users are disconnected?
0
Cancel          OK

To **reconnect** the *other* Mac to the file-sharing Mac, you can go through the process of getting the Chooser and logging on again. Or you can do this great trick:

> One day when you *are* connected, make an alias of the file server icon that represents the shared folder. To make the alias, click once on the icon, then from the File menu, choose "Make Alias."

> Keep this alias wherever you like. When you need to connect to the file-serving Mac, just double-click the alias.

> This trick will also work if you make an alias of some file in the shared folder.

You can choose to share your hard disk, then make an alias of it. You can put this hard disk alias on a floppy disk, since it is only about 2K. Then you can put this disk into any other computer that is on the network (that is, any of the computers that you have strung together with cables), double-click the hard disk alias, and be connected to your own hard disk through this other computer. Too cool. This concept is what you have probably heard of as the **office-on-a-disk**.

The only trick to this is that you can only share your hard disk if the hard disk contains no other folders that are shared.

▼ If you know which folders are being shared, select each one and turn its file sharing off, using the "Sharing…" command from the File menu.

▼ If you're not sure which folders are shared, check with the File Sharing Monitor control panel. Choose "Control Panels" from the Apple menu. Double-click on "File Sharing Monitor." This dialog box will tell you, on the right-hand side, which folders are being shared on the hard disk. You can't turn them

## Reconnecting

For Shannon    *For Shannon alias*

- *Double-clicking the alias will automatically start the file sharing without having to go through the Chooser.*

## Office-on-a-Disk

File Sharing Monitor

*Use this control panel to monitor what is being shared and by whom.*

off here—you can just make a list of the shared items, then go to each one individually and turn sharing off, using the "Sharing…" command from the File menu.

```
┌─────────────────────────────────────┐
│ □ ═══════ File Sharing Monitor ═══════ │
├─────────────────────────────────────┤
│  🖥  Big One                          │
│                                       │
│  🗂 Shared Items      📋 Connected Users │
│ ┌─────────────┐△   ┌─────────────┐△  │
│ │For Shannon  │     │ ▪  Guest   │   │
│ │Shakespeare  │     │             │   │
│ │             │▽   │             │▽  │
│ └─────────────┘     └─────────────┘   │
│  File Sharing Activity:               │
│ ▪─────────────────   [ Disconnect ]  │
│  Idle        Busy                     │
└─────────────────────────────────────┘
```

**Just the Tip**  Remember, this is **just the tip** of the networking iceberg. If you are on a serious network, you need more information than I can provide in this book. These are just the simple steps that allow several computers in close proximity to share files without having to make copies onto floppies and use SneakerNet to transport the files between computers. (SneakerNet: sharing files by walking them over to the other computer.)

# CHAPTER TWENTY-EIGHT

# OTHER FEATURES

This section explains some of the other features of the Macintosh that don't fit neatly into any other category and that don't rate a chapter of their own.

**Balloon Help** is a feature available on the Desktop. More and more applications are also incorporating Balloon Help into their programs. The idea of Balloon Help is that you can simply point to items you don't understand, like tools or menu commands or parts of a window, and a little balloon shows up explaining what that item is and sometimes what to do with it. It's nice in theory and sometimes they actually do provide answers that help. You'll find that you can't leave this feature on for very long, though, because those balloons popping up in your face all the time become quite annoying.

**Turn on Balloon Help** through the Help menu, which is that little question mark on the far right of the menu bar.

- ▼ Press on the question mark to pull down the menu (shown on the right). (If you pull down this menu in an application, it won't say "Finder Shortcuts.")

- ▼ Choose "Show Balloons."

- ▼ Move your cursor over the screen and see what pops up. You can slide down menu lists, also, and get balloons for commands. Not all applications use balloons.

- ▼ **To turn off Balloon Help**, choose "Hide Balloons" from the Help menu.

## Balloon Help

*This is an example of a helpful balloon.*

## Turn on Balloon Help

*This is the Help menu.*

*When you press on the Help menu, this is what you will see. For info on "Finder Shortcuts," see page 54.*

## Publish and Subscribe

| Edit | |
|---|---|
| Undo | ⌘Z |
| Cut | ⌘H |
| Copy | ⌘C |
| Paste | ⌘U |
| Find... | ⌘F |
| Replace... | ⌘H |
| Go To... | ⌘G |
| Create Publisher... | |
| Subscribe To... | |

*The first step is to select the text and make an edition through the "Create Publisher..." command.*

*This is an example of creating an edition in Word.*

| Editions | Subscribe to... |
|---|---|
| | Subscriber options... |
| | Stop all editions |

*Other people can choose to subscribe to this edition, which remains linked to the original.*

The feature called **Publish and Subscribe** is an interesting concept. It works like this: In your application, say your word processing application, you create a document. This document needs to be shared with several other people on the network because they need to approve it. So you select the text and **publish** it (similar to *saving* a document). When you publish the text, the text is then called an **edition**. You save the edition in a folder, just as you would any other file.

Drew, Shannon, and Scarlett need to read and approve this file. So in their applications (it does not need to be the same application or even the same type of program), they choose to **subscribe** to this edition (which is similar to importing or pasting). Now Drew, Shannon, and Scarlett each have the same information on their screens.

The magic part is that even though neither Drew, Shannon, nor Scarlett can edit the edition, they can call you and tell *you* how things need to be changed. You make the changes on the *original* edition. When Drew, Shannon, and Scarlett next see their editions on their own computers, *the changes will have already been made, automatically.* The subscribed editions remain *linked* to the original file and will continue to automatically update any changes.

Each application may have its own method and dialog boxes for publishing and subscribing, so you will have to check with your manual for the specific steps to accomplish this in your software. Not all applications take advantage of this feature yet, either.

# PART THE THIRD

This section contains information that you don't need right away to get up and running, but it is still very important. You might want to work with your Mac for a few weeks before you read this section. The solution makes much more sense if you've had the problem first.

*Experience is what you get—when you don't get what you want.*
*—Richard Thomas Cella*

# CHAPTER TWENTY-NINE

# NAVIGATING

Whenever you save a document, the Mac creates an icon to represent your file. This file has to go somewhere on the disk. Have you ever saved a document and wondered where it went? Have you lost things? Have you opened up a document only to discover that it does not contain the last several hours of your work on it, and you know you saved the document beyond that point?

The problem is that you aren't quite clear yet on how to **navigate** through the dialog boxes with all the different levels and folders on the Mac to get where you want to be, either to open the correct document or to save it where you want to find it again. Navigating is one of the most important skills you can master. It seems so befuddling at first, and then one day it will just click and make perfect sense. Once you learn how to navigate you will never misplace documents when you save them, you will always be able to find the clip art you're looking for, you will always be able to find the extra report you wanted to open along with the one currently on the screen, and you will amaze your friends and co-workers as you whip through those lists knowing exactly where you are going.

It helps to have a visual reference to show things are organized on the Mac. Let's follow the document "Scarlett's Art" through the navigation channels.

**Where is Your File?**

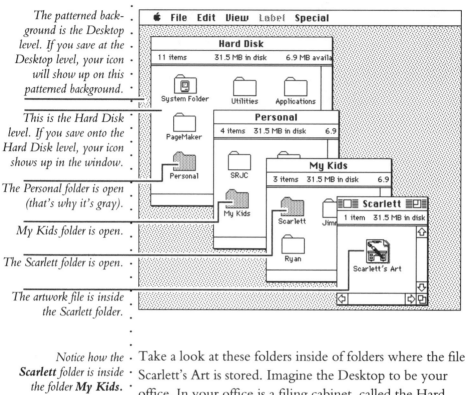

*The patterned background is the Desktop level. If you save at the Desktop level, your icon will show up on this patterned background.*

*This is the Hard Disk level. If you save onto the Hard Disk level, your icon shows up in the window.*

*The Personal folder is open (that's why it's gray).*

*My Kids folder is open.*

*The Scarlett folder is open.*

*The artwork file is inside the Scarlett folder.*

*Notice how the **Scarlett** folder is inside the folder **My Kids**.*
*   **My Kids** is inside the folder **Personal**.*
*   **Personal** is a folder in the **Hard Disk** window.*
*   The **Hard Disk** is on the **Desktop**.*

Take a look at these folders inside of folders where the file Scarlett's Art is stored. Imagine the Desktop to be your office. In your office is a filing cabinet, called the Hard Disk. In the filing cabinet are lots of folders. Each of these folders can have folders inside. Think of each of these things—the Desktop, the Hard Disk, each folder—as a separate level where you can choose to place a document. For instance, you sometimes want to file a document in a very specific and narrow compartment, nested into a number of folders with each folder getting more specific than the last, as in the case here for Scarlett's Art.

Since you have been working on your Mac for a while, you have created your own folders for organizing your own information. (Well, you *should* be creating them; read Chapter 10 on Folders, page 69). Making a folder on the computer called "Personal" is the equivalent of marking "Personal" on a manila folder and sticking it in a drawer in the filing cabinet (Hard Disk) in your office (the Desktop). When you open that folder in your real office, what do you see? You see all the documents you've stored in there, right? When you double-click on a folder on your Hard Disk, that's what you see—all the documents stored in that folder.

▼ The trick to navigating through dialog boxes is to understand that the dialog box is just a different way of looking at the contents of the folder. When you choose to see that folder in a dialog box, the list displays all those files.

**Different Ways of Looking at the Same Thing**

*Take a minute to look carefully at this menu and notice that the order is exactly like the order you see in the screen shot on the opposite page—this is a list of the folders that Scarlett's Art is nested into. This list just looks upside down compared to the one opposite. But they both lead back to the "root level," which is the Desktop.*

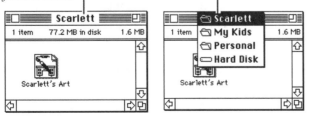

*You could view the same thing another way: At the Desktop, if you hold down the Command key and press on the name of the open folder, you see the same hierarchical list telling you where this particular folder is nested.*

### Where Does the Document Go?

!

*The document will be saved onto this disk and into this folder.*

*If the "Eject" button is black, that's a visual clue that the disk you are viewing is a floppy disk or a removable cartridge.*

So here you are in your word processor. You choose "Save As…" from the File menu.

> If you name this document and press the Save button right now, the document icon would appear on the disk whose name is shown on the right of the dialog box, and in the folder or disk whose name is in the label above the list.

The name on the right side of the dialog box is the name of the disk you are viewing. At the moment it's probably the name of your hard disk. If the icon, however, looks like a floppy disk, then you are viewing the contents of a floppy disk that is inserted into your computer.

You can save on any one of several different levels on a disk: on the Desktop (found only on a hard disk), on the disk itself (hard or floppy), or into any folder (each folder is a separate level).

**If you want to save onto the Desktop** of the Hard Disk, click the button "Desktop." Whether you were viewing a floppy disk or the Hard Disk, clicking this button will take you to the Desktop level of the Hard Disk.

> If you save onto the Desktop level, the document icon will be displayed on the far right of the screen.

**If you want to save into the Hard Disk window** (meaning you want the icon to be visible in the window of the Hard Disk, not in any folder), click the button "Desktop" to make sure you are viewing your Hard Disk. Then double-click on the name of your Hard Disk.

> If you save onto the Hard Disk, the icon for your document will be displayed in the window for the Hard Disk.

**If you want to save onto a floppy disk or a cartridge disk**, then make sure that floppy disk is inserted or the cartridge is mounted. If you don't see the name of the floppy disk on the right of the dialog box, you must first navigate over to the disk:

▼ Press Command RightArrow or LeftArrow until you see the name of your disk.

▼ *Or* click the button "Desktop." The name of any other disk should be visible in the list box. Double-click on its name.

**If you save onto the other disk,** the icon for your document will be displayed in the disk window, which is the window you see when you double-click on that disk's icon.

**If you want to save into a particular folder**, you must navigate to it.

▼ If the folder is on the Hard Disk, then first make sure you are viewing the Hard Disk: click the button "Desktop." Then double-click on the name of your Hard Disk.

▼ If the folder is on another disk, then first make sure you are viewing the other disk: follow the steps above.

Now you must find the folder. Do you see the folder listed on the disk? Yes? Then just double-click the name of that folder. Its name will appear in the label with a tiny icon of an open folder. **That open folder is your visual clue that if you were to save right now, the document would end up in that folder.**

If you save into a folder, the icon for your document will be displayed when you open the folder's window.

Is the folder you want inside another folder that you see in the list? Then double-click the other folder first. Then the one you want will be available for opening.

**On the following page is an example of the process.**

*Remember, you can only find folders that you previously created. If necessary, go back to the Finder by choosing "Finder" from the Application menu (far right of the menu bar) and creating a new folder where you need it. See page 69.*

**For Instance** · For instance, let's say you are working on a new database of the Boy Scout Roster for Jimmy. You got this new database by double-clicking on the spreadsheet program, FileMaker Pro.

**a**

```
┌─────────────────────────────────┐
│ 🖸 FileMaker Pro ▼    ⊂⊃ Hard Drive │
│ ┌──────────────────┐  ┌─────────┐ │
│ │🄰 FileMaker Pro  🖸│  │  Eject  │ │
│ │▢ Templates       │  └─────────┘ │
│ │▢ Tutorial        │  ┌─────────┐ │
│ │                  │  │ Desktop │ │
│ └──────────────────┘  └─────────┘ │
│ Create a new file named:  ┌─────┐ │
│ ┌──────────────────┐      │ New │ │
│ │Boy Scout Roster  │      └─────┘ │
│ └──────────────────┘  ┌─────────┐ │
│                       │ Cancel  │ │
│                       └─────────┘ │
└─────────────────────────────────┘
```

**a** So when you choose to save it, the Save As dialog box automatically opens to the folder in which FileMaker Pro is located. Well, you don't want to store this database file in that folder—you want to store it into Jimmy's folder. Remember where Jimmy's folder is? Right—it's in My Kids, which is in the Personal folder on the Hard Disk. So you need to navigate over to that folder.

**b**

```
┌─────────────────────────────────┐
│ 🖸 FileMaker Pro     ⊂⊃ Hard Drive │
│ ┌──────────────────┐  ┌─────────┐ │
│ │🖸 Applications   🖸│  │  Eject  │ │
│ │⊂⊃ Hard Disk      │  └─────────┘ │
│ │🖥 Desktop         │  ┌─────────┐ │
│ │                  │  │ Desktop │ │
│ └──────────────────┘  └─────────┘ │
│ Create a new file named:  ┌─────┐ │
│ ┌──────────────────┐      │ New │ │
│ │Boy Scout Roster  │      └─────┘ │
│ └──────────────────┘  ┌─────────┐ │
│                       │ Cancel  │ │
│                       └─────────┘ │
└─────────────────────────────────┘
```

**b** You know the Personal folder is on the Hard Disk so you press on the menu bar in the label and slide down to Hard Disk.

**c**

```
    ┌─ Hard Disk ▼ ─┐
┌───────────────────┐
│ ▢ Personal      ⇧ │
│ ▢ School          │
│ 🄰 SuperPaint      │
│ ▢ System Folder   │
│ ▢ Utilities       │
│ 🄰 Word          ⇩ │
└───────────────────┘
```

**c** Now in the list you see all the files on the Hard Disk. Find the folder called Personal and double-click the folder name to open it.

**d**

```
    ┌─ 🖸 Personal ▼ ─┐
┌───────────────────┐
│ ▢ BioInfo       ⇧ │
│ ▢ Love Letters    │
│ ▢ My Kids         │
│ ▢ SRJC          ⇩ │
└───────────────────┘
```

**d** Now Personal is in the label and all the files in that folder are listed. You want the folder called My Kids, so double-click My Kids to open it.

**e**

```
    ┌─ 🖸 My Kids ▼ ─┐
┌───────────────────┐
│ ▢ Jimmy         ⇧ │
│ ▢ Ryan            │
│ ▢ Scarlett      ⇩ │
└───────────────────┘
```

**e** Now in the list for My Kids you see Jimmy's folder. Double-click Jimmy to open it.

**f**

```
    ┌─ 🖸 Jimmy ▼ ─┐
┌───────────────────┐
│                 ⇧ │
│                   │
│                 ⇩ │
└───────────────────┘
```

**f** Now the label has Jimmy's name in it, and you know if you click the Save button this file will be stored into Jimmy's folder.

**g** This is just the same as digging through folders! It just looks a little bit different.

**g**

```
    ┌─ 🖸 Jimmy ▬▬┐
┌───────────────────┐
│ 🖸 My Kids      ⇧ │
│ 🖸 Personal       │
│ ⊂⊃ Hard Disk      │
│ 🖥 Desktop        │
└───────────────────┘
```

*This menu list shows the same folders inside of folders that you have on the Desktop.*

The dialog box automatically **opens to a particular folder**. There is a very clear, definite, predictable pattern that determines which folder you will see when you choose "Save As...." The following are guidelines, but there are a few variables that may affect what you see initially. If you are mildly confused at this point, ignore these guidelines. Come back to this later when you understand what it is you don't know.

- If this is a **new document** and the first one you have created today, then the dialog box will display the folder in which the application you're working with is stored.

- If this is **not a new document**, then the dialog box will display the folder in which this document was stored.

- If this is a new or an older document and you **previously opened another folder or disk** through a dialog box, perhaps in search of another file or a graphic, then the dialog box will display the same folder or disk you last looked within.

- If you using a **Performa** and the Launcher is running (see Chapter 34), then you will land in the Documents folder every time you "Save As..." or "Open...," no matter where you were before. *If this drives you nuts, just change the name of the Documents folder and it will stop going there.*

**Which Folder?**

**Keyboard Shortcuts for Navigating**

You can use **keyboard shortcuts to navigate** around the dialog boxes.

▼ **In any window on the Desktop:** If you press Command UpArrow, the window in which this folder is stored will pop forward in front of your face. For instance, if you are looking at Scarlett's folder, you can press Command UpArrow to bring the folder My Kids forward. You can keep pressing Command UpArrow all the way to the Desktop level.

▼ **In any dialog box:** If you press Command UpArrow, the dialog box will display the list of files in the folder in which this folder or document is stored (meaning you will go up one level in the hierarchy). You can keep pressing Command UpArrow all the way to the Desktop level.

- Press Command DownArrow to move one level lower in the hierarchy.

- Press the DownArrow to select files in the list.

- Type the first letter or several letters to select specific files in the list.

- Press Command D to select the Desktop level where you can find any attached hard disks or inserted floppy disks.

- Press Command RightArrow or LeftArrow to cycle through the disks or volumes you have connected or inserted.

- Press Command Period to Cancel.

- Press Return to Open or Save.

▼ **In a "Save As..." dialog box:** The default (automatic choice) is for you to type a name in the edit box.
*If you type while there is an insertion point flashing in the edit box or while the current name (which may be "Untitled") is highlighted,* then what you type will show up in the edit box.

*The edit box for giving the file a name is highlighted.*

*But* if you click in the list box, the *list box* becomes highlighted—notice the double border around it. *If you type while the list box is highlighted,* the letters you press will select any file with those letters, or the next file in the alphabet.

*The list box is selected, indicated by the double border around it.*

To bounce back and forth between the list box for selecting files and the edit box for typing a name, press the Tab key.
*This will drive you nuts for a while. Eventually, in about a year, you'll get used to it and you'll remember to hit the Tab key to switch to the mode you need—selecting files or typing a name.*

**Why Is It?**

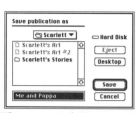

*This is a typical "Save As..." dialog box.*

**Why is it** that sometimes file names appear in a list box and sometimes they don't? It depends on which dialog box you are viewing and what program you are in.

When you view a **Save As... dialog box** in any program, the list shows you every other file that is in that folder or on that level. This lets you know what else is there and gives you a chance to make sure there is not another file by the same name. Other file names are in gray, just to let you know they are there. Folder names are in black because you can double-click to open the folder and save the document inside.

*This is the dialog box to place a graphic file or a text document in PageMaker. Even though Scarlett's Art #2 is in Scarlett's folder, it does not appear here because PageMaker cannot import that particular file format.*

When you use a dialog box to **import** or to **open** another file, such as a graphic file, the list only displays the names of files *that the current application is capable of importing or opening.* Maybe you created a graphic in SuperPaint and saved it in SuperPaint's "native" file format (meaning you just clicked the Save button in SuperPaint and didn't choose any different options). You want to place the graphic into PageMaker. When PageMaker is open and you try to bring in the graphic, you don't see its name listed, even though you know the file is in that folder. This is an indication to you that PageMaker *does not understand SuperPaint's native file format and thus cannot bring it in.* If you go back to the graphic file in SuperPaint and save it perhaps as a TIFF (another type of file format), you would then see it listed in the dialog box and PageMaker would be able to import it.

# CHAPTER THIRTY

# VERY IMPORTANT INFORMATION

It used to be so easy. And you used to not have to worry about what wasn't easy. But now you have no choice. Now you have to be conscious. Now you have to take responsibility for certain things on your Mac. Sigh.

This chapter covers several aspects of the Macintosh operating system that are all inextricably inter-related: hard disk space, memory, multi-tasking, and virtual memory. I know, you don't wanna know this stuff. But believe me, if you don't understand this particular information you will constantly find yourself frustrated and confused. Spend a few minutes here to empower yourself and gain control over your Mac.

I have worked with thousands of new and not-so-new Mac users and have heard so many people wail in confusion, "My Mac keeps telling me I'm out of memory, but I have 32 megabytes left on my hard disk!" Well, I myself have a hard time figuring out all this technical stuff so I create analogies. What follows is my personal analogy for answering the heart-breaking cry, "What the heck is the difference between **hard disk** and **memory** anyway?"

Think of the hard disk in your computer as a filing cabinet in your office. Visualize each megabyte of space as one drawer, so if you have a 40MB hard disk, your filing cabinet has 40 large drawers. Well, if you are working in your office and you need something out of the filing cabinet, you don't climb into your filing

**Very Important Information**

**Hard Disk vs. Memory**

cabinet to work on it—you take the information out of the file drawer and put it on your desk, right? Well, the computer does the same thing. The computer cannot climb into the hard disk to work any more than you can climb into your filing cabinet. It does the same thing you do—it takes things out of the hard disk and puts them on its desk, but its desk is called **memory (random access memory,** or **RAM,** to be precise). When you turn the computer on, it goes to the hard disk, just like you go to your filing cabinet, and gets the System out of the hard disk and puts a copy of it into the memory (onto its desk) to run the machine. When you open an application, such as your word processor, the computer gets a copy of that word processing application and puts the copy into memory (kind of like taking a typewriter out of the filing cabinet and plopping it onto the desk).

Well, you can see that the bigger the desk, the more things you can work on at once, or the bigger the project. The System that runs the machine, plus the typefaces and extensions you have installed, and a few other items are all automatically placed into RAM (onto the "desk") when you turn on the computer. All these things take up a certain amount of space. When you open an application, that application goes into RAM. When you work on a document, everything you haven't yet saved onto a disk floats around in RAM. When you work on large graphic files, like scans of color photos, there is an extraordinary amount of information that has to be held in RAM for the computer to be able to work on the image.

**Why do you crash?** If RAM gets full, **you will crash** (well, that's *one* reason for crashing). Sometimes you will get a warning, but often the System just goes belly up, "unexpectedly quits," or gives you some sort of "system error" message. It's like you put one thing too many on your desk and the desk just collapsed.

Here are a couple of suggestions to avoid running out of memory:

**1. Quit the application when you are finished using it (press Command Q).** Don't just *close* the document you were working on by clicking in the little close box or by choosing "Close" from the File menu. Closing makes you *think* the application is put away because you don't see it anymore. But you must actually *quit* the application (you can also Quit from the File menu) so the computer can remove it from RAM.

It's like this: If you are working in a word processing application, it's as if you pulled a typewriter out of the filing cabinet and put it on the desk. When you *close* the document you were typing, you have essentially *put the piece of paper back into the filing cabinet (the hard disk), but the typewriter itself is still sitting on your desk (in RAM).* If you then open a spreadsheet application, you have essentially pulled a large calculator out of the filing cabinet and put it on the desk. When you close the worksheet for the day, you have *put the paper documents back into the filing cabinet, but you have left the calculator itself still sitting on the desk.* Well, eventually this desk is going to get so full of applications (appliances) that it will collapse. For instance, if you still have the typewriter *and* the calculator *and* the System sitting on the desk, and then you put an easel on the desk to paint a picture (like a paint program), the desk will collapse, and you will get a message that "the application has unexpectedly quit," or the entire System may crash. SO—the point is, *quit* the application itself (which puts the appliance back into the filing cabinet); *don't just close* the current document (which just puts the piece of paper back into the filing cabinet).

So let's say you haven't been doing this and now you're getting messages or clues that you are running out of memory. You need to know how to check to see which

## Suggestions

### *Quit, don't just Close*

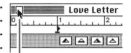

*Don't click in the close box (as shown here) and don't choose "Close" from the File menu to put an application away!*

*Do choose "Quit" from the File menu, or press Command Q when you want to put an application away.*

### *Which applications are still open?*

*This is the Application menu. This icon will change to indicate which program is currently active (open in front of you).*

Hide PageMaker 4.2
Hide Others
Show All

DeskPaint®
Finder
✓ PageMaker 4.2

*There will be a checkmark next to the application that is active right now, the one that is open in front of your face. Even if you don't see it anywhere, trust it. Look at your menu bar.*

applications are still open. In the upper right corner of the menu bar is the **Application menu**. Press on it to see a list of all the applications that are still open on your Macintosh. If you see any application program name besides "Finder" on the bottom half of that menu, *that program is still open*. Do any of the open applications in this list surprise you?

Choose one of the open applications (besides Finder) **and notice the menu bar change**. Even if you see no other change, you will see the menu bar change. You are now in that program. Really. Check the Apple menu and you'll notice that it says "About [the name of your program]." To put this application away, either choose "Quit" from the File menu, or press Command Q.

Do you ever find you are working in a program and suddenly it disappears? Or the menu bar changed? Or you closed a document and now you're back at the Desktop when you didn't want to be? That's because the Macintosh has a form of simple **multi-tasking** where you can have several things going on at once, such as having those several applications open at the same time. The important thing to know is that all it takes is a click of the mouse to pop you back and forth into the various applications. *It happens inadvertently all the time!* You may be happily working away on a letter when you accidentally click on the patterned background of your Desktop (you didn't even know it). The Mac thinks that since you clicked there, you want to go there. So suddenly all your Desktop windows flash in front of your face.

*You can go back to your open application just as easily as you left if you can see a window from the program.* Just click on the window you were working on. Now the Mac thinks you want to go back to your document and suddenly there you are. If you can't see a window, use the Application menu.

**2. Save regularly.** The entire time you work on a document, anything you do not save sits in RAM (and you know this will disappear when the computer crashes, right?). When you *save* the document, the current information is stored onto the hard disk and just the parts the computer needs still sit in RAM. It's possible to work on a document for several hours without saving and fill up RAM so it crashes. Oooh. SOS—Save Often Sweetie. Just hit Command S every couple of minutes.

**3. Check the application heap.** If you find that you crash regularly in a particular program, you may need to change the application heap for that program (details below). The application heap is the amount of memory that the computer sets aside just for that program. If the heap is set too low or just at the bare minimum, the program information gets poured into that amount and takes its chances on finding any more when it needs it, like when it needs to perform a complex maneuver such as checking spelling or flipping a graphic. You don't want to set the amount too high or you may not have enough memory for the other things the computer needs to do or for other applications that are open at the same time. Experiment to discover the amount that keeps you from crashing or "unexpectedly quitting."

- ▾ Make sure the application is not open. If its icon is gray, it is open. Check the Application menu, choose the application, and Quit.
- ▾ Click once on the application icon to select it.
- ▾ Press Command I to see the Get Info box.
- ▾ In the bottom right corner, select the "Current size" number and change it. Add about 10 to 15 percent more than the "Suggested size."
- ▾ Close the Get Info window and continue with your important work.

## Save Regularly

## Check the Application Heap

DeskDraw®

*To change the application heap, the program must be closed.*

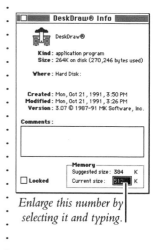

*Enlarge this number by selecting it and typing.*

## Use a Font Management Utility

**4.  If you have a large number of fonts, use a font management utility.** If you have lots of fonts, you need to get them out of the System Folder. Invest in Suitcase from Fifth Generation Systems, or in MasterJuggler from AlSoft. When fonts are in your System Folder (whether in the Fonts folder or in the System file), every one of them takes up space in RAM. Do you need every one of those fonts at every moment? No? Then manage them with a utility that lets you have open just the ones you need when you need them.

## Virtual Memory

This leads to the topic of **virtual memory**. If you don't have any interest in knowing what virtual memory is, you can ignore the rest of this chapter and still lead a very happy and productive life. If you haven't yet read the first part of this chapter, you might want to do that now because the analogy continues.

You read all the time about the miracle of virtual memory enabling you to use extra hard disk space as memory space, which many people think is the answer to the problem of not having enough memory installed in the computer. It's not. Virtual memory should only be used as a temporary stop-gap measure. This is what happens:

When you turn on virtual memory (in the Memory control panel, if your Mac allows it), you are giving the computer permission to pretend that a certain amount of hard disk space is memory. Of course, you must have that amount of hard disk space free. That is, if you have a 40 MB hard disk and you want to use 5 megs for virtual memory, you must have at least 5 megs of your hard disk available. You've probably read articles that say you shouldn't use more virtual memory than you have real memory. That is, if you have a machine with 4 megs of RAM, you shouldn't ask for more than 4 megs of virtual memory.

*If your Mac allows virtual memory, you can turn it on in the Memory control panel. Notice in this example I can't use virtual memory because there is not enough hard disk space available.*

So let's say you have four megs of RAM. When you ask for four megs of virtual memory, it's as if you are pretending that four of the drawers in your filing cabinet are part of your desk. Now, the computer cannot really use those four megabytes of hard disk space as memory any more than you can use those four drawers as part of your desk. What would you do if your desk was so full that you had to pull four drawers out and set them next to your chair so you could use them for the overflow? Wouldn't you probably put things in the drawers temporarily while you didn't need them and then switch them with something else from the actual desk when you did need it? That's exactly what the computer does.

Let's say you open your word processor and you start to work on your 563-page manuscript. That is comparable to you pulling the typewriter out of a file drawer and putting it on your desk, plus putting the entire manuscript in a pile also on the desk. Then you decide you also want to do some page layout for this manuscript so you get out your drafting table and put it on the desk; the computer gets the page layout program and puts it into memory. Now you want to paint a picture, so you get the easel out of the filing cabinet. Well, whoops, there's no more room on the desk. You don't want to pack up the typewriter and put it back into the filing cabinet, so you just plop the typewriter into one of those extra drawers you pulled out earlier and that are sitting next to your desk. The computer does the same thing— *those four drawers on the floor next to the desk are virtual memory* ("pretend" memory). If the *real* memory (the real desk) is limited, the computer has to swap things back and forth from the virtual memory to the real memory, just like you would have to swap things back and forth to make room on your desk. When you decide you need to use the typewriter again, you must swap either the drafting table or the easel to make room (this is why you don't want to use more virtual memory than you have real memory—you can't fit more in the extra boxes than you can fit on your desk).

Now, this swapping is a little faster than having to go all the way back to the filing cabinet for you, and a little faster than having to go all the way back to the hard disk for the computer, and having to set everything all up again. But it is still inefficient! What if you found you were working like this every day? Wouldn't you think that maybe you should just buy a bigger desk? You should. If you need that extra desk space, that extra memory every day, then you need to get a grip on reality, grow up, and buy the extra memory. Don't depend on virtual memory as a way of life.

**The Upshot**   So the **upshot of the analogy** is this:

▼ Your **hard disk** is like a filing cabinet where you store your work and your "appliances" (your applications).

▼ **Memory** is like your desk where you actually do your work.

▼ **Virtual memory** is like a makeshift addition to your desk, a temporary solution until you get it together to buy a bigger desk (more memory).

# CHAPTER THIRTY-ONE

# VISUAL CLUES

## What is a Visual Clue?

The Mac, with its famed graphical user interface, provides many **visual clues** to tell us what's going on. Most of these clues, though, aren't documented anywhere and we have to just kinda figure them out as we go along. Some of the clues are loud and clear, like the picture of the bomb; you might not know exactly why you bombed, but you know something is bad. The trash can is another easy visual clue, as are the icons of a hard disk or floppy disk. It doesn't take long to figure out what it means when a menu item is gray, or to notice the different cursors you get when you use different tools.

But many of the visual clues are much more subtle. And to beginners especially, there is so much information going in through the eyes that it takes a while to absorb everything. I want to point out some of the clues the Mac is constantly providing, which should help you work more efficiently.

## Ellipsis in the Menu

Whenever you see a menu item followed by an **ellipsis** (three dots …), it indicates that if you choose that menu item you will get some sort of dialog box. Dialog boxes always have a Cancel button in them, so it's a great way to explore a new program—choose any menu item with an ellipsis, check out its dialog box, then click Cancel and you'll never wreck anything. Any menu item that is not followed by an ellipsis will just execute when you choose it, which has the potential to create unexpected results if you don't know what you're doing.

| Format | |
|---|---|
| Hide Ruler | ⌘H |
| Page… | |
| Paragraph… | |
| Tab… | |
| Character… | ⇧⌘D |

*The ellipses indicate that the command will show you a dialog box.*

**Default Button** · Any button with a thick double border around it is the
· **default button** ("default" means it is the automatic
. choice). This means if you hit the Return or the Enter
· key, the button with the dark border around it is the one
· that will take effect.

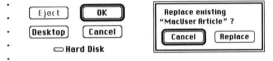

· Typically (not always) the default button is the *safest*
· option, as in the Cancel button, above.

**Highlighted Text** · When **text is highlighted** (text on a black or colored
. background), it's a visual clue to you that you are in
· typing mode and whatever you type is going to replace
· the highlighted text. *You don't need to hit the Delete key*
. *first—just type.* This is true in every dialog box, in every

*Simply type to replace* · program that uses type, in every Save As box, etc.
*any highlighted text.*

· By the way, you can hit the **Tab key** to bounce the
· selection from one edit box to another in any dialog box.
. If there is already text in an edit box, the text becomes
· highlighted. If there is no text, the Tab key sets an

*Hit the Tab key to select* · insertion point (the little flashing vertical bar), another
*each edit box in turn.* · visual clue that you are in typing mode.

**Checkboxes vs.** . The very buttons themselves are visual clues. **Radio**
**Radio Buttons** · **buttons** (the little round ones) are called radio buttons
· because they act like your car radio in that you can only
· choose one option at a time. Clicking on any radio
· button deselects any previously selected button in the
· same list. And you have to select at least one—it's not
*You can select only* · possible to have no radio button selected.
*one radio button.*

When a button is a **checkbox**, it's a clue that you can choose more than one. In fact, you can choose from none to all of them.

You can actually click anywhere in the word, not just within the tiny checkbox or circular button, to turn the buttons on or off.

In dialog boxes, whenever you see a shadow behind a little box it means if you press on the name in the box you'll get a **mini-menu**, or **submenu** (sometimes called a **pop-up menu** because it sort of pops up into your face). These are kind of subtle, so you have to know to look for them. Some pop-up menus are indicated by little arrows (a stronger visual clue), in which case you can press on the arrow itself.

Along the same lines as the previous clue, the **label above the list** in any dialog box (such as when you Save As, Open, or Export, etc.) has that little shadow behind it, indicating a menu lurks beneath. The visual clue is strengthened with a little downward arrow.

In the label there is always a tiny icon, either a Desktop icon, a disk icon (either hard or floppy), or an open folder icon. This tells you where the items visible in the list are located. For instance, if the icon is an open folder, the items in the list are found within that folder. And if you press on that label with the open folder icon, you will see the menu showing the hierarchy—that is, where that folder is located, perhaps within another folder which is within another folder which is located on the hard disk. You can, of course, select any other folder or disk in the menu to open it and display its contents.

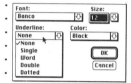

☒ Lock Text
☐ Show Lines
☒ Wide Margins
☐ Auto Tab
☒ Fixed Line Height
☐ Don't Wrap
☐ Don't Search
☐ Shared Text

*You can choose any number of checkbox buttons.*

## Mini-Menus

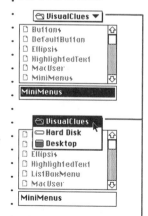

*Press on any box with a slight shadow behind it to see the mini-menu.*

## Mini-Menus Above a List

*The label above a list box tells you where the items visible in the list are located.*

**215**

*Command-press to see the hierarchy of any window on the Desktop.*

By the way, you can also see the **hierarchy of any window on your Desktop** (also known as the Finder). This feature is completely clueless: hold down the Command key and press on the name in the title bar of any active window.

## Matching Icons

DeskPaint™    PalmTrees

*Document icons usually match the application icon.*

Robin'sData

*A blank document often means the application it was created within is not in the computer.*

Robin

*Customizing icons is fun, but you lose the visual clue as to its function.*

**Icons**, of course, are major visual clues. You've probably noticed that Desktop icons can generally be grouped into several categories: disk icons, folder icons, document icons, application icons, system icons. Document icons (usually shaped like pieces of paper with the corner turned down) often match the application they were created in, which is a very thoughtful and helpful visual clue. See Chapter 9 on Icons.

If a document icon is **blank**, it is often a clue that the application in which the document was created cannot be found on the disk (see page 60 for elaboration).

You can customize any of your icons, thus potentially weakening this system of recognition. Is the icon to the left a folder, a document, an application, an init, a graphic file? Be careful. (See page 64 for details on customizing your icons.)

## Changing File Names

Publications

*The border that appears around the name of a file indicates you can now change its name. If you make a mistake, press Command Z.*

The Mac lets you know when you are about to **change the name** of a file on the Desktop/Finder. When you single click on the *name* of the icon (not on the picture) *or* select an icon and press the Return key, a border appears around the name, which is the visual clue that what you now type will replace the current name. If you wait long enough before you type, you'll notice that the pointer turns into an I-beam when you position it over the name.

A **gray icon** is a visual clue that the disk, folder, or application is already open. If you don't see its window anywhere, double-click on the gray icon to bring the window or application to the front. (You don't see any sign of your application? The visual clue that your application is active is in the menu bar; see page 61.)

Sometimes a **disk icon is gray** because you ejected the disk using the menu command or you pressed Command E. Ejecting a disk this way leaves it in the computer's memory, and it may ask for the disk again later. See page 119 for details. To prevent leaving the shadow of that disk on your screen, drag the disk out through the trash rather than use the menu command (it's perfectly safe!), *or* select the disk icon and press Command Y (the shortcut for "Put Away") to eject the disk.

When you view the items in a window in some sort of list, such as By Name, By Size, By Kind, etc., notice that the particular **view** you have chosen is **underlined** in the information bar. You can simply click on one of the other categories in the information bar to switch to that view. See Chapter 8 on Desktop Windows for details.

When you view a window By Icon or By Small Icon, the information bar tells you the **number of items in the window**, indicated in the upper left of the window, under the close box. We usually take that for granted, but I have seen countless people complain that their document is missing while the info bar says "5 items" and the window only displays 4 icons.

## Gray icons

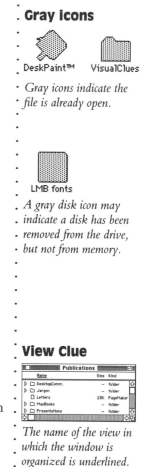

DeskPaint™    VisualClues

*Gray icons indicate the file is already open.*

LMB fonts

*A gray disk icon may indicate a disk has been removed from the drive, but not from memory.*

## View Clue

*The name of the view in which the window is organized is underlined.*

## Number of items

*Since the information bar indicates five items are contained in this window, you instantly know one is missing from view.*

## Scroll Bars

*The gray scroll bar indicates there are more items within this list that are not visible at the moment.*

Whenever you see a **scroll bar**, whether in a window or in a dialog box, the scroll bar may be white or gray. When the scroll bar is white, it's a visual clue that you are seeing all the items in that list, or viewing all the icons in that window—nothing is hidden from sight. If a scroll bar is **gray**, it indicates there are other items that are not currently visible, and you need to press the scroll arrow to display them.

On a color or grayscale monitor, the difference between white and gray scroll bars is minimal. If a scroll bar is gray, there is a scroll box in it. So **if you don't see the scroll box,** there is nowhere to scroll to.

## Scroll Box

*Check the position of the scroll box on the scroll bar— it indicates where you are in relation to the outer edges of the entire window.*

The **scroll box** shows you where you are in that list or in that window, not only at your Desktop or in dialog boxes, but within applications also. If you're typing in your word processor and your text suddenly disappears, check the scroll box—is it at the bottom of the bar? Drag it back to the top to find your text. Did you place something on the pasteboard in PageMaker and then turn the page and can't find that item on the pasteboard? Go back and check the horizontal scroll box on the other page.

## Menu Checkmark or Lack of Checkmark

*A checkmark, as you know, indicates what is selected. No checkmark in the menu indicates that there is more than one size (or font or style, etc.) within the selected text.*

You've probably already noticed that when you look at a menu, a little **checkmark** often appears to tell you what is currently selected or what is considered "on." If you pull down a font menu or a size menu and you notice there is **no checkmark** at all, it means there is more than one font or more than one size of type in the text you selected. The Mac can't tell you more than one thing at a time so it tells you nothing instead—*but that nothing is actually a valuable clue.*

You can select a smaller portion of text, or just click the insertion point within the text, to find out what the actual font or size is. Maybe *you* can't see any other font or size—remember, the Mac sees blank spaces and blank lines as characters. If even one of those selected blank spaces or blank lines is formatted in a different font or size or style than the rest of the text, you won't see a checkmark in the menu.

Sometimes you may have more than one disk in the computer, or you may be connected to more than one hard disk. You can always tell **which disk is booting**, or running, the computer: its icon is the one at the top in the upper right of the screen. (You may be surprised one day when you discover you actually need to know that bit of information. Then again, you may live a long time and never have a use for it.)

If you're not sure if you are running System 7 or not, take a quick look at the top right corner of your screen, actually in the far right corner of the menu bar. If you see a question mark inside a little cartoon-type balloon, you are running System 7.

If you're not sure if you are running System 7.1, check inside the System Folder. Is there a folder called "Fonts"? Then you are at least using 7.1.

If you see a little **diamond shape** next to an item in the Application menu (the menu at the far right), it is an indication that the progam wants to tell you something. It's usually not good news. Choose that item from the menu and take care of the problem immediately.

## The Boot Disk

*In this example, the Hard Disk is the disk that is running the computer.*

## Are You Using System 7?

*If you see a question mark in the upper right corner of the menu bar, you are running System 7.*

## Diamond in the Application Menu

**Look for Clues!** Once you become aware of these visual clues, you'll start noticing more and more of them. Every program has its own little set. Cursors change to tell you what will happen if you press now; each program has a way to indicate that an item is selected; buttons sometimes give you a clue as to what will happen if you click; etc. etc. etc. Take advantage of what they are showing you!

# CHAPTER THIRTY-TWO

# A Few Extra Tips

This is a collection of some of the tips or important notes that are imbedded in the rest of the book, as well as any other hints or fascinating bits of information or shortcuts that haven't been mentioned. Again, nothing is software-specific; it all relates to the general Mac environment.

**Compendium of Tips**
*The page number indicates where more information on that tip can be found.*

**Clean up the Desktop.** p.26

**Use the mouse left-handed.** p.29

Use the **Shift and arrow keys** to select text. p.39

To **make a window active**, click on any visible part. p.42

To **move a window without making it active**, hold the Command key while pressing-and-dragging in its title bar. p.42

To **switch window views**, click on another column header in the information bar. p.46

To **view the list by name yet still see the individual icons**, use the Views Control Panel. p.46

To **put the application itself at the top of a window list** so it's easy to find, view By Kind. p.47

To **organize the icons** according to the last list view you chose, hold the Option key down before you choose "Clean up Window." p.50

To **close every window**, hold down the Option key while you click in the active window's close box, *or* press Command Option W. p.52

To **make the previous window close instantly**, hold down the Option key while opening folders.  p.52

To **close all the Desktop windows before you even get there**, hold down the Option key while quitting.  p.52

To **make sure all previously open windows are closed when you open the disk**, hold down the Option key while inserting a disk or just before the Mac gets to your Desktop when starting up.  p.52

To **open a window as large as possible**, press Option while you click the zoom box.  p.53

To **view the hierarchy of a nested folder**, hold the Command key down and press on the title of the window.  p.52

To **expand a folder**, press Command RightArrow.  p.73

To **compress a folder**, press Command LeftArrow.  p.73

To **compress all the folders** that are expanded, press Command A to select all, then press Command LeftArrow.  p.73

To **select items from more than one folder at a time**, expand the folders.  p.81

To **put files back** where they came from, press Command Y.  p.68

To **print the contents of the active window**, choose "Print Window" from the File menu. p.55

To **print the entire screen**, choose "Print Desktop" from the File menu.  p.55

To **make the Desktop level active**, press Command Shift UpArrow.  p.54

To **select the name of an icon faster** so you can rename it, click on the name and then instantly move the mouse away; p.70. Or select the icon and press Return. p.216

To **select a file** in a window, just type the first letter or several letters of the name of the file.  p.80

To **select an icon** that is alphabetically *after* the currently selected icon, press Tab. To select the icon that is alphabetically *before* the currently selected icon, press Shift–Tab.  p.80

To **force the selected file name to appear at the top of the list window**, press the **End** key before you type the first letter of the file name.  p.81

Use **arrow keys, edit keys, the Tab key**, and **letters** to select files in windows.  p.81

To **color your icons**, use the Labels menu.  p.63, 163

Use **Find File** to find files you are too lazy to dig for.  p.82

To **make a copy of a file** on the same disk, select it and press Command D.  p.76

To **make a copy of a file** into another folder on the same disk, hold down the Option key while moving the file.  p.77

To **go back to work while copying a large file**, use the Application menu to choose the program you were previously working in.  p.75

To **make a template** out of any document, called a **stationery pad**, use the Get Info box.  p.68

To **throw away a locked file**, hold down the Option key.  p.67

**If you don't want to see the trash warning box**, hold down the Option key while trashing the item.  p.84

To **permanently remove the trash warning**, uncheck the "Warn before emptying" box in the Get Info window.  p.84

To **open a document**, drag the icon and drop it on top of its application icon.  p.87

To **open an unknown document**, drag the icon over the top of all your applications or aliases of your applications. The application icon that highlights will open the document. p.60

To **open any desk accessory**, wherever it is stored, double-click on it. p.130

To **hear a sound when you reach the Desktop**, place a sound into your Startup Items folder. p.130, 167

Use **keyboard shortcuts in Open and Save As** dialog boxes. p.202

To **see what applications are still running**, check the Application menu. p.124, 208

A **diamond symbol in the Application menu** means that program needs to tell you something. p.219

**Enlarge the application heap** if you are always running out of memory in a particular program. p.209

To create a **copy of the date and time**, press Command C while the clock is the active window. Paste the date and time into your document. p.148

Use aliases to **keep track of files** that you keep stored on floppy disks or cartridge hard disks. p.173

To **activate a default button** with a double border around it, press the Return or Enter keys. p.214

You can still **type numbers** while Caps Lock is down. p.36

To **create your own puzzle**, see p.153

To **organize your Apple menu**, see p.66

To **write notes on a file**, use the Get Info box. p.66

To **eject a disk**, press Command Y. p.120

To **eject a stuck disk** that didn't come out when the computer was turned off, hold the mouse button down while you turn the machine back on. p.121

To **eject a disk as a last resort**, use a paper clip.  p.121

To **unfreeze the screen**, try a "force quit."  p.233

To **restart after you crash** without having to turn off the power, use the Reset button.  p.240

To replace highlighted text, **just type**.  p.214

While typing, **the insertion point picks up the formatting of the character to its left**—font, style, size, alignment, and ruler settings.  p.93

To **remove all the styles** attached to characters (bold, italic, shadowed, etc.), select the text and choose Plain or Normal.  p.93

To **place accent marks over letters**, use the Option characters.  p.99

If you **change your mind** about the changes you just made, close the document and don't save those changes; when you reopen it, the document will have reverted to the last-saved version.  p.103

Look for **Easter Eggs**. An Easter Egg is a surprise, like the one mentioned on page 165.

To **avoid wasting paper and toner** every time you turn on your laser printer, pull the paper tray out a bit before you turn it on.  p.114    For a **more permanent solution**, use the LaserWriter Font Utility.  p.114–115

Three dots (**the ellipsis: ...**) after a menu item indicates that you will get a dialog box when you choose that item.  p.213

**Application Menu** Don't forget that you can choose to "Hide Others" from the Application menu to **hide all the windows you don't need** from the other programs that are running and that are visible from the Desktop.

If you hold down the Option key as you choose an application from the Application menu, **all other windows will automatically hide**. Also, if you hold down the Option key when you click to get to the Desktop, all other application windows **will be hidden** when you arrive at the Desktop.

**Tab to Select** In any dialog box that contains boxes for you to fill in, you can **press the Tab key to move the selection** from box to box. If there is data already in the box, that data will be highlighted and anything you type will replace it (you don't have to delete it first). If there is no data in the box, the Tab key will set the insertion point there, ready for you to type.

**Brightness Control** On the front of the older, compact Macintoshes, if you slip your hand right under the rainbow apple you'll find a little roller switch that will **dim or brighten your screen**. It's a good idea to dim the screen if you're going to be away from the computer for a length of time, as it's possible to burn an image into the screen, just as on video games. On larger Macs, the brightness and contrast buttons are on the monitor. Some models, however, have no controls and you must use the Brightness control panel (p.160)

**Screen Savers** There are several varieties of screen savers available to help **avoid screen burn**. A screen saver usually turns the screen black or colors and has images that constantly move, like shooting stars or geometric shapes or flying toasters. As soon as you move the mouse it disappears. Some screen savers are desk accessories that you access through your Apple menu; some you put in your System Folder and they automatically turn on after a certain period of time if the keys or mouse haven't been touched.

Type **only one space between sentences!** p.100

### One Space

Using inch and foot marks in place of the **real quotation marks** is an easily made mistake. Yes, on the typewriters we grew up with we used those marks, but we are no longer on typewriters. Also, we are attempting to come close to professional type, and you never see inch and foot marks used as quotation marks in professional type. Unfortunately, they are not located in an obvious spot, so you won't know they're there unless somebody tells you. So I'll tell you:

### Real Quotation Marks!

**" and "**
**' and '**
**not " and '**

*Each font has its own quotes designed for it.*

| To type this mark: | Press these keys: |
|---|---|
| " | Option [ |
| " | Option Shift [ |
| ' | Option ] |
| ' | Option Shift ] |

Several paint programs allow you to create a **StartupScreen**. Once you have a StartupScreen installed in your System Folder, every time you boot (start the computer), this image will show on the screen for a minute or two. This is quite fun! Simply create a paint document, or use clip art, and save the document in the PICT file format with the name "StartupScreen." It doesn't matter what letters in the name are capitalized, but it does have to be one word. Put that file *into the System Folder.* The next time you boot, you'll see it!

### StartupScreen

StartupScreen

If you have any QuickTime movie clips, you can name one **Startup Movie** (two words) and drop it into your System Folder to have it play when you boot. Too cool!

Startup Movie

**Rebuilding Your Desktop**

If you have a hard disk, you may start to notice that it slows down after a few months. This is because there is an invisible file that keeps track of all the icons that have ever been seen on your Desktop, even if you just loaded them on to see what they looked like! There is a way to **rebuild your desktop** and remove all the unnecessarily stored information. Follow these steps:

1. Turn off the Mac (or from the Special menu choose "Restart").

2. Hold down the **Command** and **Option** keys.

3. Turn the Mac back on (if you turned it off), still holding down those keys until you see this dialog box:

> ⚠ **Are you sure you want to rebuild the desktop file on the disk "Hard Disk"? Comments in info windows will be lost.**
>
> ( Cancel ) ( **OK** )

4. Click OK (or, if you read the tip on the previous page, simply hit the Return key).

▼ **Rebuild floppy disk desktop files** the same way: hold the Command and Option keys down while inserting a disk, until you see the above dialog box.

Mac will rebuild the desktop file for you and it should now open and close files and folders much faster.

The only problem with rebuilding is that it also destroys any messages you put in your Get Info boxes. Darn it. (See page 66 for info on Get Info.)

**WDEF and CDEF Viruses**

Rebuilding the Desktop will also **destroy the WDEF and the CDEF viruses**. System 7 does not have the problem with these like System 6, but you still might find the need to eradicate that virus, especially from floppy disks.

Do you want to know exactly **how much RAM** your System or any program you are running is actually using from the amount allotted to it?

▼ At the Finder, choose "Show Balloons" from the Help menu (the question mark).

▼ From the Apple menu, choose "About this Macintosh...."

▼ Position the pointer over the bar representing the largest unused block and a balloon will appear with the information.

To see what **fonts are in the System** while you are still at your Desktop, from the Apple menu choose "Key Caps." A new menu item will appear in your menu bar: Key Caps. Press on it to see your font list.

Occassionally you may find the need to **disable all the system extensions** you have installed. You might need to do this because one of them is causing problems and you have to get it out but you can't take it out while its working. **If you hold the Shift key down when you turn on your Mac or restart, none of your extensions will start up.** This is an all-or-nothing deal, though. If you have a lot of extensions, you may want to get one of the various utilities that manage these startup documents.

**Write Your Tips Here!** You can collect tips from all kinds of sources—user group newsletters, Macintosh magazines, classes, seminars, training, etc. Make a collection and share!

# CHAPTER THIRTY-THREE

This list doesn't pretend to be an all-inclusive reference for every sort of catastrophe that may befall; rather, it is just a compilation of the most common, simple problems one may encounter when first beginning to work on a Macintosh.

If the **computer doesn't turn on**, check *all* your switches and plugs. When a switch is labeled **I** or **O**, the **I** means **On**.

▼ If you have a floor surge-protector bar with an on-off switch, it may have been kicked to the *off* position—make sure it is *on*.

▼ If your hard disk is external, it has its own on-off switch that must be turned on *first* so it can boot up; then the Mac must still have its own switch turned on *also*.

▼ If your computer has a fan unit on top with buttons to push, those buttons still won't work unless the switch on the back of the computer is *also* on. The button on the left of the fan unit typically starts the Mac, while the button on the right will start your hard disk (but the hard disk itself should be turned on first).

▼ If you have any other devices attached to your computer, such as a scanner, hard disk, or CD-ROM player, sometimes they must be turned on first or sometimes they need to be turned on in a specific order. Try changing the order.

**What To Do If:**

**The Computer Doesn't Turn On**

**You Get the Question Mark, the Flashing X, or a Sad Mac on Startup**

*The Happy Mac. We like this guy.*

*The disk with the flashing question mark.*

*The disk with the flashing X.*

*The Sad Mac, better than the Dead Mac.*

Ideally, when you start the computer you see the **Happy Mac**. This means all is well. Sometimes, though, you may see another icon, like a disk with a **question mark**. This is a visual clue that the Mac cannot find the System Folder. The System Folder *must* contain the System file and the Finder file. If you are using an external hard disk, make sure the hard disk unit itself is turned on and is up and running, and make sure any extra switches are also on. If there are any other devices attached to the computer, they sometimes have to be turned on first. When you start attaching a lot of things to a Mac, they start getting fussy about the order they're turned on.

The disk with a **flashing X** means the Mac found the disk you thought was a startup disk, but it really isn't. There may even have been a System on it, but the Mac can't use it. Try your startup disk (below).

The icon you really don't want to see is the Sad Mac. This means there is really something wrong and you probably need your power user friend to help you figure it out. Even more serious is when the **Sad Mac** shows up on a black screen (rather than gray or colored or patterned) and plays the Chimes of Doom for you. On the black background, it looks like a **Dead Mac**. I, personally, have heard the Chimes of Doom five times now.

You should always keep a floppy disk around that holds a stripped-down System on it for those times when, for whatever reason, your computer won't boot. In your original disks this is called "Disk Tools." Even the Performa (which makes you create your own backup System disks) comes with a startup disk called "Utilities." You can usually at least boot from this floppy (if not, something is seriously wrong) and then take a look at your System Folder and perhaps find something obviously wrong, like a Finder missing. Or perhaps you know it is the extension you installed a half-hour ago—at least you can get to it now.

**The Screen**
**Freezes**

Occasionally the computer screen just up and **freezes**. The pointer may move around, but you can't click on anything and it doesn't respond to the keys. Very often this is the result of static electricity, or sometimes from running out of memory. You can try pressing Command Period, but it usually doesn't help.

**Force quit**

What is often effective, though, is a **force quit**. Press Command Option Escape (esc). You will get a dialog box asking if you really want to force the application to quit. Well, you have no choice. Usually this will just force quit that application and you won't have to turn off the computer (the only other option if this doesn't work). Anything you had not saved is lost. It's a good idea, if the force quit works, to save and quit in all other open applications and then restart. Also see "The Reset Switch" on page 240.

**Can't Find**
**Your Document**

In the beginning you may very often save a document dutifully, but then when you get to your Desktop you **can't find** it anywhere. This is because when you saved it you weren't paying attention into which disk and/or folder you were saving the document. Be sure to read Chapter 15 on Saving and Chapter 29 on Navigating, and carefully look at the dialog boxes pictured there so you understand how to save files where you can find them again.

Anyway, at the moment you can't find it. Use Find File (Chapter 26). When you find your document, put it in a folder you have created (page 69), just as if you were going to put it in a file folder in the filing cabinet. Press-and-drag the document icon over to the folder or disk of your choice. The folder/disk should turn *black;* when it's black, let go and the document will drop right in.

### Can't Open a File

**14 items**

*This symbol indicates the disk is locked.*

Sometimes when you click on an icon you get a message that tells you the file is locked or in use, or maybe that an application couldn't be found.

If the **disk is locked**, you'll see a little lock symbol in the upper left of its window. When a disk is locked you can't save to it, nor can you print from a locked *System* disk (if you are one who still works from a floppy System disk which you probably aren't if you're reading this book). To unlock a floppy disk, first eject it. In one of the corners is a little black tab that covers or uncovers a hole. When the hole is open, the disk is locked (seems backwards, doesn't it?). So to unlock it, switch the tab back so the hole is closed. (More info on page 14.)

If the **file is locked**, click once on it and choose "Get Info" from the File menu. In the lower left corner there is a little box called "Locked" that may be checked. If that box is checked, then click in the box to uncheck it and thus unlock the file.

If the **file is in use**, then it's in use. Usually you get this message if you try to open an icon that looks like a Macintosh; Mac icons are part of the System.

### Application can't be found

If it tells you an **application can't be found**, then one of two things is happening:

▼ The software application in which you created the document is not in the computer. Even though your document icon may *look* like SuperPaint, in order to view the document it has to go *into* the application SuperPaint to create itself.

▼ Some files cannot go straight from the Desktop to the application, even if the application is in the computer also. In this case, if you know the document was created in a certain application and you know that particular application is in your machine, then you must go into the *application* itself (double-click on its icon) and open the file you want from inside, choosing "Open" from the File menu.

Try the tip on page 87 to find another application that may open the file besides the one that created it. Most applications can usually open several file formats.

When trying to **view clip art**, often you will get the message that "An application can't be found," even when the program it was generated in is on the disk. You need to open *the actual application itself,* then open each individual document through the File menu, choosing "Open" (such as MacPaint, or SuperPaint with the MacPaint format chosen). Also see the previous suggestion for "An application can't be found."

**Viewing Clip Art Files**

If you are experiencing **system bombs** too regularly, one reason is that you have more than one System in your computer. One System is essential; two Systems is too many. Even though you don't see something called System Folder right there on your Desktop doesn't mean you don't have one tucked away in the depths of several other folders somewhere.

**System Bombs**

If you have a hard disk, don't use a floppy that also has a System on it. If the document you need is on a floppy that also contains a System Folder, *copy the document onto your hard disk, eject the floppy, and open the document from the hard disk;* you can copy the revised file back onto the floppy when you're done.

An easy way to **find all the Systems** on your hard disk and on any floppy disks you are using is to use Find File (Chapter 26). Move them all (except one—save the latest version!) to the Desktop and throw them in the trash. If you hold down the Option key while trashing them, you can avoid the nice dialog box that asks if you're sure you want to do this. *You won't be able to throw away the System that is booting the machine. That's good.*

*Find any extra Systems*

**"Not enough memory"**  Running out of RAM is another prime cause for System crashes. RAM (Random Access Memory) is the area in your computer where all the information is temporarily stored while you are working on it. When you Save, you send that information permanently to the disk and thus free up that much space in RAM. If you don't save very often, **RAM gets full** and the Mac just checks out (crashes). If you have a lot of extensions (page 258) or fonts, remember that those get loaded into RAM as soon as you turn the computer on. Then your application gets loaded into RAM. If you open more than one application at a time, they all take up RAM. Then as you work, there is not a great deal of room left. You need to read Chapter 30, Very Important Information. If you run out of RAM often, buy more (in the form of SIMMs, see the Jargon chapter). Also decide whether you *really* need all those extensions and fonts and eliminate any unnecessary ones or get extension and font manager utilities.

**Desktop File is full**  If the invisible **Desktop File gets too large**, you may run out of memory (and your computer will work slowly). At least once a month you should *rebuild your Desktop* (it's very easy; see page 228).

**Extension conflicts**  If you use **extensions** (previously called INITs, page 258), keep in mind that it is not unusual for them to be buggy, unstable, corrupted, etc., especially the free ones. It's a well-known fact that they can cause problems, including System crashes. If you think one of your INITs might be a catalyst for bombs, take them all out and put them back in one at a time, using your computer for several days between adding each one. See the tip on page 229.

**Text Formatting Unexpectedly Changed**  It's not uncommon to open your document on another *System* and find major **formatting changes.** If you created a document on your hard disk using the font Palatino, then gave a copy of the document on disk to a co-worker who opened it up and found it had trans-mogrified itself into the font Helvetica and all your formatting was thrown off, that's because Palatino was not in the co-worker's *System*. If the document can't find the font in which it was created, then it has to choose another from what is available. The solution is to make sure both Systems have the fonts from the same vendors.

Misformatting may happen occasionally even if the fonts are the same in both Systems. Another possible reason for this is that some programs create a file in the System Folder that holds the formatting for the document. When you open up the document on a different computer which of course uses a different System Folder, it can't find that document's formatting. If you know you are going to be taking the document to another computer, as soon as you quit creating it, go into the System Folder and find the formatting file; e.g., *Word Settings* if you are using Microsoft Word. Rename that file to correspond with the file you just created (though not exactly the same name), and put them both in the same folder.

▼ One of the most common reasons why **printing won't work** is because the appropriate printer icon wasn't chosen. Go to Chooser from the Apple menu and choose your printer (see pages 108).

▼ Make sure the printer is on, that it has paper, and that the paper tray, if there is one, is firmly attached.

▼ Make sure any networking cables are connected.

▼ On an ImageWriter, make sure the Select light is on. It *must* be on in order to print.

▼ Also on an ImageWriter make sure the lever on the hand roller corresponds to the way you are feeding paper—that is, friction-feed for single sheets (that's the symbol with two rollers, towards the back); and pin-feed for pin-fed labels and paper (that's the

**Printing Doesn't Work**

symbol with one roller and little pins, pulled towards the front).

▼ If the hard disk that the *System Folder is on* is running out of space, Mac cannot print. It needs some free space (like at least 100K, maybe less or more) to send over the messages for printing. You will have to free up some space on that disk by removing a file or two.

▼ Sometimes gremlins prevent printing properly. If you have checked everything and there really seems to be no logical reason for the file not to print, go away for a while, let someone else print to that printer, shut down, come back later, try again. This sometimes works. One never knows.

▼ Unusual printing problems are a common symptom of a virus attack. See page 163 for a brief explanation of viruses.

**Can't Form-Feed or Line-Feed the ImageWriter Paper**

If you want to **form-feed or line-feed the paper**, the Select light must be *off.* Be sure to turn it back on again before you try to print!

Notice that the line-feed button will feed the paper through one line at a time for four lines, then it turns into a controllable form-feed; as soon as you let go it stops. Form-feed itself will roll through an entire page length (generally 11 inches).

**There's Garbage Hanging Around Outside the Trash Can**

If **garbage piles up around your can**, it's because you didn't put it *inside* the can, but set it down *outside,* just like the kids. When the *very tip of the pointer* touches the can and turns it black, that's the time to let go. *It doesn't matter if the icon you are throwing away is positioned over the can*—it's the **pointer tip** that opens the lid.

A **gray disk icon** can mean one of two things, either it is open or it is in RAM.

**If the disk itself is still in the floppy drive**, then the gray shadow only means that you have already double-clicked on it and its window is open somewhere on the screen. If you can't see the disk's window because there are other windows in the way, simply double-click on the gray shadow and it will come forth as the active window.

**If the disk itself is not in the floppy drive**, then you most likely ejected that disk by choosing "Eject" from the File menu or by pressing Command E. This procedure does eject the disk, but also leaves its information in the Mac's *memory*. Read page 119 for an explanation of what happened and how to avoid it.

You **lost your application**? Your menu suddenly changed and you can't find "Font"? Now your window is buried under other windows? You just accidentally switched applications or perhaps you clicked on the Desktop and popped back to the Finder where all your Desktop windows are. Use the Application menu to choose the application you were previously working in: when you press on the Application menu (upper right of your menu bar) you will see a list of programs that are open. Choose the one you want. Then read Chapter 30 on Very Important Information, taking special note of the Application menu. Also see the tip on page 226 regarding hiding other windows.

If your **Desktop windows open too slowly** or perhaps everything on the Desktop seems to take longer than it should, check to see if you have told your windows to calculate the folder size. In your window in a list view,

## Gray Disk Icon is Left on the Screen

*Gray disk icon left on the screen after being ejected.*

## Lost Your Application? Other Windows Popped Up in Front of Your Face?

## Desktop Windows Open Very Slowly

under the column "Size," do you see the size of folders? That's what is slowing you down. Go back to the View control panel (found in the Control Panels folder inside the System Folder) and uncheck the box, "Calculate folder size."

**Erratic Typing or Mouse Movement**

Is the movement of the **mouse rather erratic**? Does your typing jerk around? Do your menus not show up right away? You are probably trying to do something in the background, like copy a large file or print. While the computer is doing something like printing, it has to spread its attention between you and the printer, which results in putting you on hold for seconds at a time.

**The Reset Switch**

When you crash and must restart, sometimes you cannot get to the Desktop to choose "Restart" from the Special menu and so you have to turn off the power. There is a little piece of plastic that comes with every Mac, called the **programmer's switch**. It often gets lost in the packing because it looks useless. Your manual might tell you not to install it, but do. On the side or the front of your Mac you'll see the little slots in which to install the switch.

There are two little tabs or maybe buttons to depress; one is the **reset switch** (may have a little triangle on it) and one is the **interrupt switch**. If the tabs are on the *side* of the computer, the one closest to you is the **reset switch.** If the tabs are on the *front* of the computer, the one on the left is the **reset switch.** Pushing the **reset switch** is the same as chosing "Restart." This is easier on the computer than turning off the power.

The **interrupt switch** can sometimes get you back to the Finder when your screen freezes if you type in a certain bit of code. It is easier to unfreeze with Command Option Escape (esc), called a "force quit." See page 233.

# PART THE FOURTH

This section contains information on the Macintosh model called the Performa, and also on the software from Apple called At Ease. Both create an environment on the computer that is very different from many of the Macintosh standards that I talk about in the rest of the book. You may want to stick with these differences for a while because their purpose is to make it easier for new users to learn the Mac. Eventually you will probably want to eliminate the overlying features and get down to a basic, real Macintosh. Just keep in mind that if things in the other chapters don't make sense to what you see on your screen, it is because of the Launcher or At Ease. This section explains the differences and how to work with them—*you still need to read Part the First to understand the basics.*

*If you obey all the rules, you miss all the fun.*
            —*Katherine Hepburn*

# CHAPTER THIRTY-FOUR

# THE PERFORMA

The **Macintosh Performa** is Apple's "home market" computer. If you don't know whether or not you have a Performa, check the front of the computer. There is an Apple logo and the name "Macintosh Performa" with a number indicating the model, such as 400 or 600. If you bought the computer at a retail store such as Sears, Silo, Circuit City, Office Depot, etc., then it's a Performa.

The Performa models are exactly like any other Macintoshes in that they use the same software, virtually the same operating system (with a few minor differences that won't be noticeable to you), and have the same features and friendliness. The biggest difference is in the way the Finder (the Desktop) appears and the way you can use it—the Performa automatically uses a special software program that has special features designed to make life even simpler than on a regular Mac.

In this chapter I'll explain just the special features that relate to using the Performa right out of the box (which does not include using "At Ease"— see the following chapter) that are different from a Macintosh. Everything else in this book applies to a Performa as well as to a Mac, so you can't read just this one chapter and know everything there is to know about working on the machine!

If you are accustomed to working on the Macintosh, you may wish to remove these special features from the Performa and have it work just like any other Mac. If

## The Macintosh Performa

you have never used a Mac before, these features may be just what you need to avoid some of the frustrating concepts that beginners have a difficult time with. If you ever plan to or must work with a regular Macintosh, though, you won't have these Performa features that you will come to depend on and you may be in for some surprises when you work on a Mac. If you will be using other Macs, I would recommend that you use the Performa's unique interface until you are comfortable, then remove the specialty items and learn how to do the same procedures "naturally." (The "interface" refers to what you see on the screen, what you do with what you see, and how you do it.)

**Setting it up**
The Performa comes out of the box with several software programs already loaded (installed). Just follow the directions in the manual to **set up the system**. Basically all you need to do is plug all the plugs into their matching sockets. Make sure you plug the power cord into a surge protector (available at any hardware store), not directly into a wall outlet.

**Backup the hard disk**
The manuals for the software are also in the box, but what is missing are the disks for the software that has already been installed. One of the first things you really must do is **backup your hard disk!** If you don't back it up and you have a bad system failure or crash or some sort of damage to your hard disk, you won't have any copy of all the software that came with the computer. Complete directions for backing up are in the manual, but I've also included brief directions at the end of this chapter. It's very easy.

The **Launcher**, a software program from Apple that is installed in the computer, is responsible for the unique interface of the Performa. When you turn on the Performa, you see this window at the bottom:

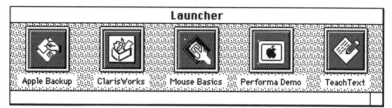

This is the Launcher window (the exact contents may be different from yours). Its purpose is to make it easier for you to find and "launch," or start, programs. The buttons in the window represent the applications (programs) that are already installed on your Performa. Click once (not twice) on any button to launch that program.

The idea is that you use the Launcher window *instead* of the hard disk window. Since the Launcher automatically opens whenever you turn on your computer, you will always have just what you need here at your fingertips with the click of a mouse.

The Launcher window acts like any other window (see Chapters 7 and 8 on Windows) in that you can scroll with the scroll bar, scroll arrows, or scroll box to see other items. You can move the window by pressing-and-dragging in its title bar (wherever you leave the window when you shut down, that is where the window will appear next time you turn on the Performa). You can use the resize box to resize the window. You can close the Launcher by clicking in the close box. (Each of these items is explained in detail in Chapter 7 on All Windows.) You can't change the view of the Launcher window except to view it horizontally or vertically.

*You can view the Launcher window vertically or horizontally.*

**Launcher Items are Buttons**

Keep in mind that the items in the Launcher are not *duplicates* of what's on your hard disk; they are just *buttons* that launch the real thing. You cannot copy items from the Launcher, either to another folder or to a disk, nor can you duplicate or print anything that is on the Launcher. You cannot organize files in folders. The Launcher window is merely a place from which to open, or launch, applications and documents. Because that is its purpose, you may want to remove items from the Launcher window that you don't use, and you may want to add items, either documents or applications, that you use regularly. See page 249 for details on adding and removing items.

**The Documents Folder**

Documents

*Everything you save will end up in this Documents folder automatically. This folder does not automatically appear on the Launcher window.*

A major feature of the Performa is that when you *save* a document you have created, the Performa automatically takes you to the Documents folder. Now, if you have never tried to figure out where a document goes when you save it, this won't mean much to you. But typically, a beginner chooses "Save As..." from the Edit menu, names the document, clicks the Save button, and then can't find the document the next day cuz he doesn't know where it went when he saved it. This *default,* or automatic feature, of taking you to the Documents folder when you save means that every document will end up in the Documents folder on the hard disk. You will always know where to look for it.

Also, if you are working on one document and want to open another, when you choose "Open..." from the File menu you will see the Documents folder. The document you want to open is probably in there, in which case you can double-click on its name to open it.

Inside the Documents folder are folders for the software programs (applications) that are already installed on your Performa. When you choose to save, you can save the document directly into the folder that holds the software itself. For instance, if you are working in GreatWorks, you might want to save your database into the GreatWorks folder instead of into the generic Documents folder.

*· **Save into the** ·**application folder***

To save the document into the GreatWorks (or other application) folder, double-click on the name GreatWorks in the Save As dialog box list. Name the document, then click the Save button.

When you want to retrieve that document, you will need to go to the hard disk window and open the Documents folder (double-click on it), then open the folder titled with the name of the program you used (double-click on the name).

*Double-click on this folder name before you save. Then when you click the Save button, your document will end up in the GreatWorks folder.*

If you are dependent on the Launcher, it becomes a minor problem that the Documents folder is not on the Launcher. If you want to depend on the Launcher for a while, have someone help you through the process of adding the Documents folder to it (details on page 249).

But you know what? You really don't *want* to store every document you ever create into the Documents folder *or* into the application folders. You need to learn how to make your own folders to organize your work; read Chapter 10 on Folders and Chapter 15 on Saving.

*· **Wean yourself** · **from the** · **Documents folder***

When you eventually start saving items into other folders you may get a little irritated with the default always popping you back to the Documents folder.

To stop the Performa from always going to the Documents folder, rename the folder. Adding a period to the end of its name is sufficient.

Documents!

*Add any character to the end of the name, or change it altogether.*

**Sanity Protection**

On a regular Macintosh it is so easy for beginners to lose applications and documents and windows in the mess that results from having several files and applications open at once. It can be difficult to understand where you are and where files disappeared to and how to get them back. But on the Performa, you can see only one application at a time, even though several may be open. It will always be clear what is open and active at the moment. Now, you may not think this is such a big deal at this moment, but really, this is for your own good and it will help you retain your sanity.

On the Mac (and thus the Performa, since it is really a Mac), remember, you can have more than one application open at a time. Even though you can't *see* any other application or the Desktop, you can always switch to any application that may be open, or switch back to the Desktop/Finder at any time: just press on the Application menu (far right of the menu bar) and choose the open application you want to switch to, *or* choose "Finder" to take you back to the Desktop and the Launcher window. For details on the Application Menu, read pages 207–208 .

**Without the Launcher, the Performa is a Mac**

If you're accustomed to working on a Mac (and if you're not, ignore this) and being able to click the Desktop to return to the Finder, you won't like having to actually go to the Application menu to get back to the Finder. **Without the Launcher, the Performa would act just like any other Mac.** You can remove the Launcher and everything else in this book will make perfect sense and you can ignore this chapter altogether, *except for backing up*. See page 252 for directions on removing the Launcher.

You can remove buttons from the Launcher that you don't use. If you are a brand-new beginner, you may want to get help for this—at least find someone who knows how to open folders and move things around and make aliases. Or you can just follow the directions.

To **remove items from the Launcher** window:

▼ Open the hard disk window by double-clicking on its icon (the hard disk icon is on the top right, just under the menu bar).

▼ Open the System Folder by double-clicking on it.

▼ Find the folder called "Launcher Items." (You can type the characters "la" to find and select the folder.) Double-click to open it.

▼ Press-and-drag any icon out of the folder. You can throw the item in the trash because it is just an "alias" of the real thing—it is not the original document or application. (Well, as long as the name is in *italic* it is not the real thing. Read about aliases in Chapter 25.)

▼ Close the Launcher Items folder and the System Folder. You'll notice that the items you removed no longer appear in the Launcher window.

You can also add buttons representing documents or applications or even folders to the Launcher. To **add items to the Launcher** window:

▼ Find the document, application, utility, etc., that you want to appear in the Launcher window. You'll probably find it on the hard disk somewhere. Click once on the file to select it.

▼ From the File menu, choose "Make Alias." This makes a copy of the icon with the same name (a copy of the *icon,* not of the file itself—read Chapter 25 on Aliases), but the new name is in italic and has the word "alias" at the end.

▼ Press-and-drag the alias icon over to the Desktop somewhere.

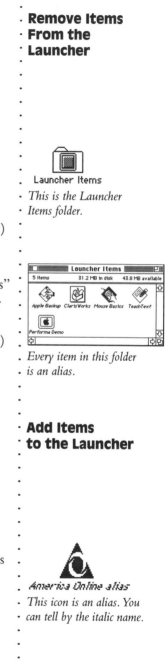

Launcher Items

*This is the Launcher Items folder.*

*Every item in this folder is an alias.*

## Add Items to the Launcher

*America Online alias*

*This icon is an alias. You can tell by the italic name.*

▾ Open the System Folder by double-clicking on it.

▾ Inside the System Folder, locate the Launcher Items folder (you can type "la" to find it quickly). Don't do anything to the folder—just make a note of where it is.

▾ Press-and-drag the alias that you put on the Desktop; drag the alias over to the Launcher Items folder and drop it in (just position the pointer over the folder so the folder turns dark, then let go).

▾ Close the window to the System Folder. This new item will now appear in the Launcher window and you can just single-click on it to launch the file.

**Alias of a folder**  You can make an alias of a folder and put it into the Launcher. When you click on the button of a folder from the Launcher window, it opens the actual folder that is on the hard disk. You cannot put items into this folder button on the Launcher—you can only put items into the real folder on the hard disk.

**Make Backups of Your Files**  Apple has made it very easy for you to **back up** your entire hard disk, just in case something goes wrong (cuz it will). You need to have 20 high-density 3.5-inch floppy disks at your side before you start if you want to copy all the files that on the computer when you buy it. If you add software before you backup, you'll need more disks. In the first step of the process, the Performa will firgure out exactly how many disks you need and let you know. Make sure the disks are *high-density,* not just double-density (see page 13). There should be two tiny square holes on the end without the metal slider, and there should be the initials "HD" somewhere on the disk.

If you just want to copy the System Folder and its data, you need just 5 disks. You will be able to choose whether to copy the System Folder or all the files. Copying the System Folder takes 15 minutes; copying all the files takes about 45 minutes.

▼ The first item in the "Launcher" (that little window that shows up at the bottom of the screen) is an icon called "Apple Backup." Click once on this icon.

If you don't see the Launcher, make sure you are at the Finder/Desktop: from the Application menu in the far right of the menu bar, choose "Finder."

If there is already a checkmark next to "Finder," then double-click on the icon for your hard disk. In the hard disk window you should find a folder icon called "Launcher." Double-click this icon and in the Launcher window you should see "Apple Backup."

If you don't see the "Launcher" icon on the hard disk, look in the folder called "Applications." The "Apple Backup" icon should be in the "Applications" folder; if it is, double-click on it.

If "Apple Backup" isn't there, use Find File to search for it (Chapter 26). If "Apple Backup" can't be found anywhere, talk to the person who could have removed it from your hard disk because it was there when you bought the machine.

▼ Whew. You've found it, right? (If you found it in the Launcher window, you can single-click on the icon. If you found it in the "Applications" folder on the hard disk, you must double-click on it.) Now all you have to do is follow the simple directions. The Performa will eject disks as they are full and will tell you when to insert a new disk. It will also tell you what to label the disk, and you should do what it says!

▼ Make sure before you begin that you have enough time and disks to complete the entire process, because if you stop in the middle you'll have to start all over again.

▼ Lock each disk when you are done (make sure the little tab that covers one of the holes is pushed so you can see through the hole; see page 14).

Apple Backup

*This is the Apple Backup button on the Launcher window.*

Apple Backup

*This is the Apple Backup file on the Hard Disk.*

*Unfortunately, the Performa does not give you any clue as to what it put on each disk. When you are done, you might want to take a few minutes to record what is on each disk. A quick way to do this is to insert a disk, double-click to open it, then choose "Print Window" from the File menu (first make sure your printer is on). Save the printouts with the disks.*

**Removing the Launcher**

Apple's software program called the Launcher is respon-sible for these special features. If you want your Performa to act just like anyone else's Mac, **remove the Launcher**.

▼ From the Apple menu, choose "Control Panels."

▼ In the Control Panels window, choose "Launcher." You can find it by just clicking the letter "L."

Launcher

*This is the Launcher control panel.*

▼ Press-and-drag the Launcher file/icon out of the Control Panels window. Put it anywhere except in the System Folder or in the Control Panels folder. Most people make a folder called "Utilities" on the hard disk for storing items like this. You don't want to get rid of it altogether yet (well, maybe you do, in which case you can of course toss it in the trash can).

▼ Close the Control Panels window.

Startup Items

*Double-click the Startup Items folder (above) to get the Startup Items window (below).*

▼ Open the System Folder. Find and double-click on the folder called "Startup Items." (Find it quickly by typing "st.") Remove the alias called "Launcher." You can throw this in the trash. If you ever want a Launcher alias again, you can always make a new one (see Chapter 25).

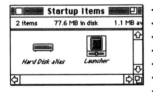

▼ Close the Startup Items folder; close the System Folder. From the Special menu, choose Restart. Et voilà, it's done.

▼ If you ever want to use the Launcher again, you can just double-click on the icon, wherever it may be, and the Launcher window will open. *But as long as the icon is not in the Control Panels folder nor the Startup Items folder, Launcher will not start automatically.* You will have the Launcher window, but the other special features, such as hiding the other applications and windows, and defaulting to the Documents folder when you save, will not be in effect. **To re-install**, put the two files back where they were and restart.

**Re-install the Launcher**

# CHAPTER THIRTY-FIVE

**At Ease** is a software program from Apple that provides an easier way for people to use the Mac or the Performa, and a way for the computer owner to control who uses what and where files get saved. It's particularly useful for schools or homes with small children, where files may accidentally get misplaced or thrown away or changed. It's great for computer labs where people have to save their documents onto floppy disks but don't quite understand how to do that so files end up getting saved in all sorts of strange places throughout the hard disk. It's great in offices where people need to be trained quickly for specific tasks, because you can ignore all the Desktop information, like using the windows and organizing files. It's great in places where you want to limit the opportunity for software pirating. You can turn At Ease on or off as the situation demands.

The following page shows what a monitor looks like when At Ease is installed and running.

## What is At Ease?

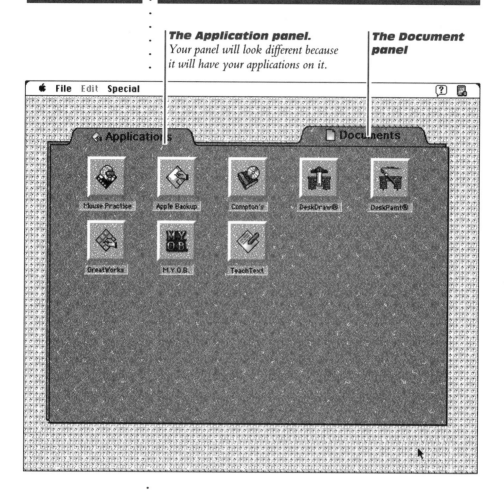

**The Application panel.**
*Your panel will look different because it will have your applications on it.*

**The Document panel**

**Limitations**  Notice there is no trash can and no hard disk icon. If you insert a disk, you won't see it on the Desktop. There is no way to copy anything while At Ease is running, either from the Applications panel or from the Documents panel. It is not possible to get to the Finder (the Desktop) unless you know the password.

The Apple menu is the same as ever, except there is no access to the Control Panels. The other **menus** are very limited, also, as shown here:

You can **customize At Ease** to suit your situation, and you can change it at any moment (*you,* that is, if you are the boss). You determine which applications show up on the Applications panel, and whether documents are saved as buttons on the Document panel or whether documents can only be saved onto a floppy disk. (See page 261–264 for details on customizing At Ease.)

**Customizing**

Each application and document that you have specified to appear in **At Ease** is displayed with a button.

**Using At Ease**

Single-click (don't double-click) on a button to open an application or a document.

If you don't specify any documents to be visible, there won't be a Documents panel. If there are more applications than will fit on one Application panel, At Ease creates more panels.

Some items that you think of as applications, such as HyperCard stacks, may show up on the Documents panel because technically a HyperCard stack is a document from the application HyperCard. If you don't see your application on the Application panel, check the Documents panel.

▼ To switch between the Applications panel and the Documents panel, just click once on the folder tab with the label on it.

▼ You can also press the Tab key to switch back and forth between panels.

**Turning Pages of the Panels**

If there is more than one page to a panel, you can **move through the pages** in several ways:

*Page 1 of 2*

*When there is more than one panel, you will see this marker on the bottom center of the panels.*

**To next page** — Single-click the arrow shown on the bottom right corner of the panel.

Or press the right arrow key on the keyboard.

**To previous page** — Single-click the arrow shown on the bottom left corner of the panel.

Or press the left arrow key on the keyboard.

**To last page** — Press Command RightArrow.

**To first page** — Press Command LeftArrow.

**Go to page 1–9** — Press Command and the number of the page you want to view.

**To a file** — Type the first character of the name of the file. This does not select the file; it only displays the panel that has that file's button. It will not select a file on the other type of panel.

**To other panel** — Press Tab.

**Opening Other Documents**

You can **open any other document** on the Mac, even if there is no button on the Documents panel. If you know the password (see page 259 for info on the password), you can use "Open Other…" from the File menu.

If you don't know the password, first open the application the document was created in (click on its button). Then from the File menu, choose "Open…" and find the document.

**From the File menu**

From the **File menu** of any application, you can open any document that was created in that application.

If there are documents that you do not want anyone to change the contents of, lock that file (see page 67). You will need to get to the Finder to find the file to lock (see page 259). Remember, locking a file does not prevent anyone from *reading* or *printing* it; locking the file just prevents anyone from *changing* it.

It's possible to **open any other application** on the Mac, *if you know the password* (see page 259 for info on the password). From the File menu, choose "Open Other...." If you have set up At Ease to require a password, you'll be asked for it. After you provide the password, you'll get a standard dialog box for opening files.

> At the bottom of this dialog box is a checkbox button, "Add to At Ease Items." If you check this box *before* you open the application, a button will be added automatically to the At Ease Applications panel. When there is a button on a panel, you won't need a password.

You can have **more than one application** or document **open at a time**, just as you can when you're not using At Ease.

▾ Click once on the button to open the first application or document.

▾ To open another document in this *same* application, just use the "Open..." command from the File menu.

To open another application or a document from *another* application:

▾ From the Application menu (far right of the menu bar), choose "At Ease." The At Ease panels will appear on top of any document that was open in the first application.

▾ Click once on the button of the second application or document.

## Opening Other Applications

*To use "Open Other..." you need to know the password.*

☐ Add to At Ease Items
*If you make a button, you don't need a password.*

## Opening More Than One Application

*This is the "Application menu."*

You will see both documents on the screen. If the open documents are from two or more different applications, you can switch back and forth between the applications by clicking in the document windows. You can also switch applications by using the Application menu (shown on the previous page).

**Saving a Document**

Sorry, your work was NOT saved. You can only save onto a floppy disk. Please save again.

OK

*Users may get deluded into thinking they can save on the hard disk because the Save button is black, but they will get this message.*

You can set At Ease so that when you or any other user **save a new document**, it cannot be saved anywhere except onto a floppy disk. This is perfect for school or office or home situations where people often end up saving documents in odd places on the hard disk and can't find them again. Or they leave junk lying all over the place.

Please insert a floppy disk.

Cancel

*This is the message users will get when they try to save a document without a floppy disk inserted.*

You can set At Ease to create a button on the Documents panel every time a document is saved.

*See page 261 for details on setting these and other options.*

If you choose both options—to save onto a floppy *and* to create a button for the document—then that floppy disk must be inserted into the computer's drive before the document can be opened. At Ease thoughtfully tells you the name of the disk you need to insert.

**Ejecting a Disk**

Special
Eject Disk ⌘E

Restart
Shut Down

*If there is a disk in the floppy drive, At Ease selects it for you so it can be ejected.*

If you cannot get to the Finder, you cannot see the disk icons. If you can't see the disk icons, how do you select and **eject a disk**? There are several ways, actually.

▼ While At Ease is active (when you can see the panels), choose "Eject Disk" from the Special menu.

▼ Or, while At Ease is active, press Command E.

▾ Or, while you are in any application, from the File menu choose "Save As...." In this dialog box is a button to eject the currently inserted disk.

▾ No matter where you are, you can always press Command Shift 1 to eject a disk from the internal floppy drive. Press Command Shift 2 to eject a disk from a second floppy drive, if you have one.

When more than one application is open, you can **choose between applications and At Ease** through the Application menu.

**Switching Between At Ease and Open Applications**

> To get to At Ease *from an application,* you will always need to choose it from the Application menu.

> If you can see the window belonging to another application, whether you are viewing At Ease or not, simply click anywhere on the window to bring that application to the front.

If the open windows of other applications or of the Finder bother you while you are viewing At Ease or any document, you can always use the Application menu and choose **Hide Others**. This will hide all the other windows that do not belong to the current application.

*"Hide Others"*

When you set up At Ease, you can set a password so no one except those in-the-know can **get to the Finder** (the Desktop). If they can't get to the Finder, they can't trash files, rearrange files, copy files, save files onto the hard disk, etc. You can choose *not* to set a password, in which case anyone can switch to the Finder at any time, which defeats the whole purpose of At Ease. Details for setting up the password are on page 265. Right here I want to explain how to move back and forth between the Finder and At Ease assuming you have (or someone has) already set a password.

**Getting to the Finder**

**"Go to Finder"**

*When you choose "Go to Finder," you will be asked to enter the password.*

While you are in At Ease, from the File menu you can choose **Go to Finder**. You will get a little dialog box in which to type the password. If a clue has been set, you'll see the clue. Thank goodness for the clue. As you type, you won't see letters—you'll see bullets (•••). That's so no one can discover the password over your shoulder.

It doesn't matter whether you type the same capital letters as the original password, but you do have to type any blank spaces that are in the original.

**"Go to At Ease"**

Once you have typed the password and are at the Finder, you can **switch back to At Ease** through the File menu, the last item. The next time you want to get to the Finder, you will have to retype the password.

If you want to be able to switch back and forth between the Finder and At Ease without repeatedly typing the password, **here is a good trick**:

▼ From At Ease, type the password and get to the Finder.

▼ Now, to get back to At Ease, *do not choose it from the File menu*. Instead, use the Application menu (far right). Notice that when you choose "At Ease" from the Application menu, *"Finder" stays in this menu*. If you choose the Finder now *from the Application menu,* you will not need to type the password.

**Create a button**

You can also **create a button for the Finder** on the Application panel so you can just click to get to the Finder. You will still need to type the password. See the section on adding buttons to the panels, page 262. To make a button for the Finder, you will need to navigate your way to the System Folder, which is where the Finder is located. You can also add a button by making an alias of the Finder (see page 170) and putting the alias inside the "At Ease Items" folder, located in the System Folder.

To **turn off At Ease**, all you need to do is click the Off button in the At Ease Control Panel.

▼ From the Apple menu, choose "Control Panels."

▼ Double-click on the At Ease Setup control panel.

▼ Click the Off button. Close the control panel (click in its close box *or* press Command W).

▼ In order for At Ease to disappear from your monitor, you need to restart. You can either choose "Restart" from the Special menu now, or you can just leave it until you're ready to quit for the day. The next time you turn on your computer, At Ease will not be active.

It is possible to turn off all extensions (page 229) when you start up. This is a common trouble-shooting technique. **To bypass** all extensions, including **At Ease**, hold down the Shift key when you turn on or restart the computer. This will take you directly to the Finder. The next time the computer starts, At Ease will kick in again.

> *You still need to know the password to get to the Finder,* even if you hold down the Shift key! If you don't know the password, At Ease will start up as usual, you will not get to the Finder, and all your extensions will be turned off.

You can **customize At Ease** through the At Ease Setup control panel. Customize it by adding buttons for the applications you want to access and for the documents you want to be able to open. Set a password that must be used whenever someone wants to get to the Finder or use the "Open Other..." command from the File menu. Determine whether a user can save documents onto the hard disk, only onto a floppy disk, and whether a button should be made and placed on the Documents panel automatically as the document is saved.

## Turning At Ease Off

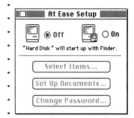

*Simply click the "Off" button in the control panel.*

## Bypassing At Ease When You Start Up

## Customizing At Ease

. If this is the first time you have used At Ease, you will
· need to **restart the computer** to put it into effect.

***Turn on At Ease***

| ▣ At Ease Setup |
| 🖥 ○ Off    🖥 ◉ On |
| *"Hard Disk" will start up with At Ease.* |
| [ Select Items… ] |
| [ Set Up Documents… ] |
| [ Change Password… ] |

*When the button is*
*"On," the three selections*
*become available.*

To customize At Ease, first turn it on. Then follow the
rest of the steps in order:

   ▼ From the Apple menu, choose "Control Panels."

   ▼ Double-click the At Ease Setup control panel.
      You can type at to find the control panel quickly.

   ▼ Click the "On" button. The three selections will
      then become available.

   ▼ If At Ease is already on, up and running, you can
      still make changes here.

***Add buttons***
***for applications***
***and documents***

Although you are now going to customize At Ease,
you won't actually see At Ease for the first time (if you
haven't used it before). After At Ease has been turned
on, it will be active automatically every time you start
the machine.

   ▼ Click the button "Select Items…."

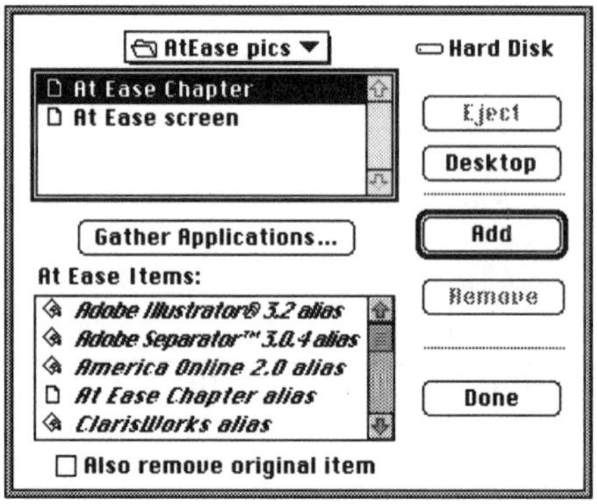

| 🗀 AtEase pics ▼ | ▭ Hard Disk |
| ▢ At Ease Chapter | |
| ▢ At Ease screen | [ Eject ] |
| | [ Desktop ] |
| [ Gather Applications… ] | [ Add ] |
| **At Ease Items:** | [ Remove ] |
| ◈ *Adobe Illustrator® 3.2 alias* | |
| ◈ *Adobe Separator™ 3.0.4 alias* | |
| ◈ *America Online 2.0 alias* | |
| ▢ *At Ease Chapter alias* | [ Done ] |
| ◈ *ClarisWorks alias* | |
| ☐ Also remove original item | |

   ▼ In the dialog box shown above, find and select the
      items, either applications (◈) or documents (▢),
      from the top list. If you click once on a folder (🗀),
      the "Add" button changes to "Open."

*If you are a very new user,* you may need help "navigating" around your hard disk to find things. See Chapter 29, or ask a friend to help.

You *can* click the **Gather Applications**... button which will gather up every application on the entire hard disk and put them on the Applications panel. If you don't know what you're doing and there is no one to help you, you can use this option. The problem is that you will end up with all kinds of weird stuff on your panel and you won't know what it is. Later, when your friend comes over, you can remove the things you don't use.

*"Gather Applications..."*

▼ Each time you make a selection, click the "Add" button. You will see the file name appear in the lower list. The word "alias" will appear at the end of the name in the list, but "alias" won't appear on the button on the panel.

▼ You can hold the Shift key down to select more than one item in the top list.

▼ Don't worry about whether the file is an application or a document. At Ease knows which is which and will place their buttons on the appropriate panels.

▼ If you add applications or documents from another disk besides your startup disk (such as a floppy or an external hard disk or a file server), that source disk will need to be available for you to use the button. The button will always appear on the panel, but that doesn't necessarily mean the button can find the application or the document. You'll get a message telling you that the computer needs the other disk.

▼ When you are finished, click the "Done" button.

If At Ease is already active and these are just changes, you will see the changes in effect on the At Ease panel immediately.

**Remove buttons** · When you **remove applications or documents** from
**for applications** · At Ease, it only removes the *button* from the At Ease
**or documents** · panel. It does not remove any part of the real application
· or document! Removing an item simply means a user
· who does not know the password cannot use the file.

▼ Click the button "Select Items...."

```
┌─────────────────────────────────────────────┐
│         ┌─ Hard Disk ▼ ┐        ⊂⊃ Hard Disk  │
│                                               │
│   □ System Folder        ⬆      ┌─────────┐   │
│   □ Applications                │  Eject  │   │
│   □ Jargon                      └─────────┘   │
│   □ LMB.3e               ⬇      ┌─────────┐   │
│                                 │ Desktop │   │
│   ┌─────────────────────┐       └─────────┘   │
│   │ Gather Applications...│      ┌─────────┐   │
│   └─────────────────────┘       │   Add   │   │
│   At Ease Items:                └─────────┘   │
│   ┌────────────────────┐ ⬆      ┌─────────┐   │
│   │ □ NUSIG alias      │        │ Remove  │   │
│   │ ⬧ Ofoto™ 1.1.1 alias│       └─────────┘   │
│   │ ⬧ PageMaker 4.2 alias│                    │
│   │ □ pc guy alias     │        ┌─────────┐   │
│   │ □ Re * * alias     │ ⬇      │  Done   │   │
│   └────────────────────┘        └─────────┘   │
│   □ Also remove original item                 │
└─────────────────────────────────────────────┘
```

▼ In the dialog box shown above, find and select the
items, either applications or documents, from the
*bottom* list. You can press the Shift key down while
you click to select more than one item.

▼ Click the "Remove" button. You won't get a
warning—the button will simply be removed
from the panel.

▼ If you check the box, "Also remove original item,"
you will remove not just the button from the panel,
but the original application or document itself from
the hard disk! Ooh la la—be careful with this!

▼ When you are finished, click the "Done" button.

If At Ease is already active and these are just changes,
you will see the changes in effect on the At Ease panel
immediately.

You can make decisions about where a user should **save documents** and whether a button should be created:

**Set up how documents are saved**

▼ Click the button "Set Up Documents...."

▼ If you leave the X in the checkbox, "Add a button to At Ease," then every time a user (or you) saves a document, a button will appear on the Documents panel. If you remove the X by clicking on the checkbox, no button will be added.

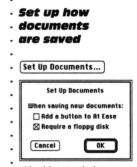

*Checkbox-style buttons mean you can have any combination of buttons selected, from none to all.*

▼ If there is an X in the checkbox "Require a floppy disk," to put an X in the box, you cannot save onto the hard disk. When you try to save, you will be asked to insert a floppy disk. You may think you can save onto the hard disk because At Ease allows you to name the document and click the Save button, but you will see a dialog box stating that the document has not actually been saved.

▼ If you select the option to require a floppy disk, check to make sure it's working. Try to save a new document. If you find that you are allowed to save a new document onto the hard disk, then restart the computer. This option will definitely go into effect when you restart and every time afterward until you change it.

The **password** you set here will be necessary every time you want to get to the Finder, and every time you want to get to a control panel or a document or an application that is not available in At Ease.

**Set a password**

▼ Click the "Set Password..." button.

▼ Type your password in the top edit box, as shown. You can use a word or phrase of up to 15 characters. Capital or lower case letters will not matter, but spaces will be recorded and will need to be remembered. After this first time, you will never again see what you actually wrote.

*Isn't it great that we get to have a clue?*

▼Type a clue of no more than 50 characters, a good enough clue to remind you of the password. Really, you don't want to forget your password. The clue will appear every time you are asked to name the password.

**Restart for changes**

Now that you have customized everything for At Ease, you need to restart the computer for all your changes to go into effect.

▼Make sure you've saved any other open documents and closed all applications.

▼From the Special menu, choose "Restart."

**Change the Password**

After you have a password, the next time you choose the At Ease Setup control panel the button will read, **Change Password**. Just repeat the process above.

Of course, you need to know the current password in order to get to the control panel to change the password.

**If You Forget the Password!**

If you **forget the password**, it is possible to start over, but it's not the simplest thing to do. Have someone who knows what they're doing help you with this. You will need a startup disk, which is a disk that has a stripped down System Folder on it. If you have a floppy disk called "Disk Tools" or "Disk Utilities," you can use that disk.

▼If you are already Shut Down, insert the startup floppy disk. If your computer is running, from the Special menu choose "Restart." As soon as you hear the beep, insert the startup floppy disk.

▼You will see a floppy disk icon at the top right of your screen. Double-click on the hard disk icon below that.

▼Open the System Folder on the hard disk. Open the "Preferences" folder. Find the "At Ease Preferences" file (type "at" to find it quickly).

▾ Press-and-drag on the "At Ease Preferences" file to remove it. Throw it in the trash.

▾ From the Special menu, choose "Restart" again. Don't insert the floppy disk.

▾ Use the "At Ease Setup" control panel and create a new password. Don't forget it.

If you want to take more radical steps than simply turning At Ease off, there is a way to **permanently remove it**. Do not simply drag At Ease files to the trash—you may not be able to restart your computer. In fact, if you remove At Ease improperly you may even need to reinstall your system software.

**If you have the disks** for At Ease, follow this method:

▾ Turn off At Ease (as above).

▾ Insert the disk called "At Ease Install 1."

▾ In the open window, double-click on the icon called "Installer."

▾ Click the button "Customize."

▾ Select "At Ease."

▾ Hold down the Option key; the "Install" button will change to "Remove." With the Option key held down, click "Remove."

**If you don't have the disks** because At Ease was already installed on your machine when you got it, as on a Performa, then follow this method:

▾ Turn off At Ease (as above).

▾ Restart the computer (from the Special menu, choose "Restart").

▾ Open the System Folder on your hard disk. Remove the following items and put them in the trash (or save them onto a floppy disk in case you ever want to reinstall At Ease):

**Permanently Removing At Ease**

***If you have the disks***

***If you don't have the disks***

At Ease Items

At Ease

Control Panel Handler

At Ease Setup

At Ease Preferences

**Remove:**

> From the System Folder:
> - a folder named "At Ease Items."
> - a file named "At Ease."
>
> From the Extensions folder
> inside the System Folder:
> - a file named "Control Panel Handler."
>
> From the Control Panels folder
> inside the System Folder:
> - a control panel named "At Ease Setup."
>
> From the Preferences folder
> inside the System Folder:
> - a file named "At Ease Preferences."

▼ While you're at it, you might want to remove the folder from your hard disk named "Mouse Practice." (Well, you can keep that if you want to.)

**Mouse Practice**

**Mouse Practice** is a cute little introduction to using the mouse, appropriate even for very young users, and enchanting for us older users. Just click once on the button to start it up, then follow the directions, which are both written and spoken.

> To quit Mouse Practice before it is finished, press Command Q or Command Period at any time.

# PART THE FIFTH

The computer world is full of all kinds of abstruse jargon and many of us are too embarrassed to ask what the unfamiliar terms mean. And then when somebody tells us what they mean, half the time it still doesn't make sense but we pretend it does. For years I pretended I knew what a SIMM was. I've made a list of the most common terms you may hear so you can look them up in the privacy of your own room. This isn't a complete list, but it should take care of most needs. **If you don't see what you want here, also look in the index.** An italicized word within the definition means it is also in the list. If you do need more complete, illustrated definitions for Macintosh terms, as well as words relating to those other computers, see the book *Jargon: An Informal Dictionary of Computer Terms*. Well, yes, I did write it.

*You can't let the seeds stop you from enjoying the watermelon.*

# CHAPTER THIRTY-SIX

# JARGON
### impress your friends

An **accelerator board** is a *card,* a circuit board with chips, that you can buy and install or have installed into your Mac. It makes the computer work faster.

**accelerator board**

An **alert box** is a message that appears on the screen to warn you of some imminent disaster.

**alert box**

**AppleTalk** is how your Mac talks to your LaserWriter or to other Macs or to other sorts of machines (provided they are hooked together with cables).

**AppleTalk**

**ASCII** (pronounced *askee*) stands for American Standard Code for Information Interchange. It's a standard code that almost all computers can read that enables them all to understand how to create numbers and letters, even though they use different programs. For instance, if you are working in FullWrite and you need to send the file to someone else, but they use MacWrite II, you can save the document as an ASCII file (which is the same as *text-only*) and their MacWrite II will be able to open the file.

**ASCII**

See *ASCII.*

**askee**

When you use a *modem* to send information from one computer to another, the information goes through the phone lines at a certain rate of *bits* per second (a *bit* being one electronic unit of information). This bits-per-second rate (bps) is commonly called the **baud rate** (pronounced "bod"). Technically, though, the baud rate is not really the same as the bps, and someone someday will surely correct you. Modems most typically send at 1200, 2400, or 9600 baud; the higher the baud rate, the faster the information flies through the phone lines and the less costly your phone bill.

**baud rate**

**BBS** **BBS** stands for Bulletin Board Service, which is a service usually set up by organizations or clubs to provide or exchange information. You access the BBS through your *modem*. You call up the number for the BBS, and on your screen you see the computer equivalent of a bulletin board. You can post messages, ask questions, answer questions, make new friends.

**beta** When a piece of *software* or *hardware* is in the testing stage, it is said to be in **beta**. Usually beta versions are sent out to people to test (called beta testers) who report back the things that are wrong or buggy or that need improvement.

**bit** **Bit** is short for "binary digit." It's the smallest unit of information that the computer works with; it's kind of like an on/off electronic pulse. See page 11.

**bitmapped** When an image or text is **bitmapped**, that means it is built out of the dots on the screen. Bitmapped graphics can be edited dot by dot. They are the simplest form of imagery on the computer.

Other kinds of graphics, *EPS,* for instance, or *PostScript* fonts, have two parts to them: They have a screen representation that is bitmapped so the computer can read and produce it on the screen. Then they also have a *PostScript,* or *outline* version of the same image that is *not* bitmapped; this is the part that the printer reads to produce it on paper.

**bomb** I don't think it's nice of them to use a **bomb** metaphor when the System *crashes*. It's very disturbing. It lays a guilt trip on us, too; we always think it's our fault.

**boot** To **boot** or **boot up** means to turn on your computer or other *hardware*. See page 17.

**bug** The B word. If a piece of *software* or *hardware* has something wrong with it, making it act weird, it is said to have a **bug** or to be **buggy.** That's something *beta* testers do— they try to find and report the bugs in new products so the bugs get exterminated before we pay lots of money for the products. The term comes down to us from the real live crawling bugs that used to get into those giant-sized computers, particularly one at Harvard in 1945.

See *BBS*.

A **bus** is a combination of software, hardware, and electrical wiring that creates a way for all the different parts of your computer to communicate with each other. For instance, you see the cables plugged into the back of your computer that connect it with the monitor or the printer or the hard disk or some other device—they all connect into the bus. If there was no bus, you would have an unwieldy number of wires connecting every part to every other part. It would be like having separate wiring for every light bulb and socket in your house.

**bus**

A **byte** is eight *bits* strung together to make a message that the computer can interpret. See page 12.

**byte**

**CAD** stands for Computer Aided Design. It actually has nothing to do with the sort of desktop publishing design projects that most of us think of—it is referring to engineering and architectural tasks.

**CAD**

A **card** is a piece of plastic with *chips* attached to it that you put inside the computer box. You can get video cards and accelerator cards and clock cards and printer cards or whole computers on a card. Some of them you can just order through the mail and then open the computer and stick 'em in, which I find to be a very frightening but empowering experience.

**card**

A **chip** is that truly amazing and remarkably tiny piece of silicon that has an entire integrated electronic circuit embedded in its surface. Chips are what make the computer. Chips are the computer. A tiny chip is one of the biggest pieces of human-made magic on earth.

**chip**

**CD-ROM** stands for Compact Disk, Read-Only Memory. A CD-ROM actually looks just like the CDs we play music with. You can get a CD-ROM player for your Mac that will read these disks. There are disks with the entire works of Shakespeare, with dictionaries, with history, with images of the works in the Louvre, etc. etc. etc. You can only read from them, you cannot store information onto them.

**CD-ROM**

**CDEV** . A **CDEV** is a control panel device. It's a little program (or *utility*) that usually makes life easier for you, like a screen saver. You can control some of their functions through the Control Panel. CDEVs are similar to *INITs* in that you just stick them in the System Folder and they work.

**CPU** The **CPU** is the Central Processing Unit. It is the one tiny little *chip* in the Macintosh, often called the microprocessor, that runs the show. Powerful magic. Sometimes people refer to the circuit board it lives on as the CPU.

**crash** . There's probably not much question about what a **crash** is. The first time it happens to you, you say, "Oh. This must be a crash. I get it now." When you see the *bomb* on the screen or when the screen freezes or when the Mac just decides to check out, that is a crash. The only thing you can do at that point is turn the computer off. Wait several minutes before you turn it back on again. Sometimes you may have a clue as to why it crashed (see page 235); sometimes you just have to accept the fact that you will never know why. Yes, everything you did not Save to your disk is gone. (Also known as "System bomb.")

**database** A **database** document is like a giant collection of 3 x 5 cards. Since they're on the computer, though, a click of a button can alphabetize those "cards," select just the names you want to invite to your party, tell you who owes how much money, etc. The term "database" can refer either to the software package you create in, or to the document itself. A database is one of the most useful tools on the Mac, and it actually is an incredible amount of fun. If you've never used one before, read Guy Kawasaki's little book, *Database 101*. Everybody needs a database.

**default** A **default** is an automatic choice. When you open a dialog box and see measurements or specifications that are already filled in for you, when a font style and size has already been chosen, these are the defaults. You can always change the actual specifications, and sometimes you can change the default itself so next time you use this dialog box or menu it has your choices as the defaults. Also, when a button has a dark border around it, that is considered the default button. Press the Return or Enter key to activate the default button.

I use the term **dialog box** loosely in this book to avoid confusing you. I refer to any of the messages you get on the screen that tell you something or ask you something as dialog boxes. Technically, some are dialog boxes and some are alert boxes and some are actually windows and there are probably a few others, but few people will argue and all will understand if you just call them all dialog boxes.

**· dialog box**

This little creature is the **Dogcow**. His name is Clarus. He says *Moof!* Sometimes he says *!fooM.*

**· Dogcow**

A **dot matrix printer** is a printer that uses coarse dots to create the text and graphics on the page, like the ImageWriter.

**· dot matrix printer**

**Dots per inch** is how the *resolution* of a printer or a scanner is measured. For instance, the Apple LaserWriter prints at 300 dots per inch. This means there are 300 rows of dots in one inch. The ImageWriter II prints at 72 dots per inch. The higher the number of dots per inch, the smoother the image.

   You may hear the resolution of a monitor spoken of in terms of dots per inch. Yes, there are a certain number of dots *(pixels)* per inch, but it is not really the **number** of dots that determine the resolution of the image on the screen. How highly-resolved an image on the screen appears is determined by how much information each pixel contains. Basically, the more colors or shades of gray your monitor can display, the more highly resolved your images will appear.

**· dots per inch**

**Download** means to send information from one source, like your computer, to another source, like another computer through a *modem*. Also, certain fonts must be downloaded, or sent to, your printer before they can be printed.

**· download**

See *dots per inch*.

**· dpi**

The **drive** is the part of the computer that takes the disks and spins them to make them work. There are floppy disk drives, the ones with the little slots where you insert a floppy disk. There are hard disk drives that are sealed inside the computer or inside the box they come in. There

**· drive**

are removable cartridge hard disk drives that have a large slot in which to insert a cartridge hard disk.

**driver**

*The LaserWriter* 🖨 *printer driver.* LaserWriter

A **driver** is a piece of *software* that tells the Mac how to communicate with or operate another piece of hardware, most commonly a hard disk or a printer. Your System Folder has a printer driver in it (if not, you can't print).

**e-mail**

**E-mail** refers to the electronic mail that you can send or receive directly on your computer. Yes, it actually means people can write you letters and send them to your computer. You can turn on your Mac and go pick up your mail. Many a love affair has begun through e-mail. I know. It's really fun, too. And useful, of course. You do need to have a *modem* or be on a *network* to send or receive e-mail.

**EPS, EPSF**

**EPS** or **EPSF** stands for Encapsulated PostScript File. This is a graphic *file format*. Graphics that are saved as EPS are made of two parts. One part is a simple *bitmapped* image that the **computer** reads and displays on the screen. The other part is a complex *PostScript* code that the **printer** reads (if the printer reads *PostScript*). EPS files are called "device independent" or "resolution independent." This means they will print at whatever resolution the printer happens to be. The same graphic will print at 72 *dpi* on the ImageWriter, at 300 dpi on a LaserWriter, at 1270 or 2540 dpi on Linotronics.

**extension**

An **extension**, previously called an **INIT** (accent on the second syllable) is a little program that does things like make extra sounds, pictures, bizarre cursors, clocks, etc. Some applications have extensions as adjuncts to the main program. Extensions work only if they are stored inside your blessed System Folder or in the Extensions folder within the System Folder; if you put them in any other folder, they don't work.

These things were called INITs because they work upon *initialization* of your computer; that is, when you start it up (they're sometimes known as Startup Documents). When you turn your machine on, all these little extensions get loaded into RAM and start working even before your System gets up and running. Those little icons that appear in the lower left portion of your screen as you *boot up* represent your extensions (some are also *cdevs,* which are like extensions except that you have some control over them through the Control Panel).

Most extensions from reputable sources will work invisibly and well. But many extensions, especially those written by individuals and sent out as *freeware* or *shareware* are a well-known source of trouble to the System. If things start acting weird after you install an extension, take the extension back out, restart (from the Special menu), and see if things are normal again. Never install more than one extension at a time; rather, put one in, work on your machine a few days, then put another one in. That way you will be able to pinpoint the one that causes trouble. (For instance, I've heard of an extension that inadvertently affects the column guides in Page-Maker. Weird.)

A **file format** simply refers to the particular structure that a document (graphics, text, spreadsheet, etc.) is saved in. For instance, in text there are file formats like *ASCII* (text-only) or RTF (rich text format), in addition to the standard file format for your particular word processor, such as MacWrite or WriteNow. In graphics there are file formats like *EPS, TIFF, PICT,* or MacPaint. Different programs can read different formats.

**file format**

A **file server** is used on a *network.* Often one Mac and its hard disk are dedicated to the job of being a file server. Everybody on the network (everybody who is connected with cables to this computer) can use the software and the hard disk belonging to that Mac, rather than everyone having their own. There is also file server *software* that controls who gets to read and use what and how many people get to do it at the same time.

**file server**

The **Finder** is the software program that runs the Desktop (see Chapter 3). Because the Desktop and the Finder are so inter-related, and when you are at the Desktop level you have access to the Finder capabilities, the two terms are often interchanged.

**Finder**

**Fkey**
**function key**
. The terms **Fkey** and **function key** are used interchange-
· ably, although there are two separate meanings.

**Fkey** is usually referring to a mini-program, or *utility,* that
can be added to your Mac (kind of like a desk accessory).
The little Fkey program makes things happen when you
press a certain key combination, like Command Shift 7.

**Function key** usually refers to the 10 to 15 extra keys
along the top of an extended keyboard, numbered F1
through F10 or F15, that you can program to perform
certain tasks, usually with a *macro* utility.

**freeware**
. **Freeware** refers to the *software* that nice people create
. and then put out into the world at no cost to the user for
· the benefit of humanity and no benefit to themselves.
· Freeware is often available on *bulletin board services,*
through *user groups,* or from friends. See also *shareware.*
People who create freeware are diametrically opposite
. to the evil people who create *viruses.*

**function keys**
. See *Fkey.*

**gigabyte**
**G**
. A **gigabyte** (G) is a unit of measure, measuring file size
. or hard disk space, etc. It's very large. Technically, one
· gigabyte is 1024 *megabytes,* which is the same as one
· billion *bytes,* which is really 1,073,741,824 bytes. Impress
your friends with this useful knowledge.

**grayscale**
· Some Macintosh screens are **grayscale**, rather than plain
ol' black-and-white, and any color monitor can be
changed to show grayscale. On a black-and-white screen
. or on printed material, gray tones are simulated by black
. and white dots that give the illusion of gray when seen
· from a slight distance. A grayscale image (a photograph,
for instance, that has been *scanned* into the computer) on
a black-and-white monitor (screen) is broken into dots to
represent the gray values. On a grayscale monitor, though,
. the same image will display in actual gray values. It's very
· beautiful to see.

**hard copy**
. **Hard copy** refers to the printed version of what you have
· in the computer. For instance, this book is a PageMaker
file stored on a disk. I printed up hard copy for editing
and for producing the pages of the book in your hands.

**Hardware** refers to the parts of the computer or of any *peripherals* you can bump into. The monitor, the external hard disk, the mouse, the keyboard, the modem, the scanner—all those things you can touch are hardware. As opposed to *software*.

The Macintosh System originally kept track of items on a disk with the Macintosh File System (MFS). Then the **HFS**, or **Hierarchical File System** was developed, which is much more efficient at keeping track of what is inside folders, and folders inside of folders

An **INIT** (accent on the second syllable) is now called an *extension*. Please see "extension" for details.

When you buy a new floppy disk or a hard disk, it is unformatted; that is, it is completely blank and doesn't have any of the tracks necessary in which to lay down the data you are going to give it. So you have to **initialize** it. Blank hard disks come with special software to use for initializing them.

When you insert a blank floppy disk, the Mac asks if you want to initialize it (see page 13). You have to, if you want to use it. If you re-initialize any disk, the process permanently erases anything that currently exists on that disk.

**Kerning** is the process of adjusting the fit between letters. You can only do it in certain programs, like the more expensive page layout or illustration applications.

To **launch** simply means to start or open an application.

**Leading** ("ledding") is the amount of space between lines of text. It is typically measured in *points*. In page layout programs and in some word processing programs you can adjust the amount of space between the lines.

A **ligature** is a typographic nicety; it is one character that is actually two single characters combined together. For instance, when you type the letter f next to the letter i, the hook of the f bumps into the dot of the i. The ligature for f and i is one character, like so: fi. Most Mac fonts includes the common ligatures for fi and fl (see the chart of the last page of this book for the keystrokes). Expert collection fonts contain many more ligatures.

**lines per inch** . **Lines per inch** is very different than *dots per inch*. Dots
per inch refers to the *resolution* of the printer, which can
get up into the 2000 dots per inch range. The lines and
curves of text appear to be perfectly smooth because the
dots are so small our eyes can't separate them.

But when a graphic that is in gray tones or in color, such
as photographs or gray bars, goes to the printing press
or a copy machine, the tones must be broken into dots
big enough to print ink or toner. The principle is the
same as in dots per inch: 85 lines per inch means that in
an inch there are 85 lines of dots. The more lines that fit
into an inch, the smaller the dots. The smaller the dots, the
higher quality the printing press must be in order to **hold**
(print clearly) the dots. Copy machines and newspapers
need graphics at 65 to 85 lines per inch. Low-cost presses
(quick printers) need 85 to 100 lines per inch. A good
press can usually print 133 lines per inch. Only very high-
quality art-type books are printed higher than 133 line.

An Apple LaserWriter has a default for grayscale
graphics of 53 lines per inch, which means that any gray
image that comes out of the LaserWriter will have the
gray values broken up into dots in lines of 53 per inch.

**log on, log off** These terms refer to the process of checking in, or
**logging on**, to a *bulletin board service* or a *network,* or to
the process of checking out, **logging off**. Typically when
you log on somewhere you have to have a password.

**macro** . The term **macro** sounds very arcane and intimidating,
but once you use them you get hooked, they are so cool.
A macro is simply a series of steps (menu commands,
mouse clicks, keystrokes, etc.) that are programmed into
one key or one key combination. Once it is programmed
and you press that key combination, the entire series of
steps is executed at high speed.

For instance, if you're creating a database of names and
addresses, you can create a macro that will type "P.O.
Box " for you so you just press one key combination and
that phrase will appear. Or if you regularly have to type
the phrase "Robin's and Janet's Private Club for the
Dissemination and Elucidation of Macintosh Magical
Mysteries," make a macro for it. If at the end of each
week you always gather up all the accounts entered,

copy them, open another spreadsheet, drop them in, then print up a report with sums and totals and balances, create a macro for it. Anything you do repeatedly, you can lighten your life by making a macro for it.

Do-it-yourself macros are very easy to create; basically, you just choose the menu command that says Do This, show the macro what you want done by doing it, Stop when the action is finished, and the macro Does It. Some applications have macro features built right in.

**Memory** is generally referring to RAM, which is Random Access Memory. Memory is temporary, volatile storage space, as opposed to the permanent storage space you have on a disk. You should read Chapter 30 to get a good grasp on this important subject.

**memory**

A **modem** is usually a little box that sits next to your computer, although you may have a modem installed directly inside your Mac, such as inside some of the PowerBooks. The external modem has a cable that plugs into your Mac, and another cord that plugs into your phone jack. With a modem hooked up, then, your computer can call any other computer that is also hooked up to a modem. You can sit at your computer and "talk" to other people who are sitting at their computers. You type a couple lines of conversation, hit the Return key, and your conversation shows up on both of your computer screens. It's really addictive. People have been known to meet and eventually marry through meeting *online* (on the screen). And many a one-night-online-stand has happened. It's a fascinating phenomenon.

**modem**

But, practically speaking, an incredible amount of business goes on through the modem. You can send any file through the phone lines. If you live out in the boonies, you can send your publication out for high-level output to a service bureau hundreds of miles away; they'll just express the finished product back to you through the mail. If your magazine column is due by 12 noon on Friday, you can finish it at 11:45 and still have it in their hands across the country by noon. You can conduct research, make plane reservations, join clubs, play long-distance chess, send faxes—oh, the possibilities are endless.

Just so you know, the word modem is derived from the terms **mod**ulator and **dem**odulator.

**modifier key** . **Modifier keys** are the ones that have no character
attached to them, but that alter the behavior of another
key. These are Macintosh modifier keys: Shift, Option,
Command, Caps Lock, and Control (if your keyboard
has it). Always when using modifier keys you press those
keys down and *hold* them, and then just *tap* the character
key that it modifies. For instance, the keyboard shortcut
for Paste is Command V. So hold down the Command
key and tap the letter V. If you *hold* the letter V down,
you'll end up pasting in more than one of the item.

**moiré** The term **moiré** refers to the bizarre patterns that result
in photographs (or other graphic images with color or gray
values), when lines of dots at one angle overlap lines of
dots at another angle (see *lines per inch*). It's not easy to
avoid them if you're trying to print directly from the
computer output, rather than high-quality separations.
How to avoid them "is beyond the scope of this book."
   (I see stuff all the time telling people to pronounce this
word "mwahr" or "mwah ´ray" but nobody says it like that. Maybe
if you're French you do, but American mouths don't work that way.
This term's been around a lot longer in printing and graphics than
computer nerds realize. [Me, I'm not a nerd; I'm a nerdette.] Just
pronounce it "**mor ay**," with the accent on the second syllable, and
you will be perfectly acceptable.)

**Moof!™** **Moof!** is what the *Dogcow* says.

**motherboard** Isn't this a nice name? It's also called a "logic board," but
**motherboard** sounds so much more earthy and close to
the heart. The motherboard contains the heart of the
Mac. It's the board, or piece of fiberglass, that contains
the most important *chips* that run the computer, including
the *RAM* and the *CPU* (Central Processing Unit).

**multimedia** **Multimedia** refers to presentations, books, proposals,
etc., that are created using a variety of media, such as
sound, video, graphics, and text. If the user can click
buttons and do things with the presentation, it is called
"interactive multimedia."

**nested** . When folders are stored inside of folders, they are said to
be **nested**. If you hold the Command key down and press
on the name of the window belonging to a folder, you will
see all the folders that this one is nested into.

When you connect computers together, either directly through cables or else through *modems* and phone lines, they are all on the same **network**. People on a network can share files, applications, e-mail, etc. Also see *file sharing*.

**network**

Some programs, like MacPaint, create everything *bitmapped,* where dots on the screen are either on or off and you can edit images dot by dot. Other programs, like MacDraw, are **object-oriented** and create images as entire objects. You can't edit the objects dot by dot; you can only change the entire object as a whole. Each object is on a separate, transparent layer, and is defined by a mathematical formula rather than bitmapped dots. Since they are not bitmapped, object-oriented graphics print much smoother, taking advantage of the resolution of the printer.

**object-oriented**

**OCR** stands for Optical Character Recognition. You can use a *scanner* and OCR *software* to take text on a printed page, *scan* it into the computer, and have the computer turn the text into the *characters,* not into a graphic image. That means you can take all the typed letters your lovers have sent you over the past ten years and input them into your computer *without retyping them*. This opens up incredible possibilities.

**OCR**

When you are talking through your computer to another computer or to an information service (see *BBS* or *modem*), you are **online**.

**online**

**Online help** is the file an application provides within itself where you can find information about the program or how to work it, without ever leaving the application or your computer. It's a manual on screen. Often they're pretty wimpy, although they can be of use. System 7 has an online Help feature (see page 191). It's pretty wimpy.

**online help**

Any *hardware* that is attached to the computer is considered a **peripheral**. Modems, scanners, CD-ROM players, printers, external hard disk drives, etc., are all peripherals.

**peripherals**

A **pica** is the unit of measure that typesetters have used for many years to measure type and line lengths. There are six picas in one inch (one pica = .167 inch), and there are 12 *points* in each pica.

**pica**

**PICT** . A **PICT** is Apple's graphic *file format*. PICTs don't take up
· much disk space, and most programs can read them.
· They're rather undependable, though, when printing to
· *PostScript printers*. If you must print a PICT to a PostScript
Pict · printer, try to avoid include any *bitmapped* graphics
. within it, and don't use any *downloadable* fonts. Even
. then, they often decide to change their appearance
· without warning you.

PICTs are more dependable if you never try to print
them. For instance, they are fine in presentations that
are meant to be presented straight from the computer.
Or you can scan a photograph as a PICT (which is much
smaller than a TIFF) with the intention of manipulating it
and then outputting it straight to slides or to Kodak film.

**pirate** · In computer jargon, **pirate** is a verb that describes
making a copy of commercial software without permission and without paying for it. It is essentially stealing.

**pixel** · A **pixel** (**pic**ture **el**ement) is the smallest dot that the
Macintosh can display on the screen. On a standard Mac
screen, each pixel (each dot) is $\frac{1}{72}^{nd}$ of an inch (remember, the *dots per inch* is 72).

**point** . A **point** is the unit of measure that typesetters have used
for many years to measure the size of type and the space
· between the lines. It is the unit of measure on the Mac
to measure type and the space between the lines. There
are 72 points in one inch. There are 72 *dots per inch* on
the standard Macintosh screen. That was not an accident.

(For type aficionados: you will be interested to know that
· 72 points on the Mac equals exactly one inch.)

**port** . **Port** is just another name for a plug (a socket, actually)
· on the back of the Mac where you plug the cords and
· cables in. You can't go wrong with plugging things in—
there is either a picture above the port giving you a clue
as to what should go in the socket, or the port is shaped
. in such a way that only one kind of plug will fit.

Port also refers to rewriting software so it works on
· another kind of computer.

**PostScript** is a page description language, developed by Adobe Systems, that has become an industry standard. It's a language that *PostScript printers* interpret (as opposed to a language that your *computer* reads) and use to create the printed pages. It is PostScript that enables complex graphics to be printed at any resolution (whatever the resolution of the printer). Also see *PostScript printer*.

**. PostScript**

A **PostScript printer** (or PostScript-compatible printer) is a printer that can interpret the graphics and fonts that are written in the PostScript page description language. Not all laser printers can read PostScript. Just because a printer has a high *resolution* does not mean it is Post-Script. For instance, the Apple StyleWriter prints at 400 *dots per inch,* but it is not PostScript. Usually if a printer is not PostScript, it is a *QuickDraw printer.*

**. PostScript**
**· printer**

Once you start using keyboard commands, install a few *extensions* and *CDEVs,* create a *macro* or two, and start throwing around words like *RAM* and *PostScript,* you can consider yourself a **power user**. Say the word *SIMM, motherboard,* or *CPU* in mixed company and you will really get respect.

**· power user**

**Public domain** is an adjective describing any kind of work, not just computer *software,* for which the public has every right to copy and use in any way they see fit. The author has retained no rights nor liabilities. Usually cuz they're dead. Public domain software is different than software that is copyrighted to the author yet distributed publicly. See *freeware* and *shareware.*

**. public domain**

**QuickDraw** is part of the Macintosh operating system that is used for creating the screen display, supporting the windows, drawing lines, handling the color, and basically taking care of all the graphics and drawing functions.

**. QuickDraw**

A **QuickDraw printer** is generally any printer that can't read *PostScript*. If a printer cannot read PostScript, then it has to just recreate what it sees on the screen. That's the big deal about ATM (Adobe Type Manager) and TrueType (see Chapter 21 on Fonts). These two things make type clean and smooth on the screen, and also make your QuickDraw printer print the text clean and smooth.

**· QuickDraw printer**

**QuickTime** . **QuickTime** is the equivalent (and beyond) of *QuickDraw* (previous page) for video, images, and animation. You don't create anything with the QuickTime *extension* itself, just like you don't create anything with QuickDraw itself. QuickTime is the "architecture," the software, that allows the Mac to display, compress, edit, create, and store video. You don't need any special hardware to run QuickTime movies on your Mac.

QuickTime is going to change how we use computers. It won't be long before any application, including your word processor and your *e-mail,* will be able to hold a picture that, when you double-click on it, will play a movie. You can cut, copy, and paste these movie clips, or even parts of these movie clips. And these movies are not just video—you can animate a slide presentation, spread-sheet charts, architectural plans. QuickTime brings us closer to the paperless office stage in history.

**read-only** When a file or a disk is **read-only**, that means you can look at and print the file or disk, but you cannot save changes onto it. Often you think you can, because the file lets you select and edit text, but when you go to Save it, you won't be allowed. Locking a disk (page 14) or a file (page 67) will make it read-only. *CD-ROMs* are read-only. A certain part of the Mac's inner workings are read-only.

**ReadMe** . You will usually see a **ReadMe** file on a disk when you get a new software package. It's a good idea to read them (how can you resist?) because they describe the product and often give you the details on any last-minute changes, additions, or *bugs.*

**redraw** When you move an object across the screen, scroll, change windows, etc., all or part of the screen has to be **redrawn**. The Mac has to figure out where everything has moved to and redraw them in their new places.

**refresh rate** . The computer screen is constantly renewing the screen, something like 65 to 75 times a second. How fast it does this is called the **refresh rate.** Faster is better, of course. It's called "refresh" because the electron beam inside the computer is re-energizing (refreshing) the phosphors on the screen.

The **resolution of a printer** is measured in *dots per inch*. The greater the number of dots per inch, the higher the resolution. The higher the resolution, the smoother the graphics and text can print. The Apple LaserWriter has a resolution of 300 dots per inch. The Apple StyleWriter has a resolution of 360 dots per inch.

The **resolution of a monitor** is not actually perceived through the number of pixels per inch. How clearly an image is "resolved" on the screen is determined by how easily the computer can fool our eyes. Our eyes get fooled when there are so many colors or shades of gray that we can't easily differentiate where one color blends into another. When there are only two colors on the screen, black and white, an image is not resolved very well because our eye can clearly see the two separate parts. When there are shades of gray, an image appears to be more resolved because our eyes can't tell as easily where one gray shade blends into the next. When there are 16 million colors, our eyes perceive that the image is in high resolution. So the same monitor with the same number of pixels per inch can actually show varying "resolutions," depending on how many shades of gray or color are displayed. The number of colors or grays available to you depends on how much memory you have, what kind of video *card* you use, and whether or not your computer uses *32-bit Color QuickDraw*.

The initials **ROM** stand for Read-Only Memory, which usually refers to the System information that is built into the *chips* inside the computer, the information that gets the System up and running. Also see *read-only*.

**RTF** is Rich Text Format, another *file format* in which you can save text. It holds onto a little more formatting, such as bold and italic, than does an *ASCII* file, and is usually capable of storing graphics. Most programs can open a file saved as RTF.

A **scanner** is a piece of *hardware*. What it does is **scan** an image: You put a photograph or a piece of drawn art or sometimes a three-dimensional object on the scanner. You close the lid and push a button, the machine views (scans) the image, and sends a copy of it to the computer. It's sort of like making a xerox copy, but instead of

## resolution

*These two screen shots are exactly the same image on the same monitor. The one on the right appears to be in higher resolution because there are more shades of gray (16). The image on the left has only 4 shades of gray to trick my eyes into thinking this object has some sort of dimension. You can imagine if the monitor had 16 million colors to fool me with.*

## ROM

## RTF

## scan, scanner

*This was a photograph.*
*I scanned it as a grayscale*
*TIFF at 210 dpi.*

coming out the other end, the copy comes out in the computer. (Not all scanners work like I described here; some are hand-held and you roll the little machine over the top of the image. There are also video scanners that can input live stuff, and slide scanners that input directly from color slides.) The image to the left was scanned in.

When you scan images, the scanning software usually offers you several *file format* options. Unless you have a clear idea and a good reason as to why you would save it in any other format, always save scanned images as TIFFs.★ TIFFs were invented for scans.

▾If the image is straight black-and-white with no gray areas, save it as a line art TIFF.

▾If the image has gray tones, such as a photograph or pencil or charcoal drawing, save it as a gray-scale or con-tone TIFF.

**Halftones:** Halftones only apply to gray or color areas. A halftone breaks the gray area into dots that a printer can print (see *lines per inch*). If the image is solid black-and-white, you don't need any sort of halftone.

▾If your scanning software can create special effect halftones that you want to use (or if your printer is not *PostScript*), save it as a halftone TIFF.

▾If there is no special effect halftone you need, then don't bother saving it as a halftone—let the Post-Script printer halftone it on the way out. (Yes, all PostScript printers will do that; they take any gray or color image and break it into *lines per inch*. The number of lines per inch varies depending on the printer. An Apple LaserWriter halftones at 53 lines per inch; a Linotronic 300 halftones at 105 to 150 lines per inch.)

★If the image you scan in will never see a printed page, then sometimes it is best to scan it as a PICT. For instance, if you are scanning a slide into the computer where you will manipulate it and then output it back to a slide, you will find a PICT image is much smaller in disk size.

If you leave an image on the screen for an extended period of time, it will eventually burn in and leave a permanent shadow. A **screen saver** is a little program (a *utility*) that prevents burn-in by creating interesting animated effects when you are not working. Effects range from simple fireworks to moving patterns to flying toasters with wings that you can hear beating if you listen closely. Some screen savers activate automatically if the keyboard or mouse haven't been touched in a certain number of minutes (those bug me; I hate to be interrupted while I'm thinking). Others you must turn on yourself. A good one lets you choose either.

**SCSI** (pronounced "scuzzy"), stands for Small Computer Systems Interface. SCSI is a connecting system, an interface, that allows computers and their *peripheral* devices (scanners, printers, etc.) to exchange information. Those big cables with the little pins in them (usually 50 pins or 25 pins) are SCSI connectors and they plug into SCSI *ports* on the back of the Mac.

See *SCSI*.

**Shareware** is copyrighted software that somebody went to the trouble to create and then distributed through *user groups, bulletin board services,* and friends. You can try the software for free, but if you like it you should pay for it. Shareware is generally pretty cheap ($5 to $20) and you really should pay it to encourage other people to create nice things for us.

Ha. Now I know what a **SIMM** is. It's a Single Inline Memory Module. Well, that's what dictionaries say it is. I say it is a little piece of plastic, usually about as long as your finger, with *chips* on it. These particular chips are *memory* chips. When you want to add more memory, more *RAM*, to your computer you buy SIMMs. Then somebody installs the SIMMs into your computer. They just pop into the little holders that are made for them.

*Hardware* is the stuff you can knock on. **Software** is the invisible stuff, the programming, the information coursing through the *chips* that makes the computer work. Software is in the form of *applications,* or *programs,* in the

**screen saver**

**SCSI**

**scuzzy**

**shareware**

**SIMM**

**software**

*memory* stored inside the Mac, it's on the disks, it's in the *System* that runs the machine. It's the big magic.

**spooler**    A **spooler** is *software* (or sometimes a combination of software and *hardware*) that allows you to work on your screen while your printer is printing. Typically what happens when you print **without** a spooler is that the computer sends the pages to the printer. The computer can send the information much faster than the printer can deal with it. So the computer has to hang around and wait while the printer processes all the information. Then it sends a little more info and waits. Sends a little more and waits. Meanwhile, you are also waiting because the computer is busy and won't let you have your screen back.

But when you use a spooler, the computer sends the information to the spooler instead of to the printer. The spooler takes it all, says thank you very much, and then funnels the information to the printer. Since the computer did its job of sending off the info, you get your screen back and you can work merrily along while the spooler finishes telling the printer what to do.

Sometimes while using a spooler your screen may get interrupted for a minute here and there while the computer takes care of details. But in general, it's painless.

**spreadsheet**    **Spreadsheet** is another one of those terms that intimidates us at first. A *database* is for making a list of items that you can then manipulate; a *spreadsheet* is generally used for number-crunching. You can do your home budget on a simple spreadsheet (I hire my teenager to do it), create invoices for your small business, project your mortgage payments, etc. etc. etc. They are so cool. It's quite a feeling of power to set one up, plug in some numbers, and watch it work.

Most spreadsheets also have a method for applying borders (lines) on the page, which means it is so incredibly easy to make great, instant forms: As you widen the page, the lines get longer; if you delete a row or a column, the lines will also be deleted; as you make the point size bigger, the space between the lines gets bigger. It's terrific, even if you don't use a single number on the page. There are always reasons to make forms.

A **stack** is a document that has been created in the application **HyperCard**. HyperCard is a very interesting and provocative program that is difficult to explain in a few sentences so I'm not going to try. The biggest single difference between something created in HyperCard and something created in almost any other program is that the document, or stack, that you create in HyperCard never leaves the computer. In almost every other program you create something on the computer and then print it up and you hand out the printed piece. In Hyper-Card, what you create is meant to be used or viewed by other people directly on the computer. It works in a series of cards (hence the term *stack,* as in stack of cards). As you flip through the cards of information, you may find sounds and animation and music and interactions. It's really an exciting and addictive program to work in, but you must keep in mind that for anyone to use your final project, they have to have a Macintosh.

Some people have more than one hard disk attached to their computer. Sometimes more than one of those hard disks has a System Folder (be careful! don't do that unless you know why and how to deal with two System Folders). The hard disk that is running the machine at the moment is the **startup volume**. Or you could call it the **startup disk** or sometimes the **boot disk**. The startup volume *boots* the computer. The startup volume will always put its icon in the top right corner.

The term **suitcase** gets confusing because two very important, closely related, but not connected items both refer to it: *suitcase icons* and the font management program called *Suitcase*™.

    **Suitcase icons** represent *screen fonts* or *desk accessories.* If you double-click on a suitcase it opens up to a window with an icon for each font size and you can double-click each one to take a look at it; see page 145.

    There is also a wonderful program called **Suitcase**™ which helps you manage a large number of fonts. It also resolves font conflicts, or identity crises, which happens regularly when a lot of fonts get together. If you're a font freak (meaning you like and collect them), it is absolutely indispensable to use a program like Suitcase or Master

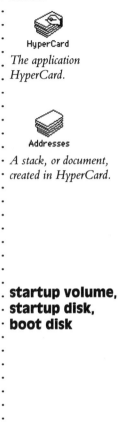

## stack

HyperCard

*The application HyperCard.*

Addresses

*A stack, or document, created in HyperCard.*

## startup volume, startup disk, boot disk

## suitcase

FuturaFamily

Desk Accessories

*Suitcase icons that hold fonts, desk accessories, Fkeys, and sounds.*

**Suitcase™**

*This is the icon for Suitcase, the font management utility.*

Juggler to manage your fonts (even with System 7, no matter what they tell ya). A font management utility allows you to store and access your fonts without having all of them in the System all the time, which can take up a lot of your memory.

But the confusion between the two items occurs because people banter around the word *suitcase* referring to either the screen font icon *or* to the font management program, and a beginner doesn't see the difference yet.

**system crash**

You'll know a **system crash**, or bomb, when you see one. Either you get a very polite yet disturbing notice on your screen with a picture of a bomb about to explode (cute, very cute), or things will just stop working. Your keys won't work, the mouse won't work. There are a couple of things you can try before turning the computer off, but no matter what you do you will have lost whatever you did not save to disk. See pages 235–236 for a couple of reasons why you might crash, how to avoid crashing, and what to do about it when it does happen (which it will).

**TeachText**

**TeachText**

*I bet you have about a dozen copies of TeachText in your Mac!*

**TeachText** is a tiny little word processing program (it only takes up 36K of disk space). Often when you get new software you will see an icon called *ReadMe*. This file has the latest info on the software, or maybe some tricks you should know about. To make sure you can read the file, since the software company has no idea what word processing program you use or even if you have one, they write the ReadMe file in TeachText, and then also send along the TeachText application on the disk so you can open ReadMe.

**telecommunications**

The term **telecommunications** refers to communicating over the phone lines through a *modem* as opposed to using your voice. It's even faster than overnight mail.

**text-only**

A document that is formatted (saved) as **text-only** is able to be read by almost any word processing or page layout program. It has no formatting, like font size or style or columns, etc. Text-only is synonomous with *ASCII*, so you should take a quick moment to look up that term.

**TIFF** stands for Tagged Image File Format. It is a format used for saving or creating certain kinds of graphics. Graphics in TIFF are always *bitmapped,* but the bitmap *resolution* can be very high, depending on the program you are working in. TIFFs can be black-and-white line art, or they can be *grayscale* images. They were invented for *scanning,* so you might want to also read the scanning information (page 269–270).

Some menu commands and keyboard shortcuts are **toggle** switches. This means if you choose it once, the command is turned on; if you choose the same command again, it is turned off. Sometimes a command that can be toggled shows up with a checkmark next to it (although a checkmark does not mean it is necessarily a toggle switch!). Sometimes a command that can be toggled changes the name of the command when you choose it (e.g., "Show Clipboard" becomes "Hide Clipboard"). See "Changing Styles Mid-Sentence" on page 94.

There are two distinct formats for *PostScript* type, **Type 1** and *Type 3* (there is no *Type 2* format). The corporation Adobe Systems, Inc., had a monopoly on Type 1 fonts; they used a secret formula to produce them and wouldn't let anybody else have the formula. So everybody else had to make Type 3 fonts.

Type 1 fonts are *PostScript,* and they are especially designed to print well at "low" resolutions (like 300 *dpi*). They print fast and clean on PostScript printers, and they can be scaled with *Adobe Type Manager (ATM)* to appear very smooth on your screen and even when output to non-PostScript printers. In 1990 Adobe decided to publicize the secret formula so everyone could create Type 1 fonts.

**Type 2** was a proposed font technology that never made it, so there are no Type 2 fonts.

**Type 3 fonts** are the typefaces that are made without Adobe System's proprietary font technology. They tend to be less expensive, and they often don't print as clean and smooth, nor as fast, as *Type 1* fonts. They also tend to be more graphic in nature; that is, many Type 3 fonts are very decorative, with gray shades and elaborate fills and fancy shadows.

**TIFF**

**toggle**

**Type 1 font**

**Type 2 font**

**Type 3 font**

**upgrade** . When a company improves their software or hardware, that improvement is called an **upgrade**. The upgrades are indicated by the *version number;* e.g., PageMaker 5.0 (pronounced "five point oh" or sometimes "five oh") is in its fifth major upgrade since it was invented. Minor little fix-its are noted by points. For instance, usually within a couple of months of releasing a new upgrade, say 4.0, a software company will release the fix-it, called 4.01 ("four point oh one") which fixes the bugs they couldn't get to in time for shipping. If you are a registered owner of the software, you can usually purchase an upgrade at a significantly reduced cost, and sometimes you even get the upgrade free.

If your *hardware* goes through an upgrade, you just have to buy the new piece. You can buy new parts for your existing computer which would upgrade your "system," your collection of hardware that you work on.

**upload** When you use your *modem* to copy information off of another computer and put it on yours, you are *downloading* (taking it down from the other computer). When you use your modem to put information onto another computer, you are **uploading** (loading it up onto the other computer).

**utility** A **utility** is an application, generally a very small application, that has a very limited function. Utilities don't create documents; they just make things work better or add a bit of sparkle or convenience to your computer. Adobe Type Manager and Disk First Aid are utilities.

**vaporware** When a company announces that their software is about to appear on the market and then it doesn't appear when it is supposed to, that software is considered **vaporware**. The term even gets loosely applied to books that don't appear on time, or blind dates.

**video card** A **video card** is the *card* (the piece of plastic with *chips* attached to it) that controls the display on your screen. You can get different kinds of video cards for different kinds of monitors that allow the monitor to display different levels of *grayscale* or colors.

Viruses are very interesting things. A **virus** is a program
that a very intelligent, very skilled, and very evil, sick
person writes. It is written to do such things as destroy
the data on your computer, corrupt your System, lock
you out of your own machine, eat your programs. They
can wipe out an entire hard disk. Viruses travel from
computer to computer through floppy disks, networks,
and even modems. You don't always know you have a
virus; they often have a delayed reaction time, so you use
the sick program for a while until one day it eats you. It
seems that a person who can write a program to do so
much evil is certainly bright enough to get a real job and
direct that energy into making people happy instead.

This is a virus scenario: You have a disk that is infected.
You put it into your Mac. As you use an application on
that disk, the virus gets into your System. You take that
disk out and insert another one. The virus jumps from
your System onto an application on the floppy disk. You
take that disk out, go to another computer in the office
and insert it. The virus jumps from that disk onto the
other person's System. Ad infinitum. The WDEF virus is
so contagious that simply inserting an infected disk into
a computer infects the computer. It's sort of comparable
to somebody with a social disease getting on a bus and
everybody on the bus automatically getting the disease.
Then everybody on the bus gets off the bus and goes into
the stores and everybody in the stores gets the disease.
Fortunately WDEF is not a terribly devastating virus, just
very irritating. See page 228 for an easy way to get rid of
this pest (System 7 is immune to WDEF and to CDEF).

How do you know when you have a virus? Things
start acting funny on your computer. Windows may not
function properly, printing might not work right, files
may be changed, programs may be "damaged." If anything starts acting weird, you can suspect a virus. (Actually,
first you should suspect any *extensions (INITs)* or *cdevs* you
may have in your System Folder, since they are a much
more likely cause of little troubles. Take out any that you
may have installed right before your problems, and put
them back in again, one at a time, over a period of a
couple of days. That way you can pinpoint the offensive
creature and remove it.) If you think the problem really

**virus**

is a virus, then get virus-protection software and disinfect your hard disk *and every single disk in your entire house and office*. And never again let anyone put a disk in your computer without checking it first.

Everyone should own virus-protection software as a normal part of computer life. The best package is one called **Disinfectant.** It has an application that will locate and kill any virus, and it comes with an *INIT* that will quietly check any disk you put in your machine. If an infected disk is inserted, Disinfectant sets off bells and whistles (literally). It is *freeware,* written by a wonderful man named John Norstad at Northwestern University. He takes the time to write this program and is constantly updating it to catch new viruses. Can you believe that? He does this out of the kindness of his heart, an intrepid soul battling the forces of evil. Write him a nice thank-you letter and tell him how wonderful he is.

Disinfectant is available on several of the *bulletin board services,* from *user groups,* or from friends. You do need to be on the lookout at all times for the latest version of it, since those evil minds are constantly striving to outsmart the current virus-protection software.

Viruses have the potential to cause catastrophic damage; however, most Macintosh viruses have been held in check by virus-protection software, and with a little knowledge you can easily protect yourself and your loved ones.

**wizziwig**    See *WYSIWYG,* just below.

**WYSIWYG**    **Wysiwyg** stands for What You See Is What You Get, which means that what you see on the screen is what will print out on paper. If you are just beginning to use a Mac and you have never used any other computer, you may wonder what the big deal is about WYSIWYG because of course that's the way it is and that's the way it should be. But it is actually a relatively new concept, and one where the Mac excels over those other machines.

**32-bit addressing**    This term, **32-bit addressing**, would take several pages to satisfactorily explain. I am going to give you just a very brief, simplified explanation here. See, your computer has a hard disk, right? It stores all the information on the hard disk. But when it wants to actually work, it has to take the information out of the hard disk and put it into memory (read Chapter 30 on Very Important Information). Memory is like all these little cubby holes, or mailboxes. Each megabyte has millions of mailboxes, but each mailbox can only hold a certain amount of information. When the computer puts stuff in a box, it remembers that particular address of that particular mailbox.

Now let's say you have a Mac with 8 megabytes of memory. Have you ever had the computer complain that you were out of memory, or maybe an application "unexpectedly quit"? That's cuz all the mailboxes were full. So you decide you need to buy more memory, and you install 8 more megabytes, for a total of 16 megs of RAM (random access memory). This is fine, but you know what? There is a bus inside the computer that drives the mail carriers around to the mailboxes. But this bus only has seats for 24 mail carriers. With only 24 mail carriers, they can only get to the mailboxes for those first 8 megs of memory. With 32-bit addressing, though, it's like using a bigger bus and putting 32 super-mail-carriers on it. The 32-bit addressing, then, lets the Mac "address" (or "get to") the information in more memory than just 8 megabytes.

So, if you install more than 8 megs of memory, you must go to your Memory control panel and turn 32-bit addressing on if you want to *use* that extra memory.

You should read the above definition for *32-bit addressing* before you read this definition for **32-bit clean** (or **32-bit dirty**). Remember that bus with the 24 mail carriers on it? Well, the Mac always had those other 8 mail carriers hanging around the office, but before the Mac got the bigger bus, some people used those other 8 mail carriers (*bits,* actually) for other things. Programmers used them and applications gave them little jobs to do and the ROMs (the read-only memory where much of the system software is kept) sometimes put them in charge of things. So when the bigger bus asked them to hop on, sometimes they were busy.

This means that when 32-bit addressing is turned on, those applications that use the extra bits for other duties cause the computer to crash—the application is not 32-bit "clean." In other words, "clean" means that those extra 8 bits have not been used for anything they weren't

**32-bit clean
32-bit dirty**

supposed to be used for. If you have "dirty" ROMs in your computer (like in the Mac SE/30, II, IIx, and IIcx), it means those ROMs have already used those extra 8 bits and so they cannot use 32-bit addressing. In other words, "dirty" means the ROMs or the applications have used the extra 8 bits for something they weren't supposed to.

**32-bit Color QuickDraw**

**32-bit Color QuickDraw** is what gives those Macs that have it its incredible color capabilities (which in turn makes a monitor appear to have a higher *resolution*). The original QuickDraw only had the capability to work with eight colors (eight colors total, not 8-bit color). Color QuickDraw can work with 16.7 million colors. Color QuickDraw is built into the ROMs (the read-only memory) of newer Macs. It's also available as a system extension.

**68000**
**68020**
**68030**
**68040**
**etc.**

These numbers designate different *chips* (designed by Motorola). These particular chips run the computers, and the higher the number the faster and more powerful the machine. For instance, the **68000** chip is the one in the older Macs, like the 128, the 512, the Plus, and the SE. The Mac II has a **68020** and runs about five times faster than the 68000. The **68030** was a big deal and was installed in the SE/30, IIx, and IIcx. And the **68040** is of course even faster and does more tricks. (Although, the speed of the computer is dependent on more factors than simply the chip.)

**68551**
**68882**
**etc.**

Other important chips have these other numbers and do things like increase the floating point mathematics speed by about 100 times, which speeds up not only math functions but complex graphic rendering as well.

# PART THE SIXTH

I wanted to do this third edition in a more tutorial format, but I realized as I was trying to organize it that we don't learn in the same organizational patterns in which a linear format such as a book needs to be organized. So to accommodate people who want to use this book as a reference and need a linear organization, and to accommodate people who want to spend as little time as possible learning how to use their wonderful Mac, I have added this chapter to give you a jump start. It follows a logical pattern that I have found to be successful in my classes.

If you follow these steps, you'll be up and running and know more than most people in a short amount of time. These steps skip around the book. After you've finished the brief tutorial, spend a few weeks working on your Mac. Then come back to the book and read the rest of it. You'll not only find a great number of tips and tricks, but you'll find that you can actually absorb the rest of the information.

*Experience teaches you to recognize a mistake—*
*when you've made it again.*

# CHAPTER THIRTY-SEVEN

You might think, in your eagerness to get right into a program and start creating something, that you want to skip all these dumb little exercises at the Desktop, like making windows smaller and larger, copying blank folders onto disks. But trust me. It's too easy to turn on the computer, find the button for your program, and go right into it. But then you're limited. You won't have complete control over your computer. Some things will always confuse you. You'll never be a Power User (your goal in Life, right?).

**Don't be Limited**

For the Jack Rabbit who wants to instantly create, save, print, and quit, the steps are quite easy:

**Jack Rabbits**

- ▾ **Open** your word processing program (or other program of your choice): double-click on its icon.

- ▾ **Save** the new document: from the File menu, choose "Save As...." Name the file and click "Save."

- ▾ **Create** something: start typing.

- ▾ **Print** the document: go up to the File menu and choose "Print...." Click OK in all the boxes.

- ▾ **Quit:** go back to the File menu and choose "Quit."

This is the same basic process you will go through in any application—it's truly that easy. But to be powerful—ahhh, that takes a little more time.

**At Ease** · **If you are using At Ease**, this tutorial won't make any sense to you—the JackRabbit steps are about all you can do because At Ease puts a "shell" over the regular Macintosh interface. Eventually, if the computer belongs to you, you may want to remove At Ease (see page 267). Then you can work through this tutorial. Take a look at the At Ease chapter, page 253.

**Performa** · **If you are using a Macintosh Performa**, you can do just about everything in this tutorial if you close the Launcher window: click in its little close box in the upper left.

**Start Here** · So here are my recommendations on what you should spend time doing if your time is very limited. Actually, this is a good way to start even if you have lots of time; there is so much information to be absorbed that it works best to absorb a little now, then come back for more later. It also helps to run into a few problems, because then when you discover the solution, the solution makes much more sense.

I'll explain a task you need to know and tell you which pages have detailed information.

**Read** · ❖ Read the first chapter on Ks, megs, and disks.
**a few things first** · C'mon—it will only take a couple of minutes and it will make everything else much more clear. And people will be impressed when you start tossing around terms like "160 meg hard disk."

❖ You've probably already done this, but just in case you haven't, learn how to turn on your computer. Read the first several paragraphs of Chapter 2, page 17.

❖ What you see when you turn on the Mac is called the Desktop. It is also called the Finder because the software program built into the Mac that runs the

Desktop is the Finder. The Desktop is kind of like home base. It would be a good idea to read Chapter 3, but **skip** the section on "Hierarchy and the Desktop Level" for now, and come back later for the section "Clean Up the Desktop."

❖ If you have never used a mouse before, read Chapter 4. Particularly take note of the hot spot of the pointer, and don't forget the part about how my terminology for "press" and "press-and-drag" differs from what you will commonly read in other documentation. (My terms are correct, of course.) If you don't have a trackball, **skip** that section, and you can come back later to figure out how to clean the mouse.

Practice using your **mouse**.

- Click **once** on items (icons) you see on the screen, such as the trash can and the hard disk icon at the top right. Notice the icons change color when you click once on them. (If you are using a Performa, don't click once on anything in the "Launcher" window, which you should have closed.)

- **Double-click** on the hard disk icon or the trash can. Notice you must position the very tip of the pointer on the picture itself, not on the name. Notice also that it takes a very quick click-click or the computer thinks it is two single clicks. And you must hold the mouse very still between the clicks.

- Point to the menu bar across the top of the screen. **Press** (press and hold the button down) on any name in the menu to see the list of menu commands. There are eight items in the menu bar—check out all of them! (Yes, the apple has a menu, as well as the two tiny icons on the far right.) Don't choose any menu commands at this moment.

**Using the mouse**

Hard Disk

*Your hard disk icon may look a little different.*

**Menus and commands**

Read the first two-and-a-half pages in Chapter 5 about **menus** and **how to choose commands**. You can read the rest of the chapter next week. Practice using your mouse to check out the menus, but be careful at this point what you choose!

- Press on any menu and slide down the list—this is a **press-and-drag**. Notice that some menu commands are black and some are grey. As you slide across the black items, the entire line highlights.

  **When choosing one of these menu commands, don't click! Just let go!** Really. This is not just a suggestion, it is a rule that will prevent trouble later. Be conscious about it—make sure you are not *clicking* in any menu.

**Using the desk accessories**

Use the **desk accessories**. Read the pages mentioned and follow the directions. This will help you feel more comfortable with the mouse, with choosing menu items, and with customizing your computer. If you press on the *name* of the open desk accessory you can drag it around the screen. To put it away, click in the little box in the upper left of the accessory.

- **Alarm clock** (page 147). Change the time. Set the alarm for about ten minutes from now. After it goes off, turn off the alarm.

- **Calculator** (page 149). Click the mouse to do the numbers, and use the numeric keypad also.

- Take a look at **Chooser** (page 149). If your computer is brand new, you'll come back here before you print for the first time. If someone has already printed from this Mac, don't choose another printer (don't click on any icons)!

- Come back to the **Control Panels** another day.

- **Key Caps** (page 150). This is a very important feature to know and understand, but don't worry

about getting the whole concept now. You will use
it again later when you work in the word processor.

- **Note Pad** (page 151). Make some notes to yourself.

- **Puzzle** (page 153). This is really fun. Don't bother
  right now about customizing the puzzle.

- **Scrapbook** (page 152). For now, just read about it
  and take a look at it.

Check out the different ways to **view a window.** Read
page 41 about what *is* a window, and pages 45 to half of
48 about viewing windows. If you do not see a window
on your screen at the moment, double-click on the icon
(the picture) of your hard disk, the top picture on the
upper right of your screen. Check out each of the views
you have in your View menu.

*Viewing windows*

Return the window view to "By Icon" so you can
follow the next few steps. When you are done, you can
turn the view into whatever method you prefer to work
in. Everything you learned while the window was
showing icons will still apply when you view as a list.

Read about icons on pages 57–63. Even if you don't see
too many icons at the moment, keep the general concept
in mind of what they are telling you, of how rich they
are in visual clues. Don't double-click on anything
except folder icons at the moment. You can open the
System Folder on your hard disk and open other folders
in there. Keep these things in mind:

*Icons*

- Folders always open to show you their
  contents in a window.

- Documents always open the application they were
  created within and display the document.

- Applications always open to a clean, blank page,
  *or* to an *option* of opening a clean, blank page.

Jargon

*It's always safe to
double-click on folders.*

*If you accidentally double-
click on an application, go
up to the File menu and
choose "Quit."*

***Manipulating*** Learn all about the windows. *Every application you will*
***windows*** *ever use will have windows in it,* so it's good to get to know
them now. Read Chapter 7. Pick out all those parts to
a window. Go through the list and use each part:

- Resize the window.

- Move the window.

- Zoom the window large and small. Hold down
  the Option key (near the Spacebar) and click the
  zoom box. What's the difference?

- Open another folder; now you should see at least
  two windows. Which window is active (very
  important!). How do you make another window
  active? What's the point of active windows anyway? *Be sure you can answer these questions!*

- Try all three methods of using the scroll bars when
  the window is sized small (ha! what *are* the three
  methods?).

- Close the window using the close box.

- Open the folder again, using the menu command
  this time (*select* the folder first). Then close it using
  the menu. (Which menu is it in? You will always
  find the "Open" command in the same menu in
  every application).

***Keyboard*** Use the keyboard commands to do some of those tasks
***commands*** you just used the mouse for. Read the second half of
page 32, "Keyboard Command Shortcuts." Using the
keyboard shortcuts is a sign of growing up. The trick to
making a keyboard shortcut work is that you must **first**
select the item you want to affect. For instance, if you
want to open a folder, first click once on the folder to
select it, *then* press Command O.

Do each of these things using a keyboard shortcut:
Open a window. Close a window. Select every item in
a window. To deselect them, click in any white space.

This is a list of several basic Desktop tasks that you will need to do everyday.

· *Folders, backing up,*
· *and the trash*

- Read page 69 about folders. Make a new folder. (What is the keyboard shortcut?!) Name your new folder.

- Make a duplicate of this new folder: click once on the folder to select it, then find the command. Which menu is it in, and what is the keyboard shortcut? Change the name of this folder (page 70).

- Read page 71. Put the second folder into the first folder. Take the second folder *out* of the first folder. You will be doing a lot of putting things into and taking them out of folders. It's exactly the same as putting items into manila folders in your office.

- If you have a new floppy disk, insert it. (If you don't have a new one, insert any one). If the floppy is new, initialize it (page 13).

- Backup your work! You should do this to every document you want to keep. Read page 75. Copy the first folder you created onto the floppy disk. *Now this floppy is your backup of that important file!* In case the file on your hard disk gets lost or trashed or your hard disk dies, you have this extra copy.

- Use the trash can (read page 83). Throw away the first folder you made. Empty the trash (page 84).

- Put your second practice folder in the trash. Oh no! That was a mistake! Open the trash can and put the folder back (read the last paragraph on page 83). Be cool—use the "Put Away" keyboard shortcut.

- Change your window view to one of the lists, such as "By Name." Read pages 72–73 about the *outline mode*. Practice expanding and compressing folders. This is just another way to look at the contents of folders, instead of opening each one to a window.

- In icon view, move the icons around: just press on them and drag. Rearrange the icons in a window.

*Word processing* — Open a **word-processing** application (double-click on its icon). Everything you learn in a word processor will apply to every other program you ever use. Any word processor is a great place to practice the most basic and valuable skills; once you feel comfortable here, you can bumble your way through any other sort of program.

❖ Read pages 89–94 in the Typing chapter. Type several paragraphs and practice using the menus, moving the insertion point, fixing typos (read "Delete" on page 90), selecting text and changing its font and style and size. *Remember, all typing and backspacing starts wherever the insertion point is flashing, not where the I-beam or the pointer is pointing!*

❖ After you've finished several paragraphs and feel comfortable with the features you've been practicing, read pages 95–97 about the **Clipboard**. **Cut** some of your text. **Copy** some of your text. **Paste** the text somewhere else. Paste it in again. Make sure you can predict *what* will be pasted and *where* it will appear. Use the keyboard shortcuts for Cut, Copy, Paste, and Undo.

*Also try using the Scrapbook! Paste a graphic onto your letter.*

❖ If you are feeling very confident, try using some of the **special characters**, such a ¢ and • and ©. Read page 98 and also page 150 (both pages talk about Key Caps). If you're really feeling sassy, try typing "résumé" with the accent marks (see page 99).

❖ **Save** this witty and intelligent report. Read pages 101–102. Eventually you should return to pages 104 and 105 and study them, but right now just go ahead and save your document: From the File menu, choose "Save As…," type a title for your document, then click the Save button. (After you lose a few documents you will appreciate pages 104 and 105.)

*Also read Chapter 29 on Navigating.*

If you are working on a *Performa* with the Launcher running, your document will automatically be saved into the Documents folder; see page 246. If you are working on any Mac with *At Ease* running, you will probably be forced to save onto a floppy disk.

❖ Now you need to **print your document**.

▪ **If no one has ever printed from this computer before,** you need to read pages 108–110 and use the Chooser to tell your Mac which printer to use. Once the Mac has printed to a printer, you never need to go back to the Chooser again unless you need to switch printers.

▪ Read pages 111–113 and just follow the steps 1–4. Basically all you're doing is choosing "Print" from the File menu and clicking the OK buttons.

❖ You need to **quit the application** if you are done for the day. Save the document again just before you quit: just use the keyboard shortcut Command S. Then from the File menu, choose "Quit." The Quit command is always the very last item, and the keyboard shortcut is always Command Q. You really should read Chapter 17 on Closing and Quitting so you understand the difference.

After you quit an application, you will usually end up back at the Desktop. There are several **very important features** you can learn that will make you the life of any party. Here are suggestions for specific things you need to be in control of:

❖ Learn how to use **Find File**. Read pages 175–178 and experiment with it. Later, another day, read the rest of the chapter and learn how to do more complex searches (when you know what you're searching for).

*You should just be able to get the Chooser from the Apple menu, click on the picture of your printer on the left, click on either the name of your printer or the printer port icon on the right, then close the Chooser and print. If it doesn't go this smooth, you might want to have someone help you through this because it can be quite confusing.*

**Other very important features**

**Control panels** ❖ Learn how to use your **control panels**. Read Chapter 24. Check out each control panel. Most of the ones you have will be explained in Chapter 24.

**Aliases** ❖ Learn how to use **aliases**. Read pages 169–172. I guarantee you will find aliases to be one of the greatest features of organization and convenience on the Mac.

**Apple menu** ❖ Learn how to take advantage of your **Apple menu**. Read the entire Chapter 23, even if customizing the menu doesn't quite make sense yet.

**Visual clues** ❖ Read the the chapter on **visual clues**. Absorb that information and keep your eyes open for other visual clues. Teach them to others. Find at least five more visual clues yourself.

**Saving and navigating** ❖ So you don't have to use Find File twenty times a day, learn how to **save** a document directly **into the folder** of your choice. It is critical that you have power over where your documents go when you save them. After you start to feel pretty competent, study the dialog boxes an pages 104–105, and read Chapter 29 on **Navigating**, page 195. Learning to navigate (getting yourself where you want to go and finding files through the dialog boxes) is one of the most important things to know, and seems to be one of the most difficult concepts to grasp.

**Very important information** ❖ After you've gotten several "out of memory" messages or had applications "unexpectedly quit" or suddenly disappear, read Chapter 30, called Very Important Information. It discusses the difference between hard disk space and memory and virtual memory, how to avoid running out of memory, and where to find those lost applications.

**p.s.** ❖ Read *The Mac is not a typewriter*.

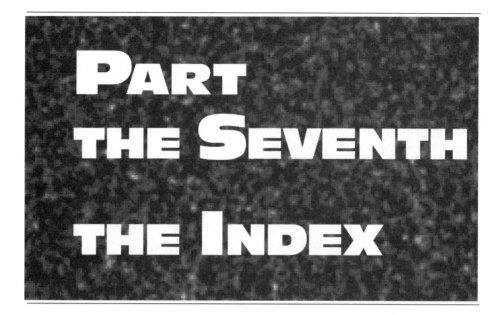

**PART THE SEVENTH**

**THE INDEX**

## Symbols

!fooM, 275
*, 38
/, 38
¶, 91
..., 33, 213
**1200,** 271
**2400,** 271
**9600,** 271
**32-bit addressing,** 164–165, 296
  check Total Memory,
    164–165
  in Memory control panel,
    164
  turn it on or off, 164
  what is it?, 296
**32-bit clean,** 165
  what is it?, 297–298
**32-bit Color QuickDraw,** 287,
  298
  what is it?, 298
**32-bit dirty**
  what is it?, 297–298
**50% page size,** 112–113

**68000,** 298
**68020,** 298
**68030,** 298
**68040,** 298
**68551,** 298
**68882,** 298

## A

**"About the ____",** 208
**accelerator board,** 271
**accent marks,** 99
**active window,** 42
  print contents of, 114
**ADB port,** 29
**Adobe Font Metrics,** 139
**Adobe Systems, Inc.,** 293
**Adobe Type Manager,** 136
**AFM file,** 139
**alarm clock**
  turn it off permanently, 149
  turn it off temporarily, 149
  what it is, how to work it,
    147–148

**alert box,** 33, 271
**aliases**
  find files on floppies or
    cartridges, 173
  find the original file of, 174
  fine points of, 171
  how to make one, 170
  in Apple menu, 169
  suggestions for using,
    171–173
  what are they?, 169
**alignment,** 94
  affects entire paragraph, 95
  what is it?, 94
**all at once in Find File,** 178
**AlSoft,** 210
**Antique Olive Black,** 146
**Any key,** 36
**Apple Backup Icon,** 251
**apple character,** 98
**Apple Color Wheel**
  with Color control panel, 161
**Apple Desktop Bus,** 29

**Apple key**, 36
**Apple LaserWriter**, 275
**Apple menu**
    aliases in, 155, 169
    alphabetizing pattern, 157
    control panels in, 159
    customizing, 156–158
    installing files in, 156
    serious customizing, 158
    suggestions for customizing,
        157
    what is it, 155
**Apple Menu Items folder**,
    129, 156
**Apple StyleWriter**, 107, 109,
    134, 136
**Appleshare file**
    extension for file sharing, 185
**AppleShare icon**, 185
**AppleTalk**, 109, 182, 271
    Active on Restart, 110
    on or off to print?, 109–110
**application**, 85
    closing vs. quitting, 117–118
    disappeared, 208
    open, 85
    quitting, 117–118
    recognizing icon, 85
    what is it?, 85
**application can't be found**
    what to do if, 234
**application heap**, 209
    changing, 209
    what is it?, 209
**application icons**, 59
    gray icons, 62
**Application menu**, 208, 219
    check for open applications,
        208
    diamond symbol in, 219
    find open apps to quit, 124
    for switching applications,
        208
    hide other windows, 226
    how and why to use,
        123–124
    illustrated, 123
    Option-click to Desktop,
        226

watch icons change, 124
    what is it?, 123
**Applications**
    still open?, 123
**applications**
    choosing between in
        At Ease, 259
    removing from At Ease,
        264
    still open?, 207–208
    which are still open?, 207–
        208
**applications folder**
    saving (Performa), 247
**arrow keys**, 39, 80
    naming conventions in
        book, 40
    navigating dialog boxes, 202
    navigating windows, 202
    selecting text with, 39
    to select files, 80
**arrows**, 215
**ASCII**, 271
**askee**, 271
**asterik**, 38
**asterisk**, 38, 40, 149
**At Ease**, 253
    add buttons for applications
        and documents, 262
    and open applications, 259
    application panel, 254
    bypassing on start up, 261
    can't use the Tutorial, 302
    changing the password, 266
    customizing, 261
    document panel, 254
    ejecting a disk, 258
    Finder in At Ease, 260
    for changes made in
        At Ease, 266
    forgetting the password,
        266
    "Gather Applications…," 263
    getting to the Finder, 259
    Go To Finder, 260
    hide others, 259
    limitations, 254
    move through pages, 256
    opening applications, 257

opening more than one
        application, 257
    opening other documents,
        256
    removing applications or
        documents from, 264
    removing items from the
        System Folder, 268
    removing permanently, 267
    restart for changes, 266
    saving a document, 258
    set up a password, 265
    set up how documents are
        saved, 265
    switch back to At Ease, 260
    turning off, 261
    turning on, 262
    using, 255
**aterisk**, 38
**ATM**, 136
    installing, 136
    residents fonts and, 141
    text, not graphics, 137
**Avant Garde**, 140–141

# B

**B word**, 272
**backup**, 15–16
    documents and disks, 15
    the Performa, 244
    files on Launcher, 250
**Background Printing**, 110
**backspace**
    to remove Return, 91
**Backspace key**, 37, 90
    and Clipboard, 97
    in typing, 90
**Balloon Help**
    Help menu, 191
    turn it off, 191
    turn it on, 191
    what is it?, 191
**baud rate**, 271
**BBS**, 272
**Bembo**, 146
**beta**, 272
**binary digit**, 272
**binary system**, 11

**bit**, 11, 272
**bitmapped**, 272
**bitmapped screen fonts**, 142, 145
**bits per second**, 271
**blank document icons**, 60
  drag-and-drop to open, 87
**blank lines**, 92
**blank space**
  indicating Spacebar, 37
**blank spaces**
  deleting them, 92
  formatting them, 92
  selecting them, 92
**blind dates**, 294
**bod**, 271
**bomb**, 272, 292
**Bookman**, 140–141
**boot**, 272
**boot disk**, 291
**boot up**, 17, 18, 232, 272
**booting up**
  from a startup disk, 232
**border**
  around buttons, 78
  around list in dialog box, 105
  colored, 161
  in "Save As…" dialog box, 203
**border around file name**, 70
**bps**, 271
**brightness**
  and contrast buttons, 226
  and dimmer switch, 226
  Brightness control panel, 226
  control, 226
**Brightness control panel**, 160
**buffer**, 110
**bug**, 20, 272
**buggy**, 272
**bulging trash can**, 83
**Bulletin Board Service**, 272
**burn in**, 289
**bus**, 273

**buttons**
  creating in At Ease, 260
  Launcher items, 246
  remove from the Launcher, 249
**by Date**, 47
**by Comments**, 48
**by Icon**, 46
**by Kind**, 47
**by Label**, 47
**by Name**, 46
**by Size**, 47
**by Small Icon**, 45
**by Version**, 48
**bypass At Ease**, 261
**byte**, 12, 273

**C**

**CAD**, 273
**Cairo**, 142
**calculate folder sizes**, 48
**Calculator**
  copy and paste calculations, 149
  what it is, how to use it, 149
**calculator keys**, 40
**Cancel**
  in dialog boxes, 33
**Can't find your document**, 233
**Can't open a file**
  what to do if, 234
**Caps Lock key**, 36
**card**, 271, 273
**cartridge hard disks**, 14, 122, 276
  mounting, dismounting, 122
**CD-ROM**, 273
**CDEF**, 295
**CDEV**, 274
**cdev. See control panel**
**Cella, Richard Thomas**, 193
**center aligned**, 94
**centering text**, 92, 95
**Central Processing Unit**, 274, 282

**change icon name**, 62
**changing**
  style of type, 93
  type styles from keyboard, 94
**character string**, 176
**checkbox, visual clue**, 215
**checkmark in menu**, 218
  no checkmark in menu, 218
**Chicago**, 142, 143
  TrueType on PostScript printer, 143
**Chicago font**
  creating Command key symbol, 36
**Chimes of Doom**, 232
**chip**, 273, 274
**choose**
  between applications and At Ease, 259
**Chooser**, 108–109
  for file sharing, 185
  network, 109
**circuit board**, 271
**city-named fonts**, 142–143
  easier to read on screen, 142
  printing, 142–143
**Clarus**, 275
**Clean Up Desktop**, 26, 51
  align on right, alphabetized, 51
**clean up selected icons**, 51
**Clean Up Window**
  by name, size, kind, etc., 50
**cleaning the mouse**, 30
**Clear**, 40
  and Clipboard, 97
**click**, 27
  as misleading term, 27
  double, 27
  in scroll bar, 44
  on icons to change name, 57
  on icons to select, 57
  single, 27
**click-and-drag. See Press-and-drag**
  as misleading term, 28
**clip art**
  viewing, 235

**Clipboard**
and RAM, 96
cut and copy, 95
icon, 95
icon in System Folder, 129
most important thing, 95
"Show the Clipboard," 95
what is it?, 95
**Close all the windows,** 52
**Close Box,** 41, 44
shortcut for, 44
**cloverleaf symbol,** 36
**Colette,** 125
**color**
icons, 63
**Color control panel,** 160
**color icons,** 163
**colors or grays**
number available determined
by, 165
**Command key,** 32, 36
keyboard shortcuts, 32
symbol, 32
**comments,** 66
destroyed, 67
search with Find File, 67
view in window, 67
**Compact Disk, Read-Only
Memory,** 273
**compress all folders,** 73
**compress folders,** 73
**compressed software,** 19
**Computer Aided Design,** 273
**computer doesn't turn on**
what to do if, 231
**connecting the mouse,** 29
**Connectix,** 165
**Control key,** 36
**control panel device,** 274
**control panels,** 129
alias of folder on Desktop,
172
alias of in Apple menu, 159
At Ease, 255
Brightness, 160
Color, 160
Date & Time, 161

File Sharing Monitor, 168
General Controls, 160
Keyboard, 162
Labels, 162
Launcher, 164, 252
Memory, 164
Monitors, 165
Mouse, 166
Network, 182
Numbers, 166
Sharing Setup, 183
Sound, 167
Startup Disk, 167
Users & Groups, 168
Views. *See* Views control
panel
what are they?, 159
**cool tricks,** 54
drag-and-drop on aliases, 172
drag-and-drop to open
documents, 87
for reconnecting file
sharing, 189
sound file in Startup Items
folder, 130
**copy**
how to do it, 96
new version based on
other, 103
what is it?, 95
**Copy of _____,** 76
**Copying**
more than one file, 78
why?, 75
**copying**
disk-to-disk, 77
Duplicate, 76
file onto same disk, 76–77
from floppy disk to hard
disk, 76
from floppy to floppy, 77
from hard disk to floppy, 75
**"could not be opened,"** 60
**Courier,** 140–141
**CPU,** 274, 282
**crash,** 206, 274, 292
one reason why, 206
reset switch, 240
unexpectedly quit, 206

**crawling bugs,** 272
**Create Publisher...,** 192
**Cronk, Drew J.,** 104, 192
**currency**
display of, 166
**customizing**
Apple menu, 157, 158
application heap, 209
At Ease, 255, 261
brightness of the screen, 160
change disk cache, 164
change startup disk, 167
colors on monitor, 160
date and time formatting, 161
Desktop pattern, 160
display of currency, 166
display of numbers, 166
icons, 64
keyboard, 162
Launcher, 249
menu blinking, 160
mouse speed, 166
rate of insertion point
flashing, 160
sounds, 167
speaker volume, 167
time and date, 160
using control panels,
159–161
**Cut,** how to do it, 96
what is it? 95

**D**

**Danger!** 102
**dark border,** 274
**DAs. See Desk accessories:**
what are they?, 147
**database,** 274
**Database 101,** 274
**date**
change the date, 148
copy and paste from
alarm clock, 148
**Date & Time control panel,** 161
**Dead Mac,** 232
**dead mouse,** 29
**default,** 274
**default button,** 214, 274

**delete**
  to remove Return, 91
**Delete key**, 37, 90
  and Clipboard, 97
  in typing, 90
**demodulator**, 281
**deselect**, 79
  icons, files, 79
**desk accessories**, 98
  closing, 154
  in System 6, 129
  installing, 154
  Key Caps, 98
  using from Desktop, 154
  what are they?, 147
**DeskJet**, 134, 137
**Desktop**, 23–26
  as office, 196
  button in dialog box, 88
  clean up, 26
  clean up on shutting down, 123
  hierarchy, 24
  level, 24
  make it active, 55
  menu, 31
  Option-click to hide windows, 226
  organizing, 25
  picture of, 23
  print the contents of, 114
  printing documents from, 113
  selecting the, 26
  switching to inadvertently, 208
  what's on it, 23
  windows at, 45–48
**Desktop file is full**
  what to do if, 236
**Desktop level**, 25
**Desktop level (illustrated)**, 196
**Desktop level in hierarchical menu**, 197
**Desktop windows**
  open too slowly, 239
**DeskWriter**, 107, 134, 137
**dialog box**, 275
  and ellipses, 33

file selection shortcuts, 80
  why do you see the files you see?, 204
**dialog boxes**
  ejecting disks, 121
  vs. folders, 197
**dim**
  the screen, 226
**Disable the Warning Box**, 84
**Disinfectant**, 296
**disk cache**
  what is it, setting it, 164
**disk capacity**, 12
**disk icon**
  double-clicking on, 58
  single-clicking on, 58
**disk is locked**
  can't open a file, 234
**disk-to-disk copying**, 77–78
**dismounting**, 122
**division symbol**, 38, 149
**document**
  blank icon, 60, 216
  cannot be opened, 86
  closing, 117–118
  opening by drag-and-drop, 87
  opening from the Desktop, 86
  print from the Desktop, 113
  removing from At Ease, 264
  saving it, 101
  stack, 291
  stationary pad, 60
  store aliases of, 172
  unknown, 60
**Document icons**, 59
  double-clicking on, 59
  drag-and-drop to open, 59
  single-clicking on, 59
**document names**
  how to pronounce, 21
**Documents folder**, 247
  and the Performa, 246
  change the name, 240
  Performa, 201
**Dogcow**, 275
**dot**, 21
**dot matrix printer**, 275

**dot sit**, 21
**dots per inch**, 275
  vs. lines per inch, 280
**double border**
  around list in dialog box, 105
  default button, 214
**double space**
  after periods, 100
**double-click**, 27
  change speed of, 166
  to open files, 27
**double-sided disk**, 13
**double-space**
  between paragraphs, 91
**DownArrow**, 40
**download**, 275
**downward Arrows**, 34
**dpi**, 275
**drag-and-drop**, 60
  make aliases for, 172
  open blank document icon, 60
  to open document, 87
  to open files, 172
**drive**, 275
**driver**, 276
**Duplicate**, 76

## E

**E-mail**, 276
**Easter Egg**
  trivia, 165
**edit box**, 34
**edit keys**, 40, 80
**edition**, 192
  example of making one in Word, 192
**eject**, 88
**eject a disk**
  in At Ease, 258
**ejecting disks**
  at any time, 121
  gray disk left behind, 119
  with a paper clip, 121
  with the mouse, 121
**ellipsis**, in button, 33
  in menu, 213

**empty the trash,** 84
**Encapsulated PostScript File,**
276
**End key,** 40, 80, 81
**Enlarge**
print on page, 112
**Enter key,** 37
**EPS, EPSF,** 272, 276
**esc,** 37, 38
**Escape key,** 37
**EtherTalk®,** 182
**expand the folders,** 73
**expanded folders,** 81
with Find File, 178
**extended keyboards**
Fkeys, 38
**extensions,** 130, 276
conflicts, 236
disable all, 229
trouble with, 277
**Extensions folder,** 130
**external floppy drive,** 19
**external hard disk,** 17
**eye-beam. See I-beam**

**F**

**F word,** 133
**FD-HD,** 13
**Fifth Generation Systems,** 210
**50% size,** 112–113
**file**
colon in name, 69–70
copying, 75
locking, 67
where did it go?, 195, 198
**file format**
**file format,** 276, 277
for scanning, 288
native, 204
tiff, 293
what is it?, 277
**file is in use**
can't open a file, 234
**file is locked**
can't open a file, 234
**file server,** 183, 277
what is it?, 183

**file serving icon,** 186–187
**file sharing**
cool trick for reconnecting,
189
connecting the computers,
182, 185
disconnecting, 188
icon, 186
reconnecting, 189
turn off for folders, 190
which files are shared?, 189
**file sharing icon,** 186
**File Sharing Monitor**
to disconnect file sharing, 188
which files are shared?, 189
**File Sharing Monitor**
**control panel,** 168
**file sharing software,** 181
installing it, 181
**filing cabinet**
as hard disk, 72
**Find Again,** 176
**find all the Systems,** 235
**Find File,** 67
all at once, 178
Find Again, 176
more complex finding, 177
narrowing your search, 179
search comments, 67
search within a search, 179
simple finding, how to, 176
suggestions for using, 180
to select files, 82
what is it?, 175
you can find it if:, 175
**Finder,** 23–26, 277
creating in a button for in
At Ease, 260
getting to in At Ease, 259
importance of, 128
interchangeable name with
Desktop, 277
printing documents from,
113
upgrades, 23
what does it do?, 18
what is it?, 23, 128
**Finder icon,** 18
**"Finder Shortcuts,"** 54

**Fkeys,** 38, 278
**flashing X,** 232
**floppy disk**
ejecting, 119–120
from the menu,
keyboard shortcut,
when shutting down
inserting, 18
**floppy disk drives,** 275
**floppy disks**
caring for, 13
disk capacity, 12
double-sided disk, 12, 13
high-density, 13
labeling, 16
locking, 14
plastic bags, 13
single-sided disk, 12
with two holes, 13, 14
**floppy disks,** 12–14
initializing, 13
what are they, 12
**folder**
change the name, 69–70
collapse, 56
colon in name, 69–70
compress, 73
compress all, 73
create your own, 69
dark bar on tab, 63
Documents, 201
error in name, 69–70
expand, 73
expanded, selecting files in,
81
expanded with Find File,
178
happy faces, 58, 187
hierarchy of, 52
name it, 69–70
nested, 52, 196, 282
open, 71, 196
organizing with, 197
outline mode, 72
project-specific, 73–74
put something inside, 71
cannot change name, 63
sharing, 184, 185
take something out, 71

triangles in front of, 72
vs. dialog boxes, 197
what are they, 69untitled
    folder, 69
which one does dialog box
    open to?, 201
**folder icons,** 41, 58
dark bar on tab, 58
double-clicking on, 58
shared, 58
single-clicking on, 58
with happy faces, 58
with wires, 58
**folder size in window,** 47
**font disk,** 135
**font downloader,** 139
icons for, 139
**font list**
at the Desktop, 229
**font management utility,**
    140, 210, 291
**font size**
in windows, 49
**font sizes,** 146
**Font Substitution,** 143
**font technology**
TrueType or PostScript,
    which one for you?, 137
**fonts,** 133
at the Destkop, 229
city-named, 142–143
in System file, 128
in windows, 48, 49
installing, 138–140
of same name, 137, 141
using Key Caps, 229
what's on a disk?, 135
**fonts at the Desktop**
finding, 229
**Fonts folder,** 128
**fonts of the same name,** 141
**force quit,** 233
**foreign language**
change keyboard layout, 162
customizing number
    display, 166
date and time, 161
display of currency, 166
**form-feed button,** 116

**form-feed the paper,** 238
**formatting**
unexpectedly changed, 236
**forward slash,** 38
**freeware,** 278
**frozen screen,** 240
**function key,** 278

**G**

**G,** 278
**garbage piles up around
    your can,** 238
**Gather Applications**
in At Ease, 263
**General Controls,** 160
Performa model, 160
**Geneva,** 136, 142, 143
**Get Info,** 66
application heap, 209
comments, 66
customize icons, 64
disable trash can warning, 84
finding original of alias, 174
info about files, 66
lock files, unlock files, 67
size of System file, 128
stationary pads, 68
tells you what kind of file,
    154
tells you what kind of file
    it is, 156
**Get Info boxes**
destroyed messages, 228
**gigabyte,** 278
**Go to**
Finder in At Ease, 260
**graphic file format. See also
    file format**
**graphical user interface,** 213
**gray,** 32, 217
disk icon, 217
disk icon after ejecting, 119
disk icon, ejected, 61–62
finding their windows, 51
left on the screen, 239
icon, 41, 51, 61, 217
menu commands, 32
scroll bars, 41, 218

**gray disk icon**
**gray menu commands,** 32
**gray scroll bar,** 41
**grayscale,** 278
**Guest,** 186

**H**

**h-menu,** 31
**Happy Mac,** 232
**hard copy,** 278
**hard disk,** 14, 14–15
as filing cabinet, 69, 72, 196
as office, 205
**hard disk back up**
on the Performa, 244
**hard disk drive,** 275
**hard disk level (illustrated),** 196
**hard disk space**
vs. memory, 205
**hard return,** 91
**hardware,** 279
**HD, on disk** 13
**header,** 41, 44, 49
show info in, 48
**Help**
Finder shortcuts, 54
**Help key,** 40
**Help menu,** 191
**Help screens,** 54
**Helvetica,** 140–141, 146
samples in sizes, 146
**HFS,** 25, 279
**hidden icon,** 41
**hidden menu,** 34
**Hide others**
in At Ease, 259
**hierarchical filing system,**
    24, 25, 279
**hierarchical menu,** 24, 31
**hierarchical menu of
    window,** 197
**hierarchy**
in menu, 24, 88
navigating with arrow keys,
    202
of a nested folder, 52
of a window, 52
of Desktop windows, 216

**highlighted. See also
    selecting: text**
  menu commands, 31
  text, 214
  text, replacing, 90
**highlighted (dark) icons**, 61
**highlighting**
  text, what is it?, 90
  to unhighlight, 90
**Home key**, 40, 80
**hot spot**, 28
**how much RAM**
  allotted to programs, 229
  allotted to system, 229
**HP DeskJet**, 134
**HP DeskWriter**, 107, 134
**HyperCard**, 291

**I**

**I-beam**, 89
  single click, 27
  using, 89–90
  what is it?, 89
**IBM PC**
  keyboard compatible with, 40
**icons**
  application, 59
  black, 61
  border around name, 62
  cannot change name, 63
  change custom back to
      original, 64
  changing name, 57–59
  color them, 63
  create your own, 64
  dark, highlighted, 61
  document, 59
  fancy, 59
  file sharing, 58
  folders, 58
  gray, 61–62
  hidden in window, 41
  matching, 59, 216
  moving, 62
  open, 61
  organizing, 49, 50
  program, 59
  renaming, 62

  select alphabetically, 80
  selected, 61
  serving platter, 58
  show in list view, 50
  snap to grid, 48
  system, 60
  undo name change, 62
  visual clues of, 57
  what are they, 57
**imagesetters**, 107–108, 133
  and TrueType, 138
**ImageWriter**, 107, 142, 275
  align the pin-fed paper, 116
  form-feed button, 116
  print quality, 112
  resolution, 275
  Select light, 116
  Tall Adjusted necessity,
      112–113
**ImageWriter paper**, 238
**information bar**, 41, 44, 49
  show info in, 48
**initialize**, 279
**initializing a new disk**, 13
**INITs**, 130, 274, 276, 279. **See
    also extensions**
  conflicts with, 236
**inserting a disk**, 18
**insertion point**, 89, 99
  customize flashing rate, 160
  formatting it, 93
  necessity for typing, 89
  picks up formatting, 93
  what is it?, 89
**Installer**, 20
**Installer disk**, 20
**installing**
  desk accessories, 154
  fonts, 138, 140
  into Apple menu, 156–158
  printer drivers, 109
**installing fonts**, 138
  the truth, 140
**installing software**
  compressed, 19
  more than one disk, 20
  on one disk, 19
**internal floppy drive**, 18

**internal hard disk**, 17
**invisible characters**, 91
**invisible space**, 92

**J**

**Jargon: An Informal
    Dictionary of
    Computer Terms**, 269
**Jimmy**, 56, 200
**justified alignment**, 94

**K**

**K**, 12
**Kawasaki, Guy**, 274
**Kelly, Walt**, 105
**kerning**, 279
**Key Caps**, 98
  fonts at the Desktop, 229
  what is it, how to use it, 150
**key repeat rate**, 162
**keyboard**, 35
  change layout, 162
  delay before repeat, 162
  disable keys repeating, 162
  extended, 35
  modifier keys, 35–38
  rate of keys repeating, 162
  standard, 35
  with numeric keypad, 35
**keyboard compatible with**
  IBM PC, 40
**Keyboard control panel**, 162
**keyboard shortcuts**, 32
  for changing type style, 94
  in dialog boxes, 105, 202
  Put Away to eject disk, 120
  saving, 102
  to eject disks, 119–120, 121
  written documentation, 32
**keys. See also modifier keys,
    keyboard**
  Any, 36
  Apple, 36
  arrows, 39
  asterisk, 38
  Caps Lock, 36
  Clear, 40
  Command, 36

Control, 36
Del, 40
Delete, 37
division, 38
Edit keys, 40
End, 40
Enter, 37
esc, 37
Escape, 37
Fkeys, 38
forward slash, 38
Home, 40
Ins, 40
multiplication, 38
Num Lock, 40
Open Apple, 36
Option, 37
PageDown, 40
PageUp, 40
Power On key, 40
Return, 37
Shift, 38
Spacebar, 37
star, 38
Tab, 39
**kilobyte**, 12

**L**

**labeling your disks**, 16
**labels**
applying, 163
changing, 163
use for organizing, 162
**Labels control panel**, 162
**landscape**, 112
**laser printers**
start-up page, 115
**LaserWriter**, 271, 275
lines per inch default, 280
**LaserWriter driver**
background printing, 110
**LaserWriter Font Utility**, 114
**last-saved version**
reverting to, 103
**launch**, 279
**Launcher**
add items/buttons, 249
alias of folder, 250

Documents folder, 201
make backups, 250
on the Perform, 244–245
remove items/buttons, 249
**Launcher control panel**, 164
**Launcher Items**, 246
**lazy tricks**
use Find File to get your
file, 82
using Find File, 180
**leading**, 279
**ledding**, 279
**left aligned**, 94
**LeftArrow**, 40
**level**
Desktop, 196, 198
disk, 198
floppy disk, 196
folder, 196, 198
hard disk, 196
**ligature**, 279
**line-feed the paper**, 238
**lines per inch**, 280
vs. dots per inch, 280
**Linotronic**, 108, 288
lines per inch default, 288
**list box**
selected; double border, 203
**list view**, 46, 50
show icons in, 50
**LocalTalk®**, 182
**lock**, 67
files, 67
throw away locked files,
67, 84
unlock files, 67
**locked**
can't change name of, 63
**locking a disk**, **14**
**log off, logging off**, 280
**log on, logging on** 186, 280
**logic board**, 282
**London**, 142
**Los Angeles**, 142
**lost your application**
what to do if, 239

**lovers**
e-mail, 276
leave love notes for, 151
leave notes in Get Info, 66
love letter labels, 163
sound file for in Startup
Items folder, 130

**M**

**Mac is not a typewriter, The**,
100, 310
**Macintosh File System**, 279
**Macintosh Performa**, 243
**MacPaint**
viewing clip art, 235
**macro**, 280
**magnetic**, 13
**make the window active**, 42
**marquee**, 78
**MasterJuggler**, 210, 291
**matching icons**, 216
**MB**, 15
**mean tricks**, 49
sound file in Startup Items
folder, 130
**megabytes**, 15
**megs**, 15
**memory**, 206–210, 281. **See
also RAM**
analogy, 206
and fonts, 210
help older Macs access
more, 165
random access memory.
*See also* RAM
suggestions to avoid
running out of, 207
vs. hard disk. *See also* RAM
**memory chips**, 289
**Memory control panel**, 164
virtual memory, 210–212
**menus**, 31
choosing commands, 31
downward arrows, 34
in At Ease, 255
other, 33
sideways arrows, 34

**menu bar**
changed?, 124, 208
flashing, 167
switch monitors, 165
**menu commands**, 32
black, 32
choosing, 32
into Apple menu, 156–158
gray, 32
highlighted, selected, 32
**MFS**, 279
**microphone**
record sounds, 167
**microprocessor**, 274
**Microsoft Word**
stupid type size menu in,
144
**mini-menu**, 215
**misformatting**, 237
**Mode32**, 165
**modem**, 271
downloading to, 275
upload, 294
what is it?, 281
**modem port icon**, 109
**modifier keys**, 35, 282
how to use, 36
**modulator**, 281
**moiré**, 282
**Monaco**, 142, 143
**monitor**
color, 63
set up two monitors, 166
**Monitors control panel**, 165
select number of colors or
grays, 165
**Moof!**, 275, 282
**More Choices, Find File**, 177
**motherboard**, 282
**mounting**, 122
**mouse**, 27, 27–28
ADB port, 29
change speed of, 166
cleaning, 30
connecting it, 29
double-click speed, 166
erratic movement, 240

left-handed, 29
movement to second
monitor, 166
run out of space, 29
why is it called, 29
**Mouse control panel**, 166
**Mouse Practice**, 268
**mousepad**, 29
**move any window**, 42
**move through the pages**
in At Ease, 256
**moving**
as opposed to copying, 71
icons, 62
**multi-disk software**, 20
**multi-tasking**
and memory, 208
**multimedia**, 282
**multiplication symbol**, 38, 149

**N**

**name**
cannot change, 63
**native file format**, 204
**navigating**
example of process, 200
to a particular folder, 199
to other disk, 198
what is it?, 195
with keyboard shortcuts, 202
**nested**, 282
**network**, 277, 283
and Chooser, 109
**Networking control panels**,
168, 182
**networking control panels.**
**See file sharing, sharing**
**files**
**New Century Schoolbook**,
140–141
**New York**, 142, 143
samples of, 143
**New...**, 87
vs. Open..., 87
**non-PostScript printer**, 135,
136
with ATM, 137

with ATM and PostScript
fonts, 137
with TrueType fonts, 137
**Norstad, John**, 296
**"Not Enough Memory"**
find extra systems, 231
what to do if, 236
**Note Pad**
icon in System Folder, 129
what it is, how to use it, 151
**Num Lock**, 40
**Numbers control panel**, 166
**numeric keypad**, 35, 40

**O**

**object-oriented**, 283
**OCR**, 283
**office-on-a-disk**, 173, 189
trick to sharing your hard
disk, 189
**on switch**, 17
**one-disk software**, 19
**online**
on a modem, 281
what is it?, 283
**online help**, 283
**Open (Gray) Icons**, 61
**open a document**, 86
**open an application**, 85
**Open Apple**, 36
**open applications**
in At Ease, 257
**open documents**
in At Ease, 256
**Open...**, 87, 88
ejecting disks, 121
vs. New..., 87
**Open... dialog box**
explained, 88
**Optical Character Recogni-**
**tion**, 283
**Option key**, 37
**organizing**
files on floppies with
aliases, 173
with aliases, 171–173
with color icons, 163

with folders, 197
with Labels, 162–163
your desktop, 25
your hard disk, 72
**orientation**, 112
**other windows pop up**
what to do if, 239
**outline**, 272
**outline character,**
**(illustrated)**, 133
**outline fonts**, 134, 135
**outline mode, outline view**,
56, 72

## P

**Page Setup**, 143
check before printing, 111
substitute fonts, 143
**PageDown**, 80
**PageUp**, 80
**Palatino**, 140–141, 141
**paper, saving**, 114
**password**
changing in At Ease, 266
forgetting in At Ease, 266
**passwords**, 186
**paste**
how to do it, 96
**Performa**, 243
backup the hard disk, 244
Documents folder, 201
Launcher control panel, 164
sanity protection, 248
setting it up, 244
using the Tutorial, 302
without the Launcher, 248
**peripheral**, 283
**peripheral devices**
SCSI exchange, 289
turning on, 231
**permanently removing**
**At Ease**, 267
**phosphors**, 286
**pica**, 283
**PICT**, 284
**PICT graphic file format,**
icon of, 284

**Picture 1**, 56, 65
**picture element**, 284
**pins**, 289
**pirate**, 284
**pirating**, 75
**pixel**, 284
**Pogo**, 105
**point (type size)**
exactly 72 per inch on
Mac, 284
what is it, 284
**point (.)**
in upgrade versions, 21
**pointer**, 28
hot spot, 28
I-beam as, 89
selection marquee, 78
**points per pica**, 283
**pop-out menu**, 31
**pop-up menu**, 215
**port**, 284
**port, printer**, 109
**portrait**, 112
**PostScript**
check icons of, 144
is it?, 144
outline character illustrated,
133
what is it?, 133, 285
**PostScript fonts**, 134–137, 272
viewing from icon, 145
**PostScript interpreter**, 134
**PostScript printer**, 133
and Chooser, 109
city-named fonts on, 142
imagesetter, 107–108
what is it?, 107–108, 285
with ATM and PostScript
fonts, 138
**PostScript printers**, 107
examples of, 134
RAM and ROM, 140–141
resident fonts in, 140–141
**Power On key**, 40
**power users**, 22, 285
muttering, 122

**PowerBooks**
and trackballs, 28
**Preferences files**
stored in folder, 131
**Preferences folder**, 131
**press**, 27
what it does, 27
**"Press any key"**, 36
**press-and-drag**, 28
scroll box, 44
**pretend memory.**
**See virtual memory**
**Print a screen shot**, 56
**Print other windows**, 56
**Print the Desktop**, 114
**Print the Screen**, 55
**Print the Window**, 55, 114
**Print... command**, 111
**printer driver**, 108, 109
installing, 109
what is it?, 109
**printer font icons**, 135
in Extensions folder, 130, 139
**printer icons in Chooser**, 108
**printer port icon**, 109
**Printers**
and fonts, 133
**printing**, 107–115
canceling in progress, 115
Chooser, 108
city-named fonts, 142–143
four steps to printing,
111–114
set a time to print, 115
spooler, 290
**printing won't work**
what to do if, 237
**PrintMonitor**, 115
background printing, 110
controlling printing with, 115
what is it?, 115
**program**
what is it?, 85
**program disk**, 20
**program icons**, 59
**Program Linking**
what is it, 184

**programmers switch**, 240
**project-specific folders**
how to create, 73–74
how to save into, 73–74
**public domain**, 285
**Publish**, 192
**Publish and Subscribe**, 192
**pull-down menu**, 31
**Put Away**, 68, 120
**puzzle**
change the puzzle, 153
what it is, how to use it, 153

## Q

**Quandt, Carole**, 104
**question mark**
on startup, 232
**QuickDraw**
programming language, 107
what is it?, 285
**QuickDraw printer**, 107, 134
city-named fonts on, 142
examples of, 134
selected in Chooser, 109
what is it?, 107, 285
**QuickTime**
what is it?, 286
**Quit**
all applications, 124
applications, 117–118
applications; how to, 207–208
closing vs. quitting, 117–118
don't just close, 207
vs. close, 207
with Option key, 118
**quotation marks**
keys for, 227
locating on the keyboard, 227
professional, 227
vs. inch and foot marks, 227
vs. typewriter marks, 227

## R

**Radio buttons (visual clue)**, 214
**RAM**, 101, 206, 282
allotted to programs, 229

allotted to system, 229
analogy with office, 101
and fonts, 210
enlarging application heap, 209
gets full, 236
running out of, 236
**Random Access Memory.**
**See RAM**
**rasterize**, 134, 136
**Read The Manual**, 19
**read-only**, 286
**read-only file**, 67
**ReadMe**, 20, 286
**ReadMe files**, 20
drop onto alias of word processor, 172
**ReadMe First**, 20
**real memory**, 211
**real quotation marks**
as professional type, 227
keys for, 227
locating on the keyboard, 227
vs. inch and foot marks, 227
vs. typewriter marks, 227
what are they?, 227
**Rebuild the desktop of**
**floppy disk**
how to, 228
**rebuild your Desktop**, 67
destroys Get Info comments, 67
why you need to, 228
**redraw**, 286
**reduce**
print on page, 112
**refresh rate**, 286
**removable cartridge**
**hard disks**, 122
**remove**
applications or documents
in At Ease, 264
At Ease, permanently, 267
items from System Folder
in At Ease, 268
items from the Launcher, 249
Returns, 91
type styles, 93

**remove the Launcher**, 252
**replace the contents**, 78
**reset**, 240
**reset button**, 240
**reset switch**, 240
**resident fonts**, 140–141
**resolution of a printer**,
275, 287
of imagesetters, 107
of printers, 133–134
of QuickDraw printers, 107
**resolution of a monitor**,
275, 287
**Restart**
for changes made in
At Ease, 266
**restart**, 240
**Return**
removing from text, 91
**Return key**, 37, 39
and word wrap, 91
hard return, 91
soft return, 91
when to use in typing, 91
word wrap, 91
**Revert**, 103
**Rich Text Format**, 277, 287
**right aligned**, 94
**RightArrow**, 40
**ROM**, 287
**root directory**, 24
**root level**, 197
**RTF**, 277, 287
**RTFM**, 19
**Rule #1**, 102
**Rule #2**, 93
**Rule #3**, 16

## S

**Sad Mac**, 18, 232
**San Francisco**, 142
**sanity protection**, 248
**sans serif font, sample**, 146
**save**
in At Ease, 258
into the Documents folder
(Performa), 247

**Save as...**
keyboard shortcut for, 103
**"Save As..." dialog box**, 102, 104, 105
edit box vs. list box selected, 203
ejecting disks, 121
explained in detail, 104
how to do it, 198
make stationery pad in, 68
using the Performa, 247
**Save As... vs. Save,** 102
**Save command,** 102
keyboard shortcut, 102
**saving,** 101–103
a document without the changes, 103
document to a different disk, 104
in different file formats, 105
into a particular folder, 199
keyboard shortcut, 102
onto Desktop level, 198
onto floppy or cartridge disk, 198
onto hard disk level, 198
onto the disk of your choice, 198
quit or close without saving changes, 118
set up how documents are saved in At Ease, 265
to avoid crashing, 209
**scalable fonts,** 135, 136
**scale,** 112
**scan,** 287
**scanner,** 287
and OCR, 283
what is it?, 287
**scanners**
hand-held, 288
slide, 288
video, 288
**scanning**
as PICT file format, 288
suggestions for saving as, 288
**Scarlett,** 192, 202, 204

**Scrapbook**
icon in System Folder, 129
what it is, how to use it, 152
**screen**
print it, 55
**screen burn**
avoiding, 226
Brightness control panel, 226
brightness control switch, 226
contrast buttons, 226
dimmer control switch, 226
screen savers, 226
**screen capture,** 65
**screen dump,** 56, 65
**screen freeze,** 240
what to do if, 233
**screen saver,** 289
as desk accessories, 226
avoiding screen burn, 226
in System Folder, 227
through the Apple menu, 227
**screen shot,** 56
how to print, 65
how to take one, 65
**scroll arrows,** 41, 43
**scroll bars,** 43
**scroll box,** 41, 44, 218
number in, 44
**SCSI,** 289
**SCSI ports,** 289
**scuzzy,** 289
**sea,** 19
**search within a search,** 179
**select**
files with Find File, 82
font, typeface, 93
more than one file in list view, 79
text, 93
text, press-and-drag, 90
with Tab key, 226
**Select First, Then Do It To It,** 93
**Select light,** 116
**selected**
icons, 61
menu commands, 31
text in color, 161

**selecting**
file names in dialog box, 105
files from expanded folders, 81
more than one file, 78
more than one icon, 78
text, 90
text with arrow keys, 39
**selection marquee,** 78
**selection shortcuts,** 80–82
**self extracting archive,** 19
**serif font, sample,** 146
**service bureaus**
what are they?, 108
**set a password**
in At Ease, 265
**"Set Up Documents..."**
how to save in At Ease, 265
**set up the system**
the Performa, 244
**shadow**
indicating menu, 34
**shadow, indicating menu,** 215
**shareware,** 289
**sharing files**
file sharing software, 181
how to do it, 187
what is it?, 181
**sharing folders,** 184
**Sharing Setup**
name that Mac, 183
password, 183
**Sharing Setup control panel,** 168, 183
**Shift key,** 38
selecting text with, 39
**Shift-Tab**
to select file alphabetically backwards, 80
**Shift-click,** 79
to de-select, 79
to select files in expanded folders, 81
to select more than one file, 79
**"Show Balloons"**
and how much RAM, 229

**Show disk info,** 49
**Show the Clipboard,** 95
**Shut Down**
  how to do it, 124
  what is it?, 123
**sideways arrows,** 34
**silicon,** 273
**SIMM,** 289
**simple networking**
  connecting the computers,
  182
**single click,** 27
  to select files, 27
**Single Inline Memory**
  **Module,** 289
**single space after periods,**
  100
**single-sided disk,** 12
**sit,** 19, 21
**size box,** 41, 42
**slash,** 40
**Snap to grid,** 48, 49, 51
  override, 49
**soft Return.**
  **See Word wrap**
**software,** 289
  networking, 182
**software program,** 85
**SOS,** 102, 209
**Sound control panel,** 167
**sound files**
  in Startup Items folder, 130
  hear in System file, 128
  listen to, 167
  stored in System file, 167
  turn it off, 167
**Spacebar,** 37
**spasms**
  during multi-tasking, 187
**special characters,** 98
**special menu**
  indicates Desktop, 25
**spooler,** 290
**spreadsheet**
  using for forms, 290
  what is it?, 290
**stack,** 291

**staggered grid,** 48, 49
**standard keyboard,** 35
**star,** 38
**startup**
  boot disk, 291
  disk, 291
  volume, 291
**startup disk,** 18
  booting from, 232
  change, 167
  using, 232
**Startup Disk control panel,** 167
**Startup Documents,** 276
**Startup Items folder,** 130
**Startup Movie**
  creating, 227
  installed in your
    System Folder, 227
  installing, 227
  saving, 227
  what is it?, 227
**StartupScreen**
  creating, 227
  installed in your
    System Folder, 227
  installing, 227
  saving, 227
  what is it?, 227
**stationery pad**
  how to make, 68
  what is it?, 68
**straight grid,** 48
**string,** 176
**style, type**
  changing, 93
  removing all styles, 93
  what is it, 93
**StyleWriter,** 107, 109, 134,
  136, 137
**submenu,** 215
**Subscribe,** 192
**substitute fonts,** 143
**Suitcase,** 210
  unalphabetized in Apple
    menu, 157
**suitcase icons,** 291
  vs. Suitcase utility, 291
**suitcases,** 134

**SuperDrive,** 13
**SuperPaint**
  viewing clip art, 235
**surge protector**
  turning on, 231
**swapping,** 212
**switch back to At Ease,** 260
**switch between At Ease**
  **and Open Applications,**
  259
**Symbol,** 141
**System**
  More than one?, 21
  removing extras, 21
  what does it do?, 18
**System** 6
  desk accessories, 129
  use *Little Mac Book,* second
    edition, 8
**System 7**
  are you using?, 8
  visual clues, 219
**System 7.0**
  storing fonts in, 139
**System 7.1**
  Fonts folder, 128, 139
**system and software**
  **Versions,** 20
**system bombs**
  what to do if, 235, 292
**system crash,** 235, 292
**system error,** 206
**system extensions**
  what are they, 130
**System file,** 127
  hear sounds in, 128
  make new sounds for, 167
  reporting high amount of
    memory for itself, 165
  to determine TrueType vs.
    PostScript fonts, 144
  view fonts in, 128
  what is it, 127–128
**System Folder,** 18
  don't copy onto hard disk,
  76
  Finder icon, 18
  installing files in, 131

removing At Ease items, 268
System icon, 18
what is it?, 127
**System icon**, 18
**system icons**, 60
**Systems**
extra, 235
removing extra, 21

# T

**Tab key**, 39
in dialog boxes, 105
in Save As dialog boxes, 203
to select edit boxes, 214, 226
to select files alphabetically,
80
**Tagged Image File Format**,
293
**Tall Adjusted**
print on page, 112–113
**TeachText**, 20, 292
ReadMe files, 20
to open screen shots, 56, 66
what is it?, 292
**telecommunications**, 292
**template**, 68
stationery pad, 68
**text**
centered, 92
removing typestyles, 93
**text formatting changed**
what to do if, 236
**text-only**, 271, 292
a.k.a. ASCII, 292
**the Performa**
Launcher, 244
**TIFF**, 293
what is it?, 293
**TIFF vs. PICT**, 284
**Tilde key**, 38
**time**
change the time, 148
copy and paste from
alarm clock, 148
**Times**, 140–141
printing TrueType on
PostScript printer, 141

samples in sizes, 146
TrueType vs. PostScript, 141
**tips**
from all kinds of sources, 230
write your own, 230
**title bar**, 41, 42
**toggle switch**, 293
**TokenTalk®**, 182
**Total Memory**, 165
**Trackballs**, 28
**trash can**, 83–84
bulging, 83
disable the warning box, 84
ejecting disks
keyboard shortcut, 120
to avoid gray disk icon,
120
opens to window, 83
Put Away command, 83
put something in, 83
take something out, 83
throw away locked file, 84
warning box, 84
**TrueType**
bitmapped font icons, 145
check icons of, 144
icon, illustrated, 145
is it?, 144
printing to PostScript
printer, 141
text, not graphics, 137
viewing from icon, 145
**TrueType fonts**, 136–137
**turning on the Mac**, 17
**Tutorial.**
See Chapter 37, 302
**type. See also Text, Typing**
changing size, 94
examples of, 146
removing all styles, 93
**Type 1 fonts**, 135, 136, 293
**Type 2 fonts**, 293
**Type 3 fonts**, 293
**type size menu**
as key to TrueType or
PostScript, 144
**typefaces**
in System file, 128

**typing**, 89
centering text, 92
change styles from
keyboard, 94
erratic, 187, 240
icon name, 62
purpose of, 89
spasms, 187, 240
when to use Returns, 91

# U

**Undo**, 97
icon name change, 62
**Undo Key**, 38
**unexpectedly quit**, 206, 209
**unlock**
files, 67
**untitled folder**, 69
where'd it go?, 70
**UpArrow**, 40
**updates**, 20–21
**upgrades**, 20
hardware, 294
software, 294
why do it, 21
**upload**, 294
**Users & Groups control panel**,
168, 186
**utility**, 136, 294

# V

**vaporware**, 294
**Venice**, 142
**version number**, 20
how to pronounce, 21
**versions**
of a document, 103
**video card**, 294
**view clip art**, 235
**View menu**
customize, 48
**views of the window**, 45
switch with click, 46
**Views control panel**, 45
size, 240

**virtual memory**, 210–212
  Memory control panel,
    210–212
  turn it on or off, 164
**virus**, 295
**visual clue**
  black Eject button, 198
**visual clues**
  blank document icons, 216
  boot disk, 219
  changing file names, 216
  checkbox buttons, 214, 215
  checkmark in menu, 218
  default button, 214
  gray or white scroll bars, 218
  highlighted text, 214
  in "Save As" dialog box, 105
  label above list, 215
  mini-menu, 214
  no checkmark in menu, 218
  number of items in
    information bar, 217
  radio buttons, 214
  scroll box, 218
  System 7?, 219
  Tab key, 214
  underlined, 217
  what are they?, 213
**volatile**, 281

# W

**warning box**
  get rid of it, 84
**watermelon**, 269
**wayward icons**, 68
**WDEF virus**, 228, 295
  rebuild desktop to destroy,
    228
**what To Do If**
  computer doesn't turn on,
    231
**what to do if**
  application can't be found,
    234
  can't form feed or line feed
    paper, 238
  Desktop file is full, 236
  desktop windows open too

  slowly, 239
  erratic typing or mouse
    movement, 240
  extension conflicts, 236
  garbage piles up around the
    trash can, 238
  gray disk icon is left on the
    screen, 239
  lost your application, 239
  "Not Enough Memory,"
    236
  other windows pop up, 239
  printing doesn't work, 237
  question mark, flashing x,
    or Sad mac, 232
  screen freezes, 233, 240
  system bombs, 235
  text formatting unexpect-
    edly changed, 236
  you can't find your
    document, 233
  you can't open a file, 234
**What You See**
  **Is What You Get**, 296
**white scroll bar**, 41
**wide**, 112
**Williams, Robin**, 288
**Williams, Shannon**, 104, 133,
  192
**window**, 41
  active, 42
  active, when does it
    become, 53
  active, making it
  active, moving without
    making it, 42
  by name, 46
  change color, 161
  change font, 48
  change font size, 48
  changed? lost? aack?, 124
  Clipboard, 95
  close every one at once, 52
  cool tricks for manipulat-
    ing, 54
  differences between
    Desktop and application,
    53
  enlarge the size, 43

  hierarchy of, 52
  moving, 42
  parts of, 42–44
  print application
    window, 56
  print contents of, 114
  print it, 55
  reduce the size, 43
  scroll by dragging file, 53
  tricks for closing, 52
  view by name, 46
  view by size, 46
**window color**, 161
**windows**
  change list view, 46
  customize the view, 48
  Desktop, 45–48
  view as list, 46
  view by comments, 48
  view by date, 47
  view by icon, 46
  view by kind, 47
  view by label, 47, 163
  view by size, 47
  view by version, 48
  view comments in, 67
  Views Control Panel, 48
**wizziwig**, 296
**Word. See Microsoft Word**:
  stupid type size menu in
**word processing**, 89.
  **See also typing**
  word wrap, 91
**Word Settings**, 237
**word wrap**, 91
**WYSIWYG**, 296

# Z

**Zapf Chancery**, 140–141
**Zapf Dingbats**, 140–141
**zones**, 185
**zoom box**, 41, 43

## Colophon

I created this book entirely within PageMaker 4.2—the writing, editing, page layout, table of contents, and indexing. PageMaker's table of contents and indexing features are incredible. I work on a Macintosh IIcx with a 21-inch grayscale monitor that I keep to black-and-white cuz I like it that way. I used Capture to create the screen shots, cleaned them up in DeskPaint, and created a separate Scrapbook for each section with SmartScrap. I proofed pages on a LaserWriter IINT.

The fonts I used are Bembo (which I will never use again) and Antique Olive Black and Compact (which I am really into at the moment but it changes regularly), both from Linotype-Hell.

The beautiful cover design (which I love even though it is a man and I am not) is by Ted Mader + Associates.

Final output was on a Linotronic 300 at Petaluma Imagesetting, Inc. Pages were nursed out of the Lino and rushed to FedEx daily by the incomparable Janet Butcher.

Cary Norsworthy spent many a frantic hour keeping track of pages in and out to the printer and getting it through the channels in the nick of time.

I've said it before but I'll say it again, this book could not have been completed on time or anywhere near on time or anywhere even close to 1993 without my sister, Shannon.

## Just in case you wanna know

I live in Santa Rosa, California, with my three kids. I run a monthly user group for new and not-so-new users. I have columns in several magazines. I usually teach at Santa Rosa Junior College but I took the semester off when I saw they were about to install System 7 on 25 networked Mac Pluses. Now I'll have more time for my drum.

# Typeface examples

| | |
|---|---|
| Avant Garde | Doch Bep, flink sexy qua vorm, zwijgt. |
| Bookman | Doch Bep, flink sexy qua vorm, zwijgt. |
| Courier | Doch Bep, flink sexy qua vorm, zwijgt. |
| Helvetica | Doch Bep, flink sexy qua vorm, zwijgt. |
| New Century Schoolbook | Doch Bep, flink sexy qua vorm, zwijgt. |
| Palatino | Doch Bep, flink sexy qua vorm, zwijgt. |
| Symbol | Δοχη Βεπ, φλινκ σεξψ θυα ϖορμ, ζωιφγτ. |
| Times | Doch Bep, flink sexy qua vorm, zwijgt. |
| *Zapf Chancery* | *Doch Bep, flink sexy qua vorm, zwijgt.* |
| Zapf Dingbats | ❖❑❋❋ ✛❋❑❧ ❋●❋■❋ ▲❋❙ ❑◆❖ ❖❑❏❍❧ |
| Garamond | Doch Bep, flink sexy qua vorm, zwijgt. |

*All of these fonts on this page are PostScript, Type 1.*
*The fonts displayed above are commonly found on most Macintoshes.*
*The fonts displayed below are the ones I used in this book.*

| | |
|---|---|
| Bembo | Doch Bep, flink sexy qua vorm, zwijgt. |
| **Antique Olive** | **Doch Bep, flink sexy qua vorm, zwijgt.** |

*I have no idea what this sentence means, but I love it.*
*It is from the Dutch translation of* The Little Mac Book.

# Zapf Dingbats

In the chart to the left, find the Zapf Dingbat you wish to type. Hold down the Shift, the Option, or the Shift-and-Option keys while pressing the text character. The dingbat in the Zapf column needs no extra keys.

| Text | Zapf | Shift | Option | Shift & Option |
|---|---|---|---|---|
| 1 | ✂ | ✂ | ② | ↗ |
| 2 | ✂ | ⌖ | ♥ | → |
| 3 | ✓ | ✂ | ❣ | ➡ |
| 4 | ✔ | ✄ | ❣ | → |
| 5 | ✗ | ☎ | ⑤ | → |
| 6 | ✖ | ✿ | ❤ | ➡ |
| 7 | ✗ | ✆ | ❧ | ➡ |
| 8 | ✘ | ☞ | ❦ | ℊ |
| 9 | ✚ | ✈ | ⑥ | ➡ |
| 0 | ✏ | ⌧ | ⑦ | ➤ |
| - | ✐ | ✾ | ⑦ | ⑧ |
| = | ✝ | ☞ | ② | ⑥ |
| q | ❏ | ✹ | ⑥ | ⑤ |
| w | ◗ | ✷ | ❷ | ➢ |
| e | ❄ | ✛ | ♠ | ♠ |
| r | ❐ | ✼ | ♣ | ➣ |
| t | ▼ | ✶ |  |  |
| y | ❙ | ✴ | ⑨ | ❘ |
| u | ◆ | ✳ | ① | ① |
| i | ❊ | ☆ | ① | ⇨ |
| o | ❑ | ✫ | ⑩ | ④ |
| p | ❒ | ✩ | ❹ | ❸ |
| [ | ✳ | ❛ | ⑨ | ❿ |
| ] | ✴ | ❝ | → | → |
| a | ❀ | ✭ | { | ) |
| s | ▲ | ✳ | ❧ | ⇨ |
| d | ❄ | ✣ | ❶ | ⇦ |
| f | ❅ | ◆ | ⑤ | ⇦ |
| g | ❆ | ◇ | ♦ | ➡➡ |
| h | ❈ | ★ | ➔ | ⇨ |
| j | ❉ | ✪ | ⑦ | ⇨ |
| k | ❋ | ☆ | ➤➔ |  |
| l | ● | ✰ | ③ | ⇨ |
| ; | ✢ | ✚ | ⑩ | ⊃ |
| ' | ⊛ | ✂ | ⑨ | ③ |
| z | ■ | ✲ | ⑧ | ➤➤ |
| x | ❘ | ✸ | ⑥ | ⇒ |
| c | ✺ | ⁙ | } | ( |
| v | ❖ | ✳ | ④ | ↕ |
| b | ✹ | ✛ | ❺ | ➢➔ |
| n | ■ | ✩ | ❞ | ➘ |
| m | ○ | ★ | ⑩ | ➡ |
| , | ✌ | ✤ | ⑦ | ➢➔ |
| . | ✎ | ✞ | ⑧ | ➹ |
| / | ✐ | ✝ | ↔ | ① |
| ` |  | ❝ | ✿ | ✿ |
| spacebar |  |  | ❶ | ❶ |
| \ | ✳ | ' | ⑧ | ⑨ |

| | | | |
|---|---|---|---|
| Sh ] | " | n (outlined) | □ |
| Sh ` | " | l (outlined) | ○ |
| Sh [ | ' | t (outlined) | ▽ |
| Sh \ | ' | s (outlined) | △ |
| | | u (outlined) | ◇ |
| | | Opt 6 (outlined) | ♡ |

| | | | |
|---|---|---|---|
| Opt Sh / | ① | Opt u space | ① |
| Opt 1 | ② | Opt = | ② |
| Opt l | ③ | Opt Sh ' | ③ |
| Opt v | ④ | Opt Sh o | ④ |
| Opt f | ⑤ | Opt 5 | ⑤ |
| Opt x | ⑥ | Opt Sh = | ⑥ |
| Opt j | ⑦ | Opt , | ⑦ |
| Opt \ | ⑧ | Opt . | ⑧ |
| Opt Sh \ | ⑨ | Opt y | ⑨ |
| Opt ; | ⑩ | Opt m | ⑩ |

| | | | |
|---|---|---|---|
| Opt d | ❶ | Opt Spcbar | ❶ |
| Opt w | ❷ | Opt ` then Sh a | ❷ |
| Opt Sh p | ❸ | Opt n then Sh a | ❸ |
| Opt p | ❹ | Opt n then Sh o | ❹ |
| Opt b | ❺ | Opt Sh q | ❺ |
| Opt q | ❻ | Opt q | ❻ |
| Opt 0 | ❼ | Opt - | ❼ |
| Opt z | ❽ | Opt Sh - | ❽ |
| Opt ' | ❾ | Opt [ | ❾ |
| Opt o | ❿ | Opt Sh [ | ❿ |

**Here is a handy chart for finding some of the special characters available that will make your work look more professional**

| | | |
|---|---|---|
| " | Option [ | Opening double quote |
| " | Option Shift [ | Closing double quote |
| ' | Option ] | Opening single quote |
| ' | Option Shift ] | Closing single quote; Apostrophe |
| - | Hyphen | Hyphen |
| – | Option Hyphen | En dash |
| — | Option Shift Hyphen | Em dash |
| … | Option ; | Ellipsis *(this character cannot be separated at the end of a line as the three periods can)* |
| • | Option 8 | Bullet |
| ❏ | o | (in font Zapf Dingbats) |
| ■ | n | (in font Zapf Dingbats) |
| □ | n (outlined) | (in font Zapf Dingbats) |
| © | Option g | Copyright symbol |
| ™ | Option 2 | Trademark symbol |
| ® | Option r | Registration symbol |
| ° | Option Shift 8 | Degree symbol: 105° F |
| ¢ | Option $ | Cents symbol |
| / | Option Shift ! | Fraction bar *(it fits fractions better and doesn't descend below the baseline as the slash does)* |
| fi | Option Shift 5 | Ligature for **f** and **i** |
| fl | Option Shift 6 | Ligature for **f** and **l** |
| £ | Option 3 | English pound sign |
| ¿ | Option Shift ? | Spanish symbol |
| ç | Option c | Cedilla, lowercase |
| Ç | Option Shift c | Cedilla, capital |
| ⌘ | Control Q | (only in the Chicago font) |

**Accent Marks**

*Refer to page 99 to learn how to type these in; this page is merely a quick reference*

| | |
|---|---|
| ´ | Option e |
| ` | Option ~ |
| ¨ | Option u |
| ~ | Option n |
| ^ | Option i |